Autonomy or Power?

Autonomy or Power?

The Franco-German Relationship
and Europe's Strategic Choices,
1955–1995

STEPHEN A. KOCS

Westport, Connecticut
London

Library of Congress Cataloging-in-Publication Data

Kocs, Stephen A.
    Autonomy or power? : the Franco-German relationship and Europe's
strategic choices, 1955–1995 / Stephen A. Kocs.
       p.   cm.
    Includes bibliographical references and index.
    ISBN 0–275–94890–0 (alk. paper)
    1. France—Military relations—Germany (West) 2. Germany (West)—
Military relations—France. 3. France—Strategic aspects.
4. Germany (West)—Strategic aspects. 5. France—Politics and
government—20th century. 6. Germany—Politics and government—20th
century. I. Title.
UA700.K63 1995
355′.031′094409045—dc20   95–7989

British Library Cataloguing in Publication Data is available.

Library of Congress Catalog Card Number: 95–7989
ISBN: 0–275–94890–0

First published in 1995

Praeger Publishers, 88 Post Road West, Westport, CT 06881
An imprint of Greenwood Publishing Group, Inc.

Printed in the United States of America

The paper used in this book complies with the
Permanent Paper Standard issued by the National
Information Standards Organization (Z39.48–1984).

10 9 8 7 6 5 4 3 2 1

Contents

Preface

With the abrupt and almost universally unexpected collapse of Communism's empire at the end of the 1980s, European politics entered into a new era. The demise of Soviet power and the accompanying unification of Germany seemed to herald a great many possibilities, some of them pleasant to contemplate, others less so. One thing that did not change with the end of the Cold War, however, was the importance of the Franco-German relationship to Europe. As two nations which felt themselves to share a common destiny, France and Germany remained the key both to European integration and to Europe's strategic potential.

In navigating the intricacies of Franco-German defense relations, I have received help from many people. Stanley Hoffmann and Robert Putnam provided crucial advice on all aspects of the project: this book would not have been possible without their guidance and enthusiasm. I am also grateful to John Goodman, Robert Keohane, Ann Tickner, Andrew Moravcsik, and David Spiro for valuable comments on all or part of the manuscript at various stages of its preparation.

I would especially like to thank the government officials, military officers, and party and industry representatives in France, Germany, and elsewhere in Europe who allowed me to interview them for this project. I have drawn heavily on their firsthand insights into the Franco-German relationship. Because many of them are still in government service or have expressed a preference not to be acknowledged by name, I do not list them here individually. I would like them to know, however, that I deeply appreciate their willingness to share their knowledge and experiences.

Many persons contributed background information or suggestions on methodology and research design to this study. An incomplete list would include Peter Berger, Yves Boyer, André Brigot, Eliot Cohen, Dominique David, Jérôme Dumoulin, Richard Eichenberg, Karl Feldmayer, Gregory Flynn, Laurence Freedman, Alfred Grosser, Pierre Hassner, Jeffrey Herf, Jolyon Howorth, Jean Klein, Ingo Kolboom, Pierre Lellouche, Eckhard Lübkemeier, Simon May, Dominique Moïsi, Philippe Moreau-Defarges, Robert Picht, John Roper, Reinhardt Rummel, Peter Schmidt, Walter Schütze, Jane Stromseth, Michel Tatu, William Wallace, Mary Weed, Wolfgang Wessels, and Steve Woolcock. I am grateful for their assistance. I would also like to thank the Ford Foundation, the Krupp Foundation, the Friedrich Ebert Foundation, and the John D. and Catherine T. MacArthur Foundation for funding much of the research and writing of this book.

Unless otherwise noted, all translations from French or German are mine. An earlier version of Chapter 8 was presented at the annual meeting of the American Political Science Association, New York, September 1–4, 1994.

Abbreviations

ANS	*Anti-navire supersonique* (Supersonic Antiship Missile)
CDU	*Christlich-Demokratische Union* (Christian Democratic Union, Germany)
CGT	*Confédération Générale de Travail* (General Labor Confederation, France)
CSCE	Conference on Security and Cooperation in Europe
CSU	*Christlich-Soziale Union* (Christian Social Union, Bavaria)
EAP	Experimental Aircraft Program
EC	European Community
EDC	European Defense Community
EEC	European Economic Community
EFA	European Fighter Aircraft
EU	European Union
FAR	*Force d'action rapide* (Rapid Deployment Force)
FDP	*Freie Demokratische Partei* (Free Democratic Party, Germany)
HAC	*Hélicoptère anti-char* (Antitank Helicopter)
HAP	*Hélicoptère d'appui et de protection* (Support/Protection Helicopter)
IEPG	Independent European Program Group
INF	Intermediate Nuclear Forces
ISL	Institut de Saint-Louis
MBB	Messerschmidt-Bölkow-Blohm
MBFR	Mutual and Balanced Force Reductions

MLF	Multilateral Force
NACC	North Atlantic Cooperation Council
NATO	North Atlantic Treaty Organization
NPG	Nuclear Planning Group
PAH	*Panzerabwehrhubschrauber* (Antitank Helicopter)
SACEUR	Supreme Allied Commander in Europe
SALT	Strategic Arms Limitation Treaty
SAMRO	*Satellite militaire de reconnaissance optique* (Optical Military Reconnaissance Satellite)
SDI	Strategic Defense Initiative
SPD	*Sozialdemokratische Partei Deutschlands* (Social Democratic Party of Germany)
TADS/PNVS	Target Acquisition and Designation System/Pilot's Night Vision System
WEU	Western European Union

Autonomy or Power?

Introduction

This book is a history of the military-strategic partnership between France and the Federal Republic of Germany. It begins in 1955, the year West Germany became a member of NATO and an official ally of France, and it follows the evolution of Franco-German strategic relations up to the beginning of 1995. Like most works of history written by political scientists, its underlying intent is broader than the specific case study it investigates. The intent is to shed light on the factors that shape the choices of states when they are forced to decide among alternative strategic priorities. From 1955 to 1995, France and West Germany repeatedly confronted hard choices in deciding whether to define their national interests primarily in terms of military power, European peace, or strategic autonomy. The decisions they made provide important insights into the relationship between international system structure and states' strategic preferences. The history of the Franco-German partnership is also important for what it reveals about Europe's destiny as a strategic actor in the post-Cold War world. The evolution of French and German perceptions of national interest provides crucial evidence for anticipating France and Germany's future strategic choices.

What are Europe's options as a strategic actor in world politics? By "strategic actor" I mean an actor willing and able to take effective political or military action to defend its vital interests and advance its principal objectives. With the end of the U.S.-Soviet Cold War, Europe's strategic destiny once again became a matter of central importance for world politics. It seemed clear that the end of the East-West divide had brought with it a new freedom of strategic action for Western Europe's key states.

The withdrawal of Soviet troops from Eastern Europe, and the demise of the Soviet Union itself, reduced the dependence on American protection that had formerly constrained West European policy choices. For Germany especially, unification and the end of Soviet occupation in East Germany greatly expanded, at least in principle, the strategic options open to it. But what would Europe, and Germany, do with this new freedom of action?

ALTERNATIVE SCENARIOS AND SUPPORTING ARGUMENTS

In the first years after the Cold War's end, scholarly analyses of Europe's prospects as a strategic actor tended to cluster around three alternative scenarios. The first scenario foresaw the evolution of Western Europe into an integrated and strategically effective actor possessing a unified defense policy. A second scenario envisaged the reemergence of a highly nationalist Germany with hegemonic ambitions in Europe. The third scenario antici-pated an evolution in which the main West European states would con-tinue to disagree over defense strategy and would thus have limited weight as strategic actors.

In this book, I evaluate the theoretical and empirical basis for each of these scenarios. In doing so I focus primarily on the defense partnership between Germany and France, which lies at the heart of Europe's destiny. I conclude that prospects for the emergence of a unified European strategic power are dim, and that the likelihood of a hegemonic and militarily assertive Germany is negligible. Germany appears fated to play an impor-tant role in international politics, but not as a strategic power in the traditional sense of the term.

Scenario 1: United Europe

The concept of a self-assertive Western Europe, acting as a unified strategic power in the international system, is not new. Throughout much of the Cold War, in fact, French leaders promoted the idea of a Europe with its own strategic identity and a capacity for strategic action independent of the United States. Over and over during the Cold War, the French denounced what they called the "Yalta system" of a Europe divided into American and Soviet spheres of interest. The Yalta system, according to the French, forced the states of Europe into dependence on their super-power protectors and thereby deprived them of strategic autonomy and control over their own destinies. Although France was itself able to regain some freedom of action in the 1960s by quitting NATO's integrated command structure, it achieved this independence at the price of frequent isolation and ineffectiveness within the Western camp. To regain true strategic leverage, France needed other West European partners to join it in defining an autonomous European strategic perspective. Confronted with the Soviet threat, however, the other major West European states— Britain, West Germany, and Italy—all preferred to nurture their relationship with the United States rather than risk American ire by going along with France.

With the end of the Cold War, the idea of a unified European strategic entity became more plausible. The end (at least temporarily) of the Russian military threat meant that a European defense entity no longer needed to be a match for the Soviet Red Army to function effectively in Western Europe's strategic environment. There was also less risk that European efforts to define a common strategic perspective would alienate the United States. In the absence of a threat of Soviet invasion, Washington became more supportive of the concept of a European defense identity.

If it were to develop a unified strategic doctrine and integrate the military forces of its separate nations under a single command structure, Western Europe could be a major strategic actor in international politics. Combined, the twelve states of the European Union (EU) had an economic product of $7.0 trillion and a population of 351 million in 1993, compared to the U.S. economic product of $6.4 trillion and population of 260 million. With nearly two million active troops, the combined armed forces of the EU were larger than those of Russia. Even if France and Germany alone were to establish a common defense, their combined annual defense budget of $65 billion would be roughly comparable to Russia's.[1]

Traditionally, American political scientists have been skeptical regarding Europe's prospects for becoming a unified and strategically effective actor on the world stage. Indeed, the predominant view among American analysts during the 1970s and 1980s could be described as "Europessimism"—the belief that European integration had reached its limits and that the obstacles to further integration could probably not be overcome. The 1986 Single European Act and the 1992 Maastricht Treaty came as surprises to most U.S. observers.[2]

Even so, many international relations analysts viewed Europe's strategic fragmentation as the result of ingrained dependence on the United States rather than the product of inherent limits on European defense integration. Scholars as diverse as David Calleo, Hedley Bull, Henry Kissinger, and Melvyn Krauss all argued in the 1980s that Europe possessed the capacity for strategic autonomy from the United States and for military viability even against the Soviet Union. Given adequate prodding by Washington, they believed, Western Europe could shake free of its strategic dependency and take responsibility for its own defense.[3]

Certainly, the very durability of the European Community (EC) provided some grounds for optimism about Europe's long-term strategic integration. During the four decades from the founding of the EC to the mid-1990s, there was never any serious reversal in existing levels of integration. From time to time the process of integration stagnated, but none of the EC's member states ever withdrew from the Community or tried to dismantle it. Integration was a process that proceeded in fits and starts, but always went in one direction only: toward further integration. Proponents of European integration had always expected, moreover, that defense would be the last and most difficult area in which to achieve it. In that sense, the fact that military integration remained largely unaccomplished even as economic integration went forward was not proof that a common European defense was impossible, but rather a sign that the process of integration was proceeding in the rightful and necessary order.

Scenario 2: Germany as a Great Power

A second and very different school of thought suggested that Germany was likely to reemerge in future years as a nationalistic and militarily assertive international actor. This scenario anticipated the erosion of European integration and the return to balance-of-power strategies like those that had prevailed in Europe prior to 1914.

Those scholars who saw Europe returning to the rivalries and conflicts of a traditional balance-of-power system tended to base their analyses on so-called "neorealist" assumptions and arguments. The neorealist school, which is closely associated with the writings of Kenneth Waltz, interprets international politics primarily in terms of a never-ending struggle among states for power and security. Neorealists view the international realm as a self-help system that creates incentives for states to maximize their military capabilities relative to those of other states. Because international politics is anarchic—meaning that individual states decide for themselves how to defend their interests and when to use force against other states—each state must remain perpetually vigilant against the possibility that another state may try to harm or destroy it. According to neorealists, no state can rely on the benign intentions of others, since intentions can always change depending on circumstances. To protect their security, therefore, states seek to protect their relative capabilities in the international system and to prevent others from achieving relative gains. They also pursue a policy of "balancing" against dominant states in order to protect against the emergence of a hegemon able to deprive them of their independence.[4]

In a series of articles appearing in the journal *International Security*, several neorealist scholars, including Waltz, John Mearsheimer, and Christopher Layne, sought to apply the logic of the neorealist model to post–Cold War Europe.[5] All three scholars predicted that, in future years, Germany would build up its military capabilities and begin to behave like a traditional great power. The basis for this prediction had little to do with the specific characteristics of German politics or society; rather, it followed directly from the neorealist assumption that in an international system based on self-help, states must seek to maximize their relative capabilities. Unified Germany had the potential to become a great power: therefore, argued Layne, the principle of self-help would ultimately "impel" it to do so.[6] "For a country to choose not to become a great power," agreed Kenneth Waltz, would be "a structural anomaly."[7] Neorealists also viewed it as likely, verging on inevitable, that Germany would eventually develop a national nuclear weapons arsenal.[8] As a state with great-power potential, they argued, Germany would want nuclear weapons both for the security offered by nuclear deterrence and for the political status a national nuclear force would provide. Neorealists also argued that as it moved toward great-power status, Germany would distance itself from the United States and pursue its own strategic agenda around the world. The Atlantic Alliance, in the neorealist analysis, had no long-run future. "Once the new Germany finds its feet," wrote Waltz, "it will no more want to be constrained by the United States acting through NATO than by any other state." Instead, neorealist logic led to the prediction that Germany, Russia, and Japan would gravitate together and act as a counterbalance to U.S. power.[9]

As the security arrangements of Cold War Europe began to break apart, neorealists emphasized, the possibility of a major European war involving Germany would reemerge. Mearsheimer, for example, considered it plausible that Germany would embark on territorial expansionism against the weaker states on its eastern boundary.[10] Layne, meanwhile, deemed it "likely" that Germany and the United States would eventually find themselves at war with each other again.[11] In short, neorealists anticipated a European future with strong echoes of the past—a continent riven by distrust and rivalry, anxious about German hegemonic ambitions, and faced with growing hostility between Germany and America.

Scenario 3: Europe as a Non-Strategic Actor

A third scenario envisaged European evolution along a path in which neither Europe as a united entity, nor Germany by itself, would emerge as a major strategic actor in world politics. According to this scenario, Germany would continue to limit its own strategic choices in a way that broadly foreclosed military options in asserting its national interests. As a result, Europe as a whole would remain an important actor in world politics, but not an independent strategic actor as the term is normally understood.

During the Cold War, West Germany's strategic policy was essentially identical with that of NATO. The Federal Republic had rearmed in the first place under agreements that subordinated its armed forces to NATO operational command. Successive German governments approved of this approach, which limited German forces to military actions undertaken within the NATO framework. In sharp contrast to the United States, Britain, and France, Germany did not employ its forces in independent national military actions. The basic rationale for this approach lay in the legacy of Hitler's aggression. German leaders and the German public perceived a special moral responsibility, imposed by history, not to repeat Hitler's use of armed violence in the service of purely national objectives. Such a policy reflected practical as well as moral considerations. German leaders understood that if Germany were to begin using its armed forces for national ends, outside the NATO framework, the result would be Germany's political isolation—precisely the outcome German leaders felt they must avoid at all costs. Given Germany's exposed position in the East-West conflict, they felt little temptation toward a nationalistic foreign policy.

With the end of the Cold War and the achievement of unification, Germany gained latitude to pursue a more nationally-oriented strategic policy. In the same way that other Western states sometimes used force to achieve what they regarded as important national objectives, Germany could (if it chose to do so) begin to include the unilateral resort to force as an option in asserting its national interests.

But what if Germany chose not to do so? Hanns Maull, in an important article in *Foreign Affairs*, argued that Germany in future years would remain what he called a "civilian power," that is, a state relying largely on cooperation and dialogue, non-military instruments of persuasion, and supranational structures to achieve its international objectives.[12] A civilian power, according to Maull, differs from a traditional great power in that it does not define its security in terms that depend on the threat or use of force to assert its strategic interests. Instead, a civilian power conceives its security in terms of preserving the collaborative relationships that allow it to interact with its external environment in self-benefiting ways. Because the resort to military force is normally irrelevant to the construction and maintenance of collaborative ties with other states, a civilian power places far less emphasis than a traditional great power on building up its military capabilities.

Although Germany originally was forced to adopt a civilian power strategy because of its situation as a defeated nation, Maull contended that there was little reason to think Germany would jettison this strategy in the post–Cold War order. On the contrary, he argued, the "civilian power" approach was better suited to the post–Cold War world than traditional great-power strategies which revolved around balance-of-power calculations and the pursuit of military strength. In a world where sustaining economic prosperity was the central problem confronting governments, and where free trade and transnational factor inputs increasingly defined the economic realm, a civilian power like Germany was the prototypical state of the future. The most likely scenario, in Maull's view, was thus not that a unified Germany would seek to become a superpower like the United States, but that the United States would in the future evolve to become a civilian power like Germany or Japan. "Neither Japan nor Germany," wrote Maull, "is about to become a new superpower, for this role no longer exists in the old sense."[13]

THEORETICAL ISSUES

These three scenarios are highly divergent. Their very incompatibility raises an interesting issue: how is it that political analysts could examine the same question—Europe's future—and arrive at such seemingly irreconcilable predictions? In fact, each scenario rested on a different set of theoretical assumptions about the nature of international politics. Predictions about where Europe was likely to go depended on which set of underlying assumptions a theorist preferred.

Scenarios 1 and 2 were actually quite similar in that they shared many of the underlying assumptions of classical realism. Both scenarios analyzed the international realm in essentially competitive, zero-sum terms and expected actors in world politics to employ strategies of power maximization and balancing to advance their interests. The key difference between the two schools was that the proponents of Scenario 1—European unity— saw national interests as transferable under certain circumstances to an entity other than the existing state, whereas neorealists tended to assume that national interests were non-transferable. Those who saw Europe as a potential military superpower began from the premise that Europe's individual states could pool their national identities to create a collective entity that would pursue the strategic interests of Europe as a whole. The creation of such an entity would permit Europe to assert its collective interests more effectively vis-à-vis the United States and Russia than a Europe that remained divided into smaller countries.

Neorealists, on the other hand, did not seem to consider it possible for Western Europe's states to redefine their identities so as to permit the pooling of national interests. Neorealism takes national identity as a given rather than a variable, and assumes that states will give their highest priority to preserving the security of the national "self" as it already exists. In cases where an existing state is too small to assert its interests effectively against larger states, neorealists generally expect it to strengthen its position through alliances (which are reversible if conditions change) or through territorial conquest (which enables it to strengthen itself without having to redefine its identity in the process). Neorealist theory simply does not make provision for the sort of supranational integration in which states would permanently yield control over national strategic policy to a supranational entity. Under neorealist assumptions, accepting such integration would mean sacrificing precisely that which national strategy exists to preserve. In the neorealist view, supranational integration can be acceptable to a state only if it is able to control the resulting supranational entity—which would, in turn, make it inherently unacceptable to the other states involved.

History, however, offers repeated examples of independent states coalescing together to preserve strategic viability vis-à-vis their international environment. The unification of the Thirteen Colonies following the American war of independence is one example; the unifications of Italy and Germany in the mid-nineteenth century are two more. Unfortunately, no existing theory of international politics adequately specifies the circumstances under which supranational integration of this sort is likely to take place. Neorealism is essentially useless in addressing this question, because it begins from assumptions that do not recognize supranational integration as a rational option for states.

Scenario 3, meanwhile, began from assumptions which rejected the realist view that the quest for security is necessarily a zero-sum game. In contrast to Scenarios 1 and 2, Scenario 3 allowed for the possibility that European states might define security in *collaborative* rather than competitive terms. As long as the leaders of any given European country remained confident that disputes with the principal states in their strategic environment could be dealt with peacefully, they might perceive no national interest in building up their own state's strategic capabilities. Instead, they might perceive the best route to security as one that involved steps such as disarmament and confidence-building measures to reinforce mutual reliance on collaborative security.

In essence, predictions about Europe's strategic destiny differed because of differences in analysts' underlying assumptions about states' strategic priorities. Those who anticipated the eventual emergence of a united and strategically effective Europe assumed that European states would put *power* above all other considerations, and would be willing to redefine their national identities in order to remain strategically effective vis-à-vis the world's other major strategic actors. Neorealists, by contrast, took states' existing identities as a given and therefore expected states in post–Cold War Europe (including Germany) to put their highest priority on maintaining strategic *independence* for themselves within the framework of their existing national identity. Finally, those who expected Germany to continue behaving as a civilian power considered it likely that states under certain circumstances would choose *peace* as their highest priority even though doing so might involve a considerable sacrifice of national power and strategic independence.

The differences between the neorealist and civilian power scenarios reflected a larger theoretical disagreement in the international relations field regarding the essential nature of international structure. Neorealists portray international politics as a Hobbesian struggle that compels states to maximize their relative capabilities in the system. In the neorealist view it would be irrational for a potential great power to pursue a civilian strategy, because great-power capability is one of the best available protections against the international dangers that surround states at all times. In other words, potential great powers can't really choose *not* to become great powers.[14] Neorealists explicitly dismissed the idea that Germany might be content to retain for the indefinite future the civilian power strategy it pursued during the Cold War. When analysts of German politics pointed out that Germany, even several years after unification, still showed no sign of seeking nuclear weapons or asserting a nationalistic military posture, neorealists responded that Germany was nonetheless likely to take such steps eventually, because the nature of international politics created strong incentives for it to do so.[15]

From a broader empirical standpoint, however, the neorealist model seems open to doubt. To begin with, it is not accurate to describe international politics as a Hobbesian state of nature in which all states must constantly fear harm or destruction at the hands of other states. Rather, international politics is a law-based realm in which most states restrain their behavior most of the time in accordance with international legal norms.[16] Because international norms generally protect states against conquest and military aggression by other states, states do not ordinarily need to base their strategic policies on the assumption that other states may at any time seek to conquer or destroy them.[17] Instead, each state can tailor its security strategy to match the demands of its strategic environment. A state bordered by a powerful renegade regime that shows little respect for international law may indeed have strong incentives to improve its relative military capabilities. A state whose strategic environment consists of law-abiding states, on the other hand, encounters little structural pressure to maximize its military potential.[18] Most states in the contemporary world therefore have much greater latitude in defining their strategic policy than the neorealist model suggests.[19]

This is particularly the case for liberal democratic states surrounded by other liberal democracies. Democracies are especially trustworthy as international neighbors because in general they are more committed to respect international legal constraints than non-democratic states; moreover, democracies have a clear historical record of not initiating or waging war against other democracies.[20] As the Cold War faded from the international scene, many scholars called attention to the "zone of peace" that had emerged among the liberal states of North America and Western Europe.[21] States in the zone of peace (including Germany) enjoyed considerable freedom to downplay the military dimension of their strategic behavior if they so chose, because with the disappearance of the Soviet invasion threat they faced few if any immediate dangers to their national territorial integrity. The security threats such states confronted were more likely to be indirect ones such as Iraq's attack on Kuwait, where collective Western action might well offer a credible substitute for traditional military self-help.

Because West European states *did* have a great deal of latitude in devising their strategic policies after the Cold War, attempts to deduce their future strategic choices from theoretical assumptions alone were of doubtful validity. From a purely theoretical standpoint, Germany in particular possessed a broad range of plausible strategic alternatives. Germany could choose to anchor Europe's emergence as a unified strategic power, or it could take the path of military nationalism, or it could decide to downgrade the military aspects of national strategy altogether. Contrary to neorealist assertions, international structure did *not* impose on Germany the path of military nationalism. Rather, the future strategic choices of all the major states in Western Europe depended on whether those states placed their highest priority on power, on peace, or on strategic independence. International structure did not, by itself, provide much insight into the future strategic policies of Germany or any other West European state.

FRANCO-GERMAN DEFENSE RELATIONS AND EUROPE'S FUTURE

On what basis, then, can predictions be made about Europe's future as a strategic actor? In my view, the best source of insight about the future strategic choices of France and Germany is the history of their *past* choices. From the 1950s to the 1990s, these states were repeatedly forced to decide among alternative strategic values. The pattern of those choices, as well as the evolution of their strategic priorities as the Cold War era progressed, provide important information regarding the underlying preferences and tendencies that will shape French and German strategic choices in future decades.

Throughout the Cold War, the key to Europe's destiny as a strategic force in world politics could be found in the defense and security relationship between France and the Federal Republic of Germany. The same is likely to be true in the future. Partnership between France and Germany has formed the essential basis for virtually every successful step in the construction of the European Union. When France and Germany have worked together to create or strengthen European institutions—whether in economic, monetary, foreign, or defense policy—their initiatives have usually succeeded. By contrast, European initiatives favored by one but opposed by the other have nearly always failed.[22]

There are several factors which make the Franco-German relationship pivotal to Western Europe's strategic options. Geographically, France and Germany are at the heart of Western Europe. Together, the two countries account for two-fifths of the EU's population and nearly half its economic product and defense spending. Individually, France and Germany each represent a considerable fraction of Europe's military, economic, technological, and cultural assets. It is difficult, even impossible, to imagine the emergence of a self-reliant European defense system without the active participation of both countries. The importance of the Franco-German relationship to Europe's destiny has been heightened by Great Britain's lingering aloofness from the Continent. From its initial reluctance to join the Common Market in the 1950s to its reservations about European monetary union in the 1990s, Britain has tended to act as a brake rather than an engine in the construction of a unified Europe.

Many analysts have recognized the importance of Franco-German defense relations to Europe's strategic destiny, and an extensive literature exists on the subject.[23] This study differs from other accounts in that it aims at a higher degree of comprehensiveness. It attempts to survey all aspects of the Franco-German defense relationship—including the diplomatic, strategic, military, weapons collaboration, and arms control dimensions— and to show the interrelationships among them. Also, it reviews the entire historical span of the Franco-German defense partnership rather than focusing on a "snapshot" view of Franco-German relations at a particular time. The advantage of this approach is that it permits one to observe changes in French and German strategic perspectives as a function of evolution in the international political context. Given the importance of Franco-German defense relations to Europe's strategic options, to understand the dynamics of the Franco-German partnership is to understand a great deal about where Germany, and Europe as a whole, are headed.

NOTES

1. These figures are drawn from *The Military Balance 1994–1995* (London: published by Brassey's for the International Institute for Strategic Studies, 1994), pp. 22, 40–72, 93, 111.

2. See Dale L. Smith and James Lee Ray, "European Integration: Gloomy Theory versus Rosy Reality," in Dale L. Smith and James Lee Ray, eds., *The 1992 Project and the Future of Integration in Europe* (Armonk, N.Y.: M. E. Sharpe, 1993), pp. 19–44.

3. See David P. Calleo, *Beyond American Hegemony* (New York: Basic Books, 1987); Henry Kissinger, "A Plan to Reshape NATO," *Time*, March 5, 1984, pp. 20–24; Hedley Bull, "Civilian Power Europe: A Contradiction in Terms?" *Journal of Common Market Studies*, September/December 1982, pp. 149–64; and Melvyn Krauss, *How NATO Weakens the West* (New York: Simon and Schuster, 1986).

4. The principal source for these neorealist arguments is Kenneth N. Waltz, *Theory of International Politics* (New York: Random House, 1979). Other neorealist works which usefully restate Waltz's analysis include Joseph M. Grieco, *Cooperation among Nations* (Ithaca: Cornell University Press, 1990), and Fareed Zakaria, "Realism and Domestic Politics," *International Security*, Summer 1992, pp. 177–98.

5. See Kenneth N. Waltz, "The Emerging Structure of International Politics," *International Security*, Fall 1993, pp. 44–79; John J. Mearsheimer, "Back to the Future: Instability in Europe after the Cold War," *International Security*,

Summer 1990, pp. 5–56; and Christopher Layne, "The Unipolar Illusion: Why New Great Powers Will Arise," *International Security*, Spring 1993, pp. 5–51.

6. Layne, "The Unipolar Illusion," p. 47; also note pp. 9–11.

7. Waltz, "Emerging Structure," p. 66.

8. Waltz, "Emerging Structure," pp. 64–67; Layne, "The Unipolar Illusion," p. 37; Mearsheimer, "Back to the Future," pp. 36–39.

9. Waltz, "Emerging Structure," pp. 75–76.

10. Mearsheimer, "Back to the Future," pp. 32–33.

11. Layne, "The Unipolar Illusion," p. 42.

12. Hanns W. Maull, "Germany and Japan: The New Civilian Powers," *Foreign Affairs*, Winter 1990/91, pp. 91–106.

13. Maull, "Germany and Japan," p. 92.

14. See Layne, "The Unipolar Illusion," p. 11.

15. See, for example, the exchange between Elizabeth Pond and Kenneth Waltz in *International Security*, Summer 1994, pp. 195–99.

16. See Christopher G. Joyner, "The Reality and Relevance of International Law," in Charles W. Kegley, Jr. and Eugene R. Wittkopf, eds., *The Global Agenda: Issues and Perspectives* (New York: McGraw-Hill, 1992), pp. 202–15; Ian Brownlie, "The Reality and Efficacy of International Law," in *The British Year Book of International Law 1981* (Oxford: Clarendon, 1982), pp. 1–8; and Thomas M. Franck, *The Power of Legitimacy among Nations* (New York: Oxford University Press, 1990).

17. On this point see David Strang, "Anomaly and Commonplace in European Political Expansion: Realist and Institutional Accounts," *International Organization*, Spring 1991, pp. 143–62, and Robert H. Jackson, *Quasi-states: Sovereignty, International Relations, and the Third World* (Cambridge: Cambridge University Press, 1990).

18. For an extended discussion of this point, see Stephen A. Kocs, "Explaining the Strategic Behavior of States: International Law as System Structure," *International Studies Quarterly*, December 1994, pp. 535–56.

19. Indeed, as Paul Schroeder points out in an important article, even states confronting immediate threats to their security and independence have many strategic options other than power maximization and balancing. Schroeder notes that the neorealist model seems unable to account for the variety of states' actual strategic behavior throughout history, and concludes that neorealist theory offers a fundamentally false portrayal of international political dynamics. Paul Schroeder, "Historical Reality vs. Neo-realist Theory," *International Security*, Summer 1994, pp. 108–48.

20. For a survey of the extensive empirical literature on this point, see Bruce Russett, *Grasping the Democratic Peace* (Princeton: Princeton University Press, 1993).

21. Francis Fukuyama, *The End of History and the Last Man* (New York: Free Press, 1992); Carl Kaysen, "Is War Obsolete? A Review Essay," *International*

Security, Spring 1990, pp. 42–64; John Mueller, *Retreat from Doomsday: The Obsolescence of Major War* (New York: Basic Books, 1989); James Lee Ray, "The Abolition of Slavery and the End of International War," *International Organization*, Summer 1989, pp. 405–39; and Max Singer and Aaron Wildavsky, *The Real World Order* (Chatham, N.J.: Chatham House, 1993).

22. On this point see, for example, Haig Simonian, *The Privileged Partnership: Franco-German Relations in the European Community, 1969–1984* (Oxford: Clarendon, 1985); also Karl Kaiser and Pierre Lellouche, eds., *Deutsch-französische Sicherheitspolitik: Auf dem Wege zur Gemeinsamkeit?* (Bonn: Europa Union Verlag, 1986).

23. See, for example, David G. Haglund, *Alliance within the Alliance? Franco-German Military Cooperation and the European Pillar of Defense* (Boulder, Colo: Westview, 1991); Urs Leimbacher, *Die unverzichtbare Allianz: Deutsch-französische sicherheitspolitische Zusammenarbeit 1982–1989* (Baden-Baden: Nomos, 1992); Robbin F. Laird, ed., *Strangers and Friends: The Franco-German Security Relationship* (New York: St. Martin's Press, 1989); David S. Yost, "Franco-German Defense Cooperation," *Washington Quarterly*, Spring 1988, pp. 173–95; Philip Gordon, "The Franco-German Security Partnership," in Patrick McCarthy, ed., *France-Germany, 1983–1993: The Struggle to Cooperate* (London: Macmillan, 1993), pp. 139–60; and Kaiser and Lellouche, *Deutsch-französische Sicherheitspolitik*.

CHAPTER 1 ————————————————

Prelude to Cooperation, 1955–1962

The early years of the postwar era found French and German leaders confronting immediate and urgent problems rather than plotting grand strategies for the return of their nations to great-power status. In the case of the French Fourth Republic, the national government found its decision-making powers limited by weak institutions and decentralized political authority.[1] Foreign policy consisted almost entirely of trying to fend off the crises that thrust themselves upon France. These included the anticolonial insurgencies emerging in Indochina and Algeria as well as the extremely unwelcome U.S. proposal in September 1950 to rearm Germany and include the Germans in the North Atlantic Alliance.

West Germany had come into existence in 1949, the same year in which NATO was formed. The new West German state was created by fusing together the occupation zones controlled by the United States, Britain, and France. The creation of West Germany came about only after lengthy resistance on the part of the French, who had instead favored dismembering Germany and instituting quasi-permanent occupation controls. The intensification of the Cold War in 1948, however, and the deepening division of Europe into two armed camps, left France isolated in its determination to limit Germany's recovery. The French were heavily dependent on American military and economic assistance, and Washington had decided to insist on German rearmament. Including West Germany in the Alliance defense perimeter was vital, the Truman administration believed, to prevent it from falling into Soviet hands through Communist aggression or internal defeatism. As beneficiaries of allied defense, moreover, the Germans should contribute troops to NATO. Doing so would serve the double function of helping reduce the West's disadvantage in the East-West troop balance and of anchoring the Federal Republic to the side of the Western democracies.

The rearmament question was tremendously important to West German leaders because it greatly enhanced their political leverage vis-à-vis the occupation powers. Since Washington increasingly regarded German rearmament as indispensable for the containment of Soviet power in Europe, the promise of German troops was a potent bargaining chip for Konrad Adenauer, West Germany's first federal chancellor. Adenauer's immediate foreign policy priorities encompassed three interlocking goals: first, to bind West Germany irrevocably to the Western democracies through the progressive unification of Western Europe; second, to regain equality of rights (Gleichberechtigung) for Germany among Western nations; and third, to obtain a guarantee from the United States, Britain, and France for the security of West German territory.[2] Germany's prospective contribution to Western military defense was the key to each of these goals.

Because French political leaders found German rearmament a horrifying prospect, the government of René Pleven countered the American proposal with its famous suggestion for a fully integrated European army, which came to be referred to as the European Defense Community (EDC).[3] The basic rationale for the EDC was to incorporate German troops into Western Europe's defense while preventing the West German state from possessing an independent national army or national defense policy, or from exerting significant influence in Alliance decision-making bodies. The EDC proposal, impractical for a variety of reasons and never translated into a genuinely feasible program, nevertheless became the basis for European negotiations on German rearmament. The governments of Germany, France, Italy, and the Benelux states spent an extraordinary amount of effort on the proposal in the period 1951–1954, first in negotiating the EDC treaty and then in considering amendments to the treaty which successive French governments demanded. The French were not only dissatisfied with the safeguards against the reemergence of German military power, but became increasingly uneasy about the threat the EDC posed to France's own national independence and to the traditions and identity of France's national armed forces. Finally, in August 1954 the French National Assembly rejected the European army altogether. Soon afterward, the United States revived its earlier proposal that Germany be rearmed and given full membership in Alliance defense organizations. This time the French gave way.

A series of agreements in October 1954 established the framework for German rearmament. The Western allies agreed to end the occupation regime and to admit West Germany to full membership in NATO. Germany would also become a member of the Brussels Treaty Organization, a mutual defense pact established in 1948 by Britain, France, and the Benelux countries. However, termination of the occupation regime in West Germany did not affect the rights of the three Western occupation powers in Berlin, nor did it alter their legal authority in any question involving Germany as a whole, such as reunification or a general peace settlement.[4]

West Germany, for its part, declared that it would "refrain from any action inconsistent with the strictly defensive character" of the North Atlantic and Brussels Treaties, and undertook never to "have recourse to force to achieve the reunification of Germany or the modification of [its] present boundaries."[5] In addition, Adenauer offered a voluntary pledge that the Federal Republic would renounce the production on German territory of atomic, biological, or chemical weapons. Germany would also renounce the production of certain types of heavy weapons including long-range missiles, strategic bombers, and large warships. Further, the German government would accept inspections by a standing authority within the Brussels Treaty Organization to verify that the prohibitions were observed.[6] On May 5, 1955, West Germany gained formal membership in NATO and the restructured Brussels Treaty Organization (which was renamed the Western European Union, or WEU). Simultaneously, the American, British, and French governments revoked the Occupation Statute and declared the Federal Republic of Germany to be a sovereign state with full authority over its domestic and foreign policies.

The new arrangements represented a major improvement in Germany's status, but in several respects West Germany remained politically and militarily disadvantaged within the Alliance. For one thing, all of West Germany's armed forces were to be assigned to NATO's Central Europe Command, which was headed by a French general. Germany, in contrast to its major allied partners, would have no national general staff for its armed forces. Operational planning for the deployment and use of the Bundeswehr would take place within NATO, not at the national level. Also, alone among NATO members, Germany was bound by the October 1954 agreements to accept foreign troops on its soil "of the same nationality and effective strength" as when the agreements took effect.[7] Although Bonn actively desired the presence of forces from other NATO countries on West German territory as an assurance for its security, the troop stationing provision represented in some sense a continuation of the postwar occupation.

FRENCH DISENCHANTMENT WITH NATO

Tenacious French opposition had delayed the rearmament of West Germany for nearly five years. Once rearmament began to take place, however, Paris seemed to reconcile itself quickly to the idea. In fact, by 1956 the French government was already beginning to consider ways in which it could turn bilateral cooperation with a rearming Germany to its own advantage. The impetus for cooperation arose from France's growing dissatisfaction with NATO. It is one of the ironies of Franco-German relations that West Germany achieved its long-awaited admission to NATO at virtually the same time that France began to pull away from the organization.

A number of factors contributed to France's accumulating discontent in the Alliance during the Fourth Republic's final years.[8] Two major French complaints were that the United States dominated Alliance policymaking and military planning, and that the United States gave favored treatment to Britain while discriminating against France (particularly in the sharing of nuclear technology). The French were also unhappy over the lack of American or Alliance support for France during its successive colonial wars in Indochina and Algeria. What good was NATO, the French asked bitterly, if it did nothing to protect France's vital interests outside Europe? A major catalyst for French dissatisfaction with the Alliance was the 1956 Suez crisis, which brutally exposed France's limited foreign policy independence vis-à-vis Washington.

French leaders became determined to find means of increasing France's leverage in international politics. One way to do so, a growing number believed, was through the possession of nuclear weapons. In the months after Suez, support for the development of a national nuclear force began to coalesce among French policy elites.[9] While much of this support came from those who viewed nuclear weapons in terms of national prestige and diplomatic influence, others favored the nuclear program on military or industrial grounds. Within the French military, an influential group of officers led by General Charles Ailleret had begun to press for acquisition of nuclear weapons to enhance the firepower and battlefield effectiveness of French armed forces in Europe. Some scientists and government officials, meanwhile, favored a nuclear weapons program for the contribution they believed it would make toward France's industrial strength and technological advancement.

The enormous budgetary burden caused by the expanding war in Algeria, however, created increasing financial difficulties for the French nuclear weapons program. To reduce the financial strain involved in developing nuclear weapons, Fourth Republic governments repeatedly sought technical information from the United States and Britain. But whereas the United States had provided substantial aid to the British nuclear weapons program, both Washington and London rebuffed the French requests for assistance. Paris reacted to this treatment with outrage, interpreting Washington's refusal to share nuclear information, together with U.S. actions designed to thwart French interests in North Africa, as part of an "Anglo-Saxon" conspiracy aimed at monopolizing nuclear weapons in the Western Alliance and reducing France to second-class status.[10]

It was against this backdrop of frustration and anxiety that Paris began in 1957 to look for a "Continental" response to the perceived threat of technological and political domination by the "Anglo-Saxons." The French initiative took the form of a proposal to coordinate armaments production and advanced weapons research among France, West Germany, and Italy. As the initiative took shape during 1957 and early 1958, two separate components emerged—one publicly acknowledged, the other secret. The public component, announced in January 1958, involved efforts to create a Franco-Italo-German "armaments triangle" for the joint development and production of conventional weapons such as tanks, fighter airplanes, and short-range missiles (see Chapter 3).

A second, highly secret component of the French initiative related to cooperation with Germany and Italy on the production of nuclear warheads and long-range missiles. In January 1957, German Defense Minister Franz Josef Strauss and a high-level delegation of German military officers went to Paris for lengthy discussions with French Defense Minister Maurice Bourgès-Maunoury. The talks, which were followed by a tour of the French missile-testing installations at Colomb-Béchar in the Sahara, led to a series of secret agreements concerning the development and production of "modern weapons" by France and Germany.[11] France followed up the Colomb-Béchar accords with proposals to Germany and Italy for studies on the possible joint construction of "modern, sophisticated arms, including the nuclear sector."[12] In a conversation with Konrad Adenauer in November 1957, Maurice Faure, then a high official in the French Foreign Ministry, suggested total integration of funding among West European countries for weapons research.[13] By implication, the French nuclear development program would be able to draw on funds supplied by the German government.

The French government's proposals reflected its dual objective of alleviating its uncomfortable dependence on the United States while not sacrificing the political advantages it continued to hold over Germany. The proposed nuclear cooperation was to take a form such that none of the three participants would hold a monopoly on the conception or construction of nuclear weapons, but that the contribution of each would be indispensable.[14] Prime Minister Gaillard provided an insight into French intentions when he stated in an interview that Germany might "contribute scientific cooperation or certain manufactures not in themselves nuclear but which enter into the construction of atomic missiles."[15] It appears that the French government hoped to induce Germany and Italy to share the costs and technical problems faced by the French nuclear program, but in a way that would prevent Germany from developing its own independent nuclear capability. Franco-German nuclear collaboration held evident risks for France: for one thing, it might whet the German appetite for a national nuclear force; for another, it might provoke a hostile Soviet reaction. Proponents of the initiative were apparently convinced, however, that France needed German assistance—especially financial assistance—for its nuclear program to succeed.[16]

A secret "protocol of agreement" on the French proposals was signed in November 1957 by France, Germany, and Italy.[17] The possibilities for cooperation in both conventional and nuclear armaments were further explored at meetings of the three defense ministers in January and April 1958, and at several bilateral meetings between Strauss and French Defense Minister Jacques Chaban-Delmas during the same period.[18] It is not clear what Germany was supposed to obtain in return for its financial and technical contribution to the French nuclear effort. According to one account, Germany was to receive French-produced nuclear warheads, which would be stored in peacetime on French soil under German ownership and supervision.[19]

As events would have it, however, the accords were never implemented. In France, opposition within Gaillard's cabinet to the idea of nuclear weapons cooperation with Germany blocked moves to put the accords into effect.[20] At the same time, the Algerian crisis which would soon destroy the Fourth Republic increasingly dominated the government's attention. In Germany, the political leadership was wary of committing itself too deeply on nuclear weapons cooperation until it had a clearer idea what the American reaction would be. Strauss, for his part, seems to have regarded cooperation with France as a useful option to keep open, but considered nuclear control-sharing arrangements with the United States to be a more direct and effective route to nuclear codetermination for Germany.[21] In both France and Germany, moreover, the nuclear agreements had the potential to provoke violent public reactions, making it necessary to proceed with caution. The hesitations in Paris and Bonn about implementing the nuclear accords were resolved by de Gaulle's return to power on June 1, 1958. On being briefed about the Franco-Italo-German arms production plans, de Gaulle assigned his Armies Minister, Pierre Guillaumat, to inform the German and Italian governments that the parts of the agreements dealing with nuclear weapons collaboration were no longer valid.[22]

Taken as a whole, the last years of the Fourth Republic were a period of ambiguity and ambivalence in Franco-German defense relations. Preoccupied with its remaining imperial commitments and increasingly dissatisfied with its place in the Atlantic Alliance, France in 1955–1958 was beginning to grope toward a policy that would regain for it a more powerful and independent place on the world stage. Short-lived governments, organizational disarray, and a certain lack of self-confidence were obstacles to such a policy, however, and led Paris to begin looking toward Germany as a technological and financial prop for French aspirations. Certainly the French did not want to give up the various political advantages they enjoyed over Germany; even so, in their dismay at existing circumstances they apparently were willing to contemplate something as risky and ambitious as cooperation with Bonn in the development of nuclear weapons.

West Germany, for its part, was acutely conscious throughout the 1950s that its political rehabilitation and military security depended entirely on continuing American aid and goodwill. Some German leaders, above all Strauss, were aware of the severe limitations on West Germany's autonomy implicit in its status as an American client state. These leaders were sympathetic to European-level cooperation, including military cooperation, that could in some way counterbalance U.S. domination of Germany's foreign policy environment and function as a surrogate for a nationalistic German foreign policy. At no point, however, did Adenauer appear willing to jeopardize Germany's relationship with the United States in the pursuit of relations with the Fourth Republic.

The situation inherited by de Gaulle in 1958 was thus one in which France and West Germany had only begun, with caution and hesitation, to explore the possibilities for increased international influence offered by their bilateral relationship. This was soon to change, as de Gaulle raised the Franco-German relationship to one of the cornerstones of his sweeping plan to restore French national grandeur.

CLASHING VISIONS OF INTERNATIONAL ORDER

De Gaulle's return to power in June 1958 was destined to have profound consequences for the Franco-German relationship. Even more important than the substantive policy differences between de Gaulle and the governments of the Fourth Republic, perhaps, was the change in French diplomatic style ushered in by the institutions of the Fifth Republic under de Gaulle's leadership. De Gaulle's ability to mold French foreign policy to his own long-term aims for France created both opportunities and risks for Bonn in its relations with Paris. To the extent that de Gaulle's ultimate goals coincided with those of Adenauer, the new clarity of purpose in Paris would be to West Germany's advantage. To the extent that they did not, Germany would be seriously hampered in its foreign policy objectives.

De Gaulle was deeply dissatisfied with France's place in the postwar world, and his tenure as French president from 1958 to 1969 can be viewed as an unceasing effort to win back influence and weight for France in international politics. For de Gaulle, the most threatening aspect of the postwar order was the division of Europe into rival blocs under the domination of the two superpowers. The Cold War polarization of Europe, by forcing medium-sized countries like France into close alignment with their giant ally, deprived them of a foreign policy of their own and hence undermined their domestic authority and legitimacy. If the superpower quarrel grew too intense, the smaller countries risked being drawn into a deadly conflict against their will. No less dangerous was the possibility of superpower collusion, which would most likely take the form of a Soviet-American condominium achieved by sacrificing the interests of lesser states.[23]

De Gaulle's short-term solution for the dangers of the bloc system was his famous proposal for an American-British-French "directorate" to coordinate the military strategy of the Western Powers around the world. If France must accept the United States as its protector for the time being, at least it could try to limit the risks of such an arrangement by joint planning that would constrain American freedom of action. Meanwhile, France could take steps to decrease its dependence on American security guarantees, above all by acquiring its own nuclear deterrent.

In the longer term, de Gaulle believed, peace could be secured only by defusing the ideological antagonisms underlying the "Yalta system" and replacing the superpower blocs with looser coalitions. In the restructured system, each state would have substantial autonomy to define its own security network. A stabilized European order would also have to include the Soviet Union, on the basis of a reasoned recognition of Soviet interests within Europe. Unlike the American presence in Europe, which (viewed in historical perspective) was probably only temporary, the Russian presence was permanent. As an integral part of Europe's geography, Russia could not simply be locked away on the other side of the Western palisade and excluded forever from the company of civilized peoples. Ultimately one had to seek a modus vivendi embracing all of Europe "from the Atlantic to the Urals," in one of de Gaulle's favorite phrases.

Adenauer's strategy for European peace took the opposite tack from de Gaulle in nearly every respect. Germany, unlike France, could not demand participation in a global "directorate." Any hint of global ambitions would rekindle suspicion and resistance on the part of Germany's enemies and friends alike, as well as from large segments of German public opinion. German nationalism, discredited by the verdict of two world wars, could not provide the basis for German influence in the world at large. For the sake of peace, the German nation must pursue its goals from within integrated organizations such as NATO and the Common Market. Only in this way, believed Adenauer, was it possible to insure that German energies were channeled constructively. Also, it was only in the context of integrated organizations that Germany could hope to exert political influence commensurate with its economic and military capabilities.[24]

Since Germany had no international influence except through its part in Atlantic and European institutions, it followed that these institutions must be kept as strong and cohesive as possible. Divisions in the Western camp must be counteracted, because they offered the Soviet Union opportunities to accomplish its prime objective of isolating West Germany. The only route to durable peace, Adenauer believed, lay in solidifying Western strength and unity until the Soviet leaders gave up their dreams of European conquest and accepted German reunification on the basis of sovereignty and self-determination. Simply accepting the European status quo could not provide a foundation for peace because it would leave Berlin and East Germany as hostages in Soviet hands, condemning Germany's Eastern inhabitants to permanent Soviet overlordship and the Federal Republic to permanent insecurity. Thus where de Gaulle was prepared to recognize legitimate Soviet security needs in Europe, Adenauer believed in consolidating Western strength until the Soviets redefined their security needs more modestly. Where de Gaulle favored "loosening up" NATO as a first move toward overcoming Europe's division into blocs, Adenauer insisted on the need for Western solidarity.

The stage was accordingly set for a long tug-of-war between the French and German leaders over the best strategy for surviving the Cold War. It was only two days after his first meeting with Adenauer, held at General de Gaulle's home in Colombey-les-deux-Eglises, that de Gaulle introduced his directorate idea in the form of a memorandum to Eisenhower and to British Prime Minister Harold Macmillan.[25] The memorandum, dated September 17, 1958, proposed the formation of a tripartite organization to coordinate strategic policies around the world and to formulate plans governing the use of nuclear weapons by any of its three members. De Gaulle justified his request by pointing out that the NATO alliance was limited to the North Atlantic region, and was thus unable to cope with problems arising elsewhere around the globe. Since France, like the United States and Britain, had responsibilities in many regions of the world, and since American actions outside the Atlantic treaty area could have repercussions for European interests, global coordination of military strategy was necessary.

A notable feature of de Gaulle's initiative was that the general insisted on establishing a formal, highly visible structure for tripartite decision making rather than a discreet, informal system of three-way consultations. A conspicuous organization would have a higher political payoff for de Gaulle. At home, it would increase his freedom of maneuver on Algeria by providing French pride with a focus other than doomed colonial ventures. Internationally, creation of the directorate would confirm France's status as a major, independent world actor, enhancing French power in the Alliance and increasing de Gaulle's leverage in his chosen role as mediator between East and West and between North and South.

The West German government opposed de Gaulle's directorate proposal quietly but energetically.[26] The directorate idea ran directly counter to Adenauer's goal of equal status for Germany within the Alliance. A directorate of the three Western Powers would reinforce existing French and British advantages over Germany. Symbolically, it would recall the Allied High Commission that had ruled Germany during the Occupation. Many Germans particularly resented de Gaulle's request for a bigger French role in Alliance decision making at a time when most of France's armed forces were in Algeria fighting a war that, in the German view, contributed nothing to Alliance goals.[27]

Adenauer reports in his memoirs that de Gaulle raised the subject of the directorate proposal during their July 1960 meeting at Rambouillet.[28] The general contended that his initiative did not aim at reshaping decision making within NATO, but was only concerned with strategic coordination in regions not covered by the Atlantic Pact. While this was perhaps not entirely false, it was surely less than a candid assessment. Inevitably, a directorate of the sort de Gaulle proposed would transform strategic planning inside as well as outside NATO and reduce German influence over NATO strategy.[29] Herbert Blankenhorn, Bonn's ambassador to Paris, believed that implementing the French proposals would create such resentments in the Alliance that it "would probably mean the end of NATO."[30] As it turned out, however, the Americans were unwilling to accept any binding arrangements concerning the use of American military force outside Europe. De Gaulle followed up his 1958 memorandum in private conversations and further exchanges of letters with Eisenhower and, after 1960, with Kennedy.[31] But the American leaders only responded with counterproposals that fell far short of what the French leader had in mind. De Gaulle finally abandoned his directorate idea early in 1962.

During the same period that he promoted his directorate concept, de Gaulle also attempted to position France as the principal intermediary between the Soviet Union and the West—a role that would magnify France's leverage vis-à-vis both the United States and Germany. The first opportunity for action in this regard arose from the international crisis which Soviet Premier Khrushchev precipitated in 1958 with his demand that Western occupation rights in Berlin be renegotiated. In the drawn-out crisis that followed, de Gaulle repeatedly hinted at France's availability as a mediator. At his press conference of November 10, 1959, for example, de Gaulle claimed to discern a reduction in the "virulence" of Soviet communism and a new realism on the part of the Soviet leadership which, he implied, could open the way to East-West détente.[32] In a televised address on May 31, 1960, the French president stated that France, for its part, was favorably disposed to cooperative East-West relations. Asserting that "no direct dispute" divided France from the Soviet Union, and that France was bound to Russia by a "traditional attraction," de Gaulle conveyed a clear impression of the role he envisaged for France in bringing détente about.[33]

But the circumstances of the situation proved ill-suited to de Gaulle's aspirations. The British government, and to a lesser extent the American government, gave indications of willingness to negotiate with Khrushchev on the Berlin question. As a result, de Gaulle found himself forced to adopt a hard line on Berlin to preclude the possibility of a U.S.-Soviet deal. De Gaulle sided with Adenauer repeatedly in rejecting any negotiations until Moscow withdrew its ultimatum, a stance that won him Adenauer's deep gratitude.[34] The chancellor had been haunted by fear that his allies would give way on Berlin in the face of Khrushchev's threats. For de Gaulle, however, a compromise on Berlin was out of the question. France's role as one of Berlin's occupying powers was, like its permanent seat on the United Nations Security Council, an indispensable component of French international prestige and influence. As such, de Gaulle was not about to see French rights bargained away in a U.S.-Soviet arrangement that would merely consolidate Europe's subjection to superpower dictates. Ultimately, the only East-West deals de Gaulle could trust were those arranged by the nations of continental Europe themselves, led by France.

For a French-led détente to succeed, however, there had to be at least some willingness on the Soviet side to proceed by negotiation rather than by bluster and intimidation. As the Berlin crisis dragged on year after year, it became clear that Moscow was not yet prepared to negotiate in good faith over a European settlement. De Gaulle had little choice but to shelve his blueprint for détente until more favorable circumstances arose.

DIVERGING STRATEGIC OUTLOOKS

Another important area of disagreement between Adenauer and de Gaulle concerned the question of what military strategy best responded to Western Europe's needs. During the latter half of the 1950s, France and West Germany had both become discontented with NATO policymaking processes. Despite the internationally integrated staff of NATO's planning and command structures, all major decisions were in fact made by Americans. Much to their frustration, European staff officers assigned to NATO (with the partial exception of the British) found themselves systematically excluded from information on American nuclear targeting and strategy.[35]

If France and Germany shared a common grievance about American domination of NATO, however, they were far from agreed on the appropriate remedy. For the German government, the problem was one of gaining more control over NATO decision making—above all where decisions on the use of nuclear weapons were concerned. Lacking the option of building its own national nuclear force, Bonn depended on arrangements within NATO to assure that American nuclear forces would stand behind Germany when needed. New developments in 1956 and 1957, however, began to call into question the reliability of the American nuclear guarantee. Rumors circulated regarding possible American troop cuts in Europe (the so-called Radford Plan), which Bonn interpreted as portending a decreased U.S. strategic commitment to the Alliance. Even more worrisome to Bonn was the launching of Sputnik in October 1957, which presaged a Soviet capability to strike directly at the United States with nuclear missiles. Amid the doubts inspired by these events, German defense officials became increasingly anxious to complete one of the various arrangements for nuclear control-sharing then under discussion in NATO. The idea behind control-sharing was to insure that the European members of NATO, who except for Britain lacked nuclear forces of their own, would nevertheless have access in wartime to American tactical nuclear warheads through NATO procedures still to be determined.

The nuclear control-sharing debate had originated in NATO in the mid-1950s. As the Western allies began to come to terms with the impossibility of meeting the conventional force goals established by NATO at Lisbon in 1952, the alternative which imposed itself was for NATO to increase its reliance on tactical nuclear weapons as a substitute for the manpower it lacked.[36] But if NATO military strategy in Europe was to be heavily dependent on the resort to tactical nuclear arms, European governments naturally did not want their own armed forces to be excluded from access to nuclear weapons. At the December 1956 meeting of the NATO Council, several governments (including those of Britain, France, and Germany) requested that American tactical nuclear weapons be made available to them.[37] In response, Washington decided to permit the sale of U.S.-made nuclear-capable weapon systems to certain allies including Germany. In addition, the United States would stockpile tactical nuclear warheads in Europe; warheads from these stockpiles would be made available to the allies under agreed circumstances for use with their nuclear-capable weapon systems.

The nuclear stockpile arrangement was formally approved at the December 1957 NATO Council meeting, and Germany began buying nuclear-capable weapon systems from U.S. manufacturers. During Franz Josef Strauss's tenure as defense minister, in fact, West Germany was among the most avid of the NATO allies in acquiring nuclear-capable systems. These included the F-104G fighter aircraft, the Nike surface-to-air missile, the Honest John and Sergeant tactical missiles, and the 203–millimeter howitzer.[38] In principle, the Europeans were to have access to U.S. tactical warheads only under emergency authorization from the Supreme Allied Commander in Europe (SACEUR), an American general. In practice, however, prior authorization effectively gave European armed forces (including the Bundeswehr) peacetime custody of warheads designated for use in their nuclear-capable systems.[39] The warhead-sharing arrangement thus turned Germany into a de facto nuclear power, at least in a limited sense.

For Germany, the political stakes of nuclear control-sharing were exceedingly high.[40] Given its exposed geographic position as well as its vulnerability to political isolation, the Federal Republic viewed nuclear control-sharing both as a vital demonstration of the U.S. commitment to Germany's defense and as a crucial assurance of the Bundeswehr's combat effectiveness if confronted by nuclear-equipped Soviet forces. In view of Germany's pledge not to develop its own nuclear weapons, moreover, control-sharing was an indispensable symbol of Germany's equality of status within NATO.

The French Fourth Republic, like Germany, had participated eagerly in NATO nuclear control-sharing arrangements. Under de Gaulle, however, French policy changed. In de Gaulle's view, the true solution to American domination of NATO lay not in nuclear control-sharing but in French self-help. The overriding priority of de Gaulle's defense policy was to reorganize France's defense effort on the basis of the greatest possible national self-reliance and autonomy. In de Gaulle's view, taking responsibility for national defense was "the first duty of the State," even "its raison d'être."[41] For a nation like France, self-reliance was "an absolute imperative." A great people could never leave the responsibility for its defense to a larger ally, because "if one spontaneously loses, even for a while, the free disposition of oneself, there is a strong risk of never regaining it."[42] It was therefore essential that France regain its strategic independence, or it would be "in contradiction with all that it is since its origins: with its role, with its self-esteem, with its soul."[43] Self-reliance was both an end in itself and a precondition for national grandeur. De Gaulle considered it vital that France be in a position to assert its own personality in world affairs, convinced as he was that "France is not really herself unless in the front rank; that only vast enterprises are capable of counterbalancing the ferments of dispersal which are inherent in her people; that . . . France cannot be France without greatness."[44] De Gaulle had good reason to fear that France, as a nation, was losing the self-confidence necessary for strategic independence. Having endured successive defeats by Hitler and in Indochina, and facing a prospective defeat in Algeria, France needed urgently to recover its self-respect.

De Gaulle had not been back in power long before he began to reorganize French defense policy in line with his stated principles. In March 1959, he withdrew the French Mediterranean fleet from assignment to NATO on the grounds that NATO's area of coverage did not extend south to regions where French interests might be at stake. If France found it necessary to act independently of NATO in Africa or the Middle East, de Gaulle said, it would need to have its fleet under its own control.[45] In June, the French government rejected a 1958 American request to station tactical nuclear weapons in France on the grounds that the weapons would not be under exclusive French control. As a consequence of the French refusal, the United States had to remove two hundred of its bombers from France and redeploy them in Britain and West Germany.[46] Then, on November 3, 1959, de Gaulle made his famous announcement at the Ecole Militaire that France would acquire its own national nuclear force. Although the governments of the Fourth Republic had been moving in this direction for several years before de Gaulle's return, the general's announcement marked the first time that possession of a national nuclear force was officially declared a goal of the French government.

The German government observed the trend of French defense policy with great misgivings. The more troops and ships France reassigned from NATO to roles in Algeria and elsewhere around the world, the fewer would remain for the defense of Central Europe; and the more difficulties France created for NATO planning, the less effectively Western defenses would function. As he repeatedly emphasized in private meetings with de Gaulle, Adenauer feared that France's uncooperative behavior in NATO would encourage the Soviet Union in its belligerent designs and feed isolationist sentiment in American public opinion.[47] As for French nuclear ambitions, Adenauer initially regarded the creation of independent European nuclear forces as a highly disadvantageous development for Germany. The more money France and Britain spent on their own nuclear forces, the less they would have available to meet their NATO obligations. Also, the likely refusal of Britain and France to subordinate their nuclear forces to NATO command would create major problems for Alliance strategy.[48]

In addition to the military drawbacks of Gaullist defense policy, West German leaders discerned substantial political disadvantages as well. From the outset, it was clear that the French government intended to use a national nuclear force as a means of enhancing its international prestige and increasing its influence in Alliance decision making. The possession of nuclear weapons would provide a further justification for the tripartite directorate de Gaulle had requested.[49] A French nuclear force would reinforce the political distinctions between Germany and France, emphasizing Germany's dependent status in the Alliance.

From the German perspective, in other words, each step de Gaulle took toward a more nationalistic defense strategy amounted to a net loss of security and prestige for Germany. The German government's frustration over de Gaulle's behavior was all the greater because Bonn could afford neither to retaliate against the French president nor to imitate him. De Gaulle, meanwhile, conscious of the potential difficulties involved in taking a foreign policy course independent of Washington, attempted to win German support for the French position. At a meeting with Adenauer late in 1959, the general argued that the United States would someday withdraw its troops from Europe. The preparation of an independent European defense, led by France and Germany, was indispensable. Adenauer countered with the view that Europe could not possibly defend itself against the Soviet Union without American assistance. Rather than taking steps that might alienate the United States, Western Europe should instead do all it could to convince the Americans that the defense of Europe was in their own best interest.[50]

THE IMPACT OF FLEXIBLE RESPONSE

The Franco-German disagreement over NATO was further intensified by the modifications to U.S. strategic nuclear doctrine introduced by the Kennedy administration. American nuclear planning during the final years of Eisenhower's presidency had envisaged rapid, virtually automatic escalation to the use of tactical nuclear weapons in the event of Warsaw Pact military aggression in Europe. At the strategic nuclear level, existing operational plans included only one option: for the United States to launch all its strategic weapons at the Soviet bloc in a single, all-out "spasm." This situation had been widely criticized in the latter 1950s by American strategic analysts, who doubted both the credibility and the wisdom of a policy that depended so heavily on immediate recourse to tactical nuclear weapons, and which seemed to lead directly to full-scale strategic nuclear war.[51] In the face of growing Soviet nuclear capabilities, the need to devise procedures to limit a nuclear conflict necessarily began to assume greater importance in American strategic thought. During their first months in office, Kennedy and Secretary of Defense Robert McNamara undertook a comprehensive review of U.S. defense policy.[52] What emerged from this review was a basic reformulation of U.S. strategic doctrine in line with the heightened American concern over the dangers of uncontrolled nuclear escalation.

McNamara spelled out the new policy to the Allies in a pivotal speech at the NATO Ministers' Conference held in Athens in May 1962.[53] Henceforth, stated McNamara, the United States would develop options for different degrees of nuclear response depending on the situation faced by NATO armed forces. Recourse to tactical nuclear weapons should not come automatically in the event of Soviet military aggression, but should be limited to situations involving "massive commitment of Soviet force." In other words, the earlier American doctrine of massive retaliation was being replaced by a policy of "flexible response." This in turn implied an expanded role for NATO conventional forces, which must be strong enough to withstand a "quick or ambiguous aggression" by Warsaw Pact forces without resorting to nuclear arms.

McNamara's presentation also reflected increasing American anxiety over the possibility of accidental nuclear war, as well as worry that a limited nuclear engagement could escalate out of control. To minimize the risk of accidental war, the defense secretary argued, it was essential to centralize "to the greatest extent possible" all decisions over whether to use nuclear weapons. A failure to coordinate allied nuclear actions would invite catastrophe. In other words, allied nuclear forces operating autonomously of the American arsenal were a danger to the West. Small, independent nuclear forces, said McNamara, wasted resources, invited preemptive attack, and could serve no useful deterrent function because "the use of such a force against the cities of a major nuclear power would be tantamount to suicide, whereas its employment against significant military targets would have a negligible effect on the outcome of the conflict."

The revisions to American strategy announced by McNamara posed a major challenge to French and German foreign policy goals. For the German government, the revisions seemed to call into question the nuclear control-sharing arrangements on which Germany depended. For de Gaulle, the new U.S. doctrine signaled a hardening of Washington's resistance to the independent course he had charted for France. Rather than pushing Paris and Bonn closer together, however, the shift in U.S. nuclear doctrine drove an additional wedge between them.

In the end, the Germans came out the losers. Because nuclear control-sharing was so important to Bonn as a symbol of its equal status and full partnership in the Alliance, McNamara's moves to tighten access to U.S. nuclear stockpiles threatened to deprive West Germany of the tenuous political equality in the Alliance it had gained only a few years earlier. But the French, far from showing solidarity with German concerns, instead viewed the changes in U.S. doctrine as vindication for their earlier arguments about the need for a national French nuclear force. Thus for all the acrimony of their disagreement, Washington and Paris were headed in the same direction: toward a policy that emphasized the distinction between nuclear haves and have-nots, with Germany consigned more solidly than before to the have-not category.

The American adoption of flexible response had the further, unintended effect of pushing France toward a strategic nuclear doctrine that could not be reconciled with Germany's needs. Prior to 1962, the French government had not articulated anything that could properly be called a nuclear strategy. At bottom, the French government sought to have its own nuclear weapons for the simple reason that the Americans and Soviets possessed nuclear weapons. McNamara's vehement criticism of independent nuclear forces, however, had demonstrated the need for a formal doctrine to justify France's policy of independence.[54] In defensive reaction to McNamara's critique, therefore, French theorists after 1962 developed a nuclear doctrine that exaggerated both the strategic value of a national nuclear force and the impossibility of subordinating nuclear deterrence to multilateral decision-making processes. In later decades, it proved all but impossible to revise this doctrine in response to evolving international conditions. Having elaborated their nuclear strategy in a traumatic context of U.S. criticism and political isolation within the Alliance, the French became acutely sensitive on the subject. In French policymaking circles, serious debate on nuclear strategy all but ceased by the late 1960s; suggestions for revising French nuclear doctrine became politically taboo. Rigid French insistence on nuclear independence was to cast a long shadow over Franco-German military cooperation after de Gaulle's departure. Because no French leader dared propose any real changes to the existing strategic doctrine, Franco-German defense cooperation became limited to those few aspects of military operations and weapons production that had no implications for overall strategy.

NOTES

    1. See Alfred Grosser, *La IVe République et sa politique extérieure* (Paris: Armand Colin, 1961).

    2. See Arnulf Baring, *Im Anfang war Adenauer: Die Entstehung der Kanzlerdemokratie* (Munich: Deutscher Taschenbuch Verlag, 1971), pp. 86–109, and Wolfram F. Hanrieder, "West German Foreign Policy, 1949–1979: Necessities and Choices," in Hanrieder, ed., *West German Foreign Policy, 1949–1979* (Boulder, Colo.: Westview, 1980), pp. 16–18.

    3. On the history of the EDC, see Gerhard Wettig, *Entmilitarisierung und Wiederbewaffnung in Deutschland, 1943–1955* (Munich: R. Oldenbourg, 1967); Edward Fursdon, *The European Defence Community: A History* (New York: St. Martin's Press, 1980); Daniel Lerner and Raymond Aron, eds., *France Defeats EDC* (New York: Praeger, 1957); and F. Roy Willis, *France, Germany and the New*

Europe, 1945–1967, rev. and expanded ed. (Stanford: Stanford University Press, 1968).

4. See Paul B. Stares, *Allied Rights and Legal Constraints on German Military Power* (Washington, D.C.: Brookings, 1990), especially pp. 3–9.

5. Declaration reprinted in Stares, *Allied Rights*, p. 109.

6. See especially the account in Konrad Adenauer, *Erinnerungen*, 4 vols. (Stuttgart: Deutsche Verlags-Anstalt, 1965–1968), *1953–1955*, pp. 346–48.

7. Convention on the Presence of Foreign Forces in the Federal Republic of Germany, Article 1.1. Reprinted in L. Radoux, *France and NATO* (Paris: Assembly of Western European Union, 1967), p. 22.

8. See Frédéric Bozo, *La France et l'OTAN* (Paris: Masson, 1991), pp. 51–62.

9. Wilfrid L. Kohl, *French Nuclear Diplomacy* (Princeton: Princeton University Press, 1971), pp. 16–47.

10. See, for example, *The New York Times*, December 3, 1957.

11. These agreements were presumably of a purely exploratory nature. Cf. Catherine M. Kelleher, *Germany and the Politics of Nuclear Weapons* (New York: Columbia University Press, 1975), p. 149; Walter Schütze, *Frankreichs Verteidigungspolitik, 1958–1983* (Frankfurt am Main: Haag & Herchen, 1983), p. 5; and Kohl, *French Nuclear Diplomacy*, p. 55.

12. Giuseppe Walter Maccotta, "Alcune considerazioni sulla Force de frappe: Le sue origini ed il suo significato politico," *Rivista marittima*, April 1982, p. 24. Maccotta, later the Italian ambassador to Moscow, was posted at the Italian embassy in Paris at the time of these events.

13. Adenauer, *Erinnerungen, 1955–1959*, p. 331.

14. Maccotta, "Alcune considerazioni," p. 24.

15. *U.S. News and World Report*, January 3, 1958, pp. 60–63.

16. This interpretation is supported by the author's interviews in Paris with former French foreign ministry officials.

17. Maccotta, "Alcune considerazioni," p. 24.

18. Kohl, *French Nuclear Diplomacy*, pp. 57–59.

19. Hans-Peter Schwarz, *Die Ära Adenauer: Epochenwechsel, 1957–1963* (Stuttgart: Deutsche Verlags-Anstalt, 1983), p. 97. Such an arrangement would, at least technically, have been permissible under the 1954 London accords, in which Germany had renounced the production but not the possession of nuclear weapons.

20. Cf. Schütze, *Frankreichs Verteidigungspolitik*, p. 5; note also the remarks by Pierre Guillaumat in Institut Charles-de-Gaulle, ed., *L'aventure de la bombe: De Gaulle et la dissuasion nucléaire, 1958–1969* (Paris: Plon, 1985), p. 68.

21. Kelleher, *Germany*, p. 151.

22. Maccotta, "Alcune considerazioni," p. 25; also see the remarks by Ernst Weisenfeld in Hans-Peter Schwarz, ed., *Adenauer und Frankreich: Die deutsch-französischen Beziehungen 1958 bis 1969* (Bonn: Bouvier, 1985), p. 35.

23. Stanley Hoffmann, *Decline or Renewal? France since the 1930s* (New York: Viking, 1974), p. 288, and Edward A. Kolodziej, *French International Policy under de Gaulle and Pompidou: The Politics of Grandeur* (Ithaca: Cornell University Press, 1974), pp. 42–46.

24. On Adenauer's foreign policy strategy in the late 1950s and early 1960s, see the excellent analysis by Hans-Peter Schwarz, "Das aussenpolitische Konzept Konrad Adenauers," in Klaus Gotto et al., *Konrad Adenauer: Seine Deutschland- und Aussenpolitik, 1945–1963* (Munich: Deutscher Taschenbuch Verlag, 1975), pp. 97–155.

25. The text of the memorandum, long kept secret, appeared in *Espoir*, no. 15, June 1976. For an English translation see Alfred Grosser, *The Western Alliance* (New York: Continuum, 1980), p. 187.

26. See, for example, Herbert Blankenhorn, *Verständnis und Verständigung: Blätter eines politischen Tagebuches, 1949 bis 1979* (Frankfurt am Main: Propyläen, 1980), pp. 327–29, and Gerd Schmückle, *Ohne Pauken und Trompeten: Erinnerungen an Krieg und Frieden* (Munich: W. Heyne, 1982), pp. 248–49.

27. *The Times* (London), September 7, 1960.

28. *Erinnerungen, 1959–1963*, p. 59.

29. Kolodziej, *French International Policy*, p. 83.

30. Blankenhorn, *Verständnis*, p. 328.

31. See Michael M. Harrison, *The Reluctant Ally: France and Alliance Security* (Baltimore: Johns Hopkins University Press, 1981), pp. 86–95.

32. Charles de Gaulle, *Major Addresses, Statements and Press Conferences, May 19, 1958 to January 31, 1964* (New York: French Embassy, Press and Information Service, 1964), pp. 57–59.

33. De Gaulle, *Major Addresses*, pp. 75–76.

34. See the account in Adenauer, *Erinnerungen, 1959–1963*, pp. 24–26, 48–51.

35. Grosser, *Western Alliance*, pp. 157–58; Harrison, *Reluctant Ally*, pp. 21–22; André Beaufre, *NATO and Europe* (New York: Knopf, 1966), pp. 32–36.

36. See Robert E. Osgood, *NATO: The Entangling Alliance* (Chicago: University of Chicago Press, 1962), chapter 5.

37. James L. Richardson, *Germany and the Atlantic Alliance* (Cambridge, Mass.: Harvard University Press, 1966), p. 50.

38. Kelleher, *Germany*, p. 99.

39. John D. Steinbruner, *The Cybernetic Theory of Decision* (Princeton: Princeton University Press, 1974), p. 182.

40. Kelleher, *Germany*, p. 123.

41. Press conference of June 30, 1955. Charles de Gaulle, *Discours et messages* (Paris: Plon, 1970), vol. 2, p. 645.

42. Press conference of January 14, 1963. *Major Addresses*, p. 216.

43. Speech at the Ecole Militaire, November 3, 1959. *Discours et messages*, vol. 3, p. 126.

44. Charles de Gaulle, *War Memoirs* (New York: Viking, 1955), vol. 1, p. 3. See also de Gaulle's remarks along these lines to Adenauer as reported in the latter's *Erinnerungen, 1959–1963*, pp. 140–41, 228–29.

45. Press conference, March 25, 1959. *Major Addresses*, p. 49.

46. Maurice Couve de Murville, *Une politique étrangère, 1958–1969* (Paris: Plon, 1971), p. 65.

47. Adenauer, *Erinnerungen, 1959–1963*, pp. 60, 64, 102, 229.

48. Adenauer, *Erinnerungen, 1955–1959*, p. 295.

49. Charles de Gaulle, *Mémoires d'espoir: Le Renouveau, 1958–1962* (Paris: Plon, 1970), pp. 214–15.

50. Adenauer, *Erinnerungen, 1959–1963*, p. 21.

51. Particularly influential in this regard was General Maxwell D. Taylor, *The Uncertain Trumpet* (New York: Harper and Brothers, 1959).

52. See Jane E. Stromseth, *The Origins of Flexible Response* (New York: St. Martin's Press, 1988).

53. McNamara's speech was declassified in 1979. Parts of it, including the sections quoted here, are reprinted in David N. Schwartz, *NATO's Nuclear Dilemmas* (Washington, D.C.: Brookings, 1983), pp. 156–65.

54. Lothar Ruehl, *La politique militaire de la Ve République* (Paris: Fondation Nationale des Sciences Politiques, 1976), p. 168.

CHAPTER 2

France, Germany, and the Europe That Wasn't, 1962–1966

An integral part of de Gaulle's long-term vision for Europe was his plan to achieve "political union" among the six members of the Common Market.[1] Political union, as de Gaulle pictured it, would revolve around periodic meetings of the government heads and foreign ministers of the Six. Their consultations would aim at reaching a common policy in the fields of foreign policy, defense, economic policy, and cultural affairs. A European union along these lines would serve two major purposes. First, it would redirect the construction of Europe away from the economic, supranational emphasis reflected in the creation of the Common Market toward a more political, intergovernmental approach. De Gaulle supported the Rome Treaty which created the European Economic Community (EEC), despite the fact that the treaty had been negotiated under the Fourth Republic. However, de Gaulle considered the EEC's supranational aspects to be unworkable and illegitimate for a European entity that went beyond the narrow technical questions involved in regulating a common market area. In a Europe composed of nations, each of which had "its own spirit, its own history, its own language, its own misfortunes, glories, and ambitions," European unification could only proceed on a basis that respected the full national sovereignty of the participating states.[2] It was one thing to have a supranational commission set a tariff, but quite another to have it decide matters of high politics involving foreign and defense policy.[3]

Second, political union of the Six would establish the conditions for a more independent, self-reliant Europe capable of supporting de Gaulle's nationalistic strategic objectives. Political union as de Gaulle envisaged it would work to French advantage in several ways. To the extent that a political union of the Six defined foreign and defense policies of its own, France's influence in the West would increase. When they were in agreement, the Six—and hence France—could act as a counterweight to the United States within NATO, launching European policy initiatives and forcing the United States to reach accommodation with European viewpoints. In the absence of political union, France (like other European countries) could do little more than watch in frustration as Washington imposed its preferences unilaterally.

Even when the Six could not reach agreement on a given policy, the mere existence of a political union along Gaullist lines would provide indirect support for France's independent defense strategy. Existing arrangements, in which Alliance defense policy was discussed only under NATO auspices, left France isolated whenever it took a position at odds with that of the United States on an important issue.[4] Political union, by creating a forum where Alliance defense policy could be discussed from a purely European viewpoint, would promote the articulation of European interests in the Alliance as distinct from American interests, opening the way for a diversity of strategic conceptions in NATO and thus reducing the political costs to France of standing up for its own position.

Political union on de Gaulle's principles would also serve the goal of "overcoming Yalta." If it pursued a common foreign policy, Western Europe would have the political weight to resist U.S.-Soviet dealings aimed at perpetuating the division of Europe into blocs. De Gaulle believed that a politically independent Europe would be a more attractive partner for the Soviet Union in negotiating the terms of détente than a Europe that was merely an appendage of Moscow's principal world rival.[5]

De Gaulle outlined a framework for political union at his meeting with Adenauer at Rambouillet in July 1960. The French president envisaged a framework for political union consisting of regular meetings of the government heads of the Six, coordinated action in the areas of cultural, economic, foreign, and defense policy, periodic meetings of the relevant ministers charged with achieving this coordination, and, eventually, referendums in all of the member nations to obtain popular assent for these measures.[6] De Gaulle revealed his plan publicly at a press conference on September 5, repeating in general terms the proposals he had made at Rambouillet.

The government heads of the Six met in two conferences, in February and July 1961, to consider de Gaulle's proposals. Assurances from de Gaulle that the proposed union was compatible with the existing Common Market, and that it would not undermine the Atlantic Alliance, made it possible for the leaders to reach tentative agreement on the plan. A committee of representatives of the six governments, chaired by Christian Fouchet of France, was assigned to work out the specific provisions of the agreement. The ensuing negotiations, on what was now referred to as the "Fouchet Plan," were derailed by British Prime Minister Harold Macmillan's July 31 announcement that Britain intended to apply for membership in the EEC. From this point on, the Fouchet discussions revolved essentially around the problem of Britain's relation to Europe. The Dutch delegation made British participation in the Fouchet negotiations a precondition for their own acceptance of political union, a stance which put them sharply at odds with the French. The negotiations ceased to make headway, and were finally adjourned indefinitely in April 1962. De Gaulle's design for European political union had failed.

In terms of the Franco-German relationship, the most notable feature of the Fouchet episode was Adenauer's enthusiastic reception of de Gaulle's initiative and his consistent support for it throughout the negotiations.[7] That Adenauer was such a strong advocate of de Gaulle's plan for European political union may at first glance seem puzzling. Given the chancellor's devotion to the cause of Western unity, why would he so enthusiastically favor a Gaullist design aimed above all at enhancing French national power and independence? The apparent paradox dissolves on closer inspection. From Adenauer's perspective, the Fouchet Plan offered tangible gains to Germany that it would be foolish to let slip away just because de Gaulle's motives for political union were not identical to Bonn's. Adenauer could not afford to waste the opportunity offered by the French proposals. Always fearful of reawakening suspicion about German motives among Germany's allies, the chancellor realized that he was not in a position to launch major initiatives of his own to advance European integration. If he wanted to assist the process of European unification he would have to make the most of initiatives offered by others, promoting them while seeking whatever modifications were necessary to insure that the initiatives corresponded to Germany's own interests. This was precisely Adenauer's tactic in the negotiations on political union. Adenauer's consuming obsession was to cement Western unity against the Soviet danger. The progressive unification of Western Europe, in his view, was an indispensable element of this unity. Whether the construction of Europe took place according to the supranational or the Gaullist recipe was less important, in Adenauer's eyes, than the simple fact of doing something to keep the process of unification in motion.[8]

From Adenauer's perspective, European political union offered two major attractions. First, it offered a fallback in the event of a weakening of the American engagement in Europe. In his later years as chancellor, Adenauer was deeply pessimistic about America's long-run determination to uphold its European commitments. Adenauer most assuredly did not wish for the Americans to depart from Europe; but if they did, it would be all the more important to have a European political entity already in place.[9] Second, the proposed political union offered Germany the prospect of a voice—even if only an indirect one—in world politics. For a Germany overshadowed by the United States within the Alliance, excluded from membership in the United Nations, and barred from a nationalistic foreign policy, European union offered as much international influence as Germany could aspire to for the immediate future.

Thus, although the political union envisaged by de Gaulle would undoubtedly work to France's advantage, Adenauer favored it because it would benefit Germany as well. Moreover, Adenauer was careful to proceed in such a way that supporting the French plan would not come at the expense of Germany's relations with its other European partners or with the United States. In his meetings with de Gaulle, Adenauer always insisted that the plan for political union include clauses showing that its goals were compatible with those of the Atlantic Alliance and the EEC.[10]

THE ELYSÉE TREATY

The Franco-German Treaty of 1963, also known as the Elysée Treaty, arose as a direct consequence of the breakdown of negotiations on European political union. The idea of a Franco-German agreement as a partial substitute for the stalled Fouchet Plan evolved in the course of conversations between Adenauer and de Gaulle during the last half of 1962. Adenauer, on a state visit to France early in July 1962, proposed to de Gaulle an informal bilateral arrangement under which the French president and the West German chancellor would agree to consult with each other on all world events related to the Communist danger.[11] In the face of what he saw as a continual weakening of American and British resolve to stand up to the Communist threat, it is not surprising that the German leader sought to institutionalize in some way the French support he had so welcomed during the Berlin crisis. Adenauer also intended his proposal as a constructive means of recovering from the breakdown of the Fouchet negotiations, which he viewed as a grave setback to the cause of European unification. A Franco-German accord would help sustain momentum in the process of European political union; it would also preempt Soviet efforts to exploit the temporary disunity of the Six. In response to Adenauer's proposition, de Gaulle asked his guest whether he would be willing to make a bilateral agreement along the lines of the French proposals for European political union, if it should prove impossible to revive the Fouchet negotiations. Adenauer readily agreed.[12]

In September de Gaulle visited West Germany, reciprocating Adenauer's visit to France. The idea of a bilateral accord came up again, and de Gaulle suggested several areas where closer diplomatic coordination was possible: Berlin, East-West relations, Africa, and policy toward the developing countries. Bilateral relations should also be better organized in the areas of armaments planning and military cooperation. Lastly, de Gaulle suggested, the agreement could include provisions for youth exchanges and closer cultural relations. The two leaders agreed that the French government would draw up a draft agreement. Both leaders felt it unnecessary to formalize the agreement as a state treaty; a simple "gentlemen's agreement" would suffice.[13] During the fall of 1962, an interministerial committee negotiated the specific details of the accord on the basis of the French draft.

A few days before de Gaulle and Adenauer were due to sign the agreement, legal experts from the German foreign ministry advised Adenauer that unless it were ratified by the Bundestag as a formal treaty, the pending accord might be vulnerable to a constitutional challenge under Article 59 of the Basic Law. It was Foreign Minister Gerhard Schröder, apparently, who first called into question the constitutionality of the planned agreement. He did so two days after de Gaulle's renowned press conference of January 14, 1963, at which the general announced his determination to refuse Great Britain entry into the Common Market. Very probably the German foreign minister, known to take a highly critical view of de Gaulle, was motivated by political as well as legal considerations. Coming on the heels of the French president's veto against Britain, signature of a bilateral agreement with France might give Germany's other allies the impression that Bonn had supported de Gaulle's action. A ratification debate in the Bundestag would make clear that although Germany strongly favored reconciliation and good relations with France, it strongly disagreed with France's current policy.[14]

Adenauer had hoped to avoid a public debate over the details of the Franco-German text; but Schröder apparently persuaded the chancellor that since the agreement would easily gain approval in the Bundestag, the best course of action would be to submit it for ratification as a treaty.[15] Given the lack of sympathy for de Gaulle's policies prevalent among the

Social Democrats, the Free Democrats, and even in parts of Adenauer's own Christian Democratic party, this was the most likely way of assuring that the agreement would survive under future governments.[16] At Adenauer's request de Gaulle agreed to the idea of making the accord into a formal treaty, even though the French leader had originally hoped for an agreement in the form of a private exchange of letters. After last-minute changes to put the agreement into proper legal form, the treaty was signed by Adenauer and de Gaulle at the Elysée Palace on January 22, 1963.

The provisions of the Elysée Treaty reflected its lineage as the descendent of de Gaulle's plans for European political union. The treaty incorporated measures to establish closer bilateral cooperation in foreign policy, defense, education, and youth exchanges. Under the treaty terms, the French president was to meet with the German chancellor at least twice a year, and the two foreign ministers were to meet at least once every three months. The two governments were to "consult each other, prior to any decision, on all important questions of foreign policy . . . with a view to arriving . . . at a similar position."[17]

On the question of defense relations, the treaty provided detailed instructions. The two defense ministers were to meet at least every three months; the armed forces chiefs of staff, or their representatives, were to meet every two months. The treaty defined the following objectives for defense cooperation:

On the level of strategy and tactics, the competent authorities of both countries will endeavor to harmonize their doctrines with a view to arriving at mutual concepts. . . . Exchanges of personnel between the armed forces will be increased. These particularly concern professors and students from the general staff schools. They may include temporary detachments of entire units. . . . With regard to armaments, both Governments will endeavor to organize a joint program from the time of drafting appropriate armaments projects and formulating financing plans. To this end, joint committees will . . . submit proposals to the Ministers, who will examine them during their quarterly meetings and will give the necessary directives for implementation.

That the French and German governments could aspire to such ambitious goals for defense cooperation seems almost startling in view of their emerging disagreements on so many aspects of defense policy, as detailed in Chapter 1. It is evident from the treaty's cautious wording that its drafters recognized the obstacles to agreement on defense strategy: the two governments did not pledge to harmonize but to *endeavor* to harmonize their strategic and tactical concepts; similarly, they would *endeavor* to organize a joint program for armaments planning. As far as defense cooperation was concerned, in other words, the Elysée Treaty was not a treaty of substance but of procedures. It committed the two sides to a good-faith effort at coordinating their defense efforts, but contained no concrete obligation for them actually to do so.

If the two governments implicitly recognized the difficulties standing in the way of the treaty's stated goals, however, then why did de Gaulle propose the clauses on defense cooperation at all, and why did the German government accept their inclusion in the treaty? The best explanation seems to be that each side continued to overestimate its ability to win its partner to its own views by a sustained effort at persuasion. This was especially true in the case of de Gaulle, who seemed convinced that world developments such as the American adoption of flexible response and the growth of the Soviet nuclear arsenal gave West Germany an objective national interest in accommodating itself to French strategic concepts.[18]

As it turned out, however, the military clauses of the treaty were not destined to be applied in the spirit de Gaulle intended. In the weeks after the treaty was signed, it became apparent that ratification of the accord would not be a straightforward matter. Anger in Germany over de Gaulle's high-handed rejection of the British application for EEC membership, which had enjoyed strong support from all the major political parties in the Bundestag, was still fresh.[19] A widespread sentiment developed among the deputies that ratification of the Elysée Treaty must not imply any change in Germany's policy toward the EEC or any lessening of German determination to see Britain and other West European countries included in the Community. The pursuit of cooperation with France must not extend to the point of accepting de Gaulle's vision of Europe.

In Washington, meanwhile, the Elysée Treaty met with deep suspicion bordering on outright hostility.[20] The American government asked Bonn repeatedly for clarification of the treaty's content. Washington's anxiety focused on the sections of the agreement concerning coordination of French and German defense policies. Given that West Germany's military strategy was determined within the framework of NATO, U.S. officials asked, how did Bonn plan to harmonize its strategic concepts with Paris? Washington was also incensed by the timing of the treaty. Having taken a strong position in favor of the British EEC application, the American government saw de Gaulle's veto as a damaging blow to Kennedy's "grand design" for Europe. That Adenauer should sign a treaty of friendship with the French president under such circumstances seemed an act of purposeful disloyalty. Throughout February 1963, the American government let it be known through multiple channels and in the strongest possible terms that it favored a clear declaration from the Bundestag that the Elysée Treaty would not interfere with Germany's close defense ties to the United States.[21]

In the reigning atmosphere of German and American displeasure with de Gaulle, the Social Democratic party (SPD) proposed that a preamble reaffirming West Germany's commitment to NATO and the EEC be added to the treaty. The SPD proposal, which offered a way for the Bundestag to mollify Washington, assert its own views on Europe, and still preserve the treaty with France, was quickly taken up by the Free Democratic party (FDP) as well. The idea of a preamble also enjoyed considerable support in the Christian Democratic Union (CDU) even though Adenauer furiously opposed it, insisting that the treaty did not in any way contradict Germany's existing obligations.

As the ratification process in the Bundestag got under way, it became clear that the FDP would insist on a preamble as a condition for remaining part of the governing coalition with the CDU and its Bavarian ally, the Christian Social Union (CSU). Rather than risk the collapse of his government, Adenauer reluctantly gave in to pressure from the FDP and from leading figures in his own party. The preamble approved by the Bundestag took the form of an inventory of West Germany's major foreign policy objectives. On the subject of NATO, the preamble stated Germany's will to promote "the common defense in the framework of the North Atlantic Alliance and the integration of the armed forces of the states in this alliance." On the EEC, Germany's goals were defined as "the unification of Europe along the path taken with the creation of the European Community, including the admission of Great Britain and of other states willing to accede, and the further strengthening of this Community."[22] The Bundestag ratified the treaty and preamble by an overwhelming majority on May 16, 1963. On June 14 the French National Assembly followed suit, ratifying the treaty (without any preamble) by a large majority.

Although the Elysée Treaty had won a clear vote of approval from the parliaments of its two signatories, the preamble attached by the Bundestag insured that the harmonization of foreign and defense policies envisaged in the treaty would not take place. Germany's foreign policy aims, as defined in the preamble, were irreconcilable with a Gaullist conception of Europe. De Gaulle, enraged by the Bundestag's action, hinted publicly that he regarded the treaty as a dead letter.[23] In the years following the accord, both Paris and Bonn were careful to respect most of the major terms of their agreement. Bilateral meetings of the French and German heads of government, foreign ministers, and defense ministers took place regularly as prescribed by the treaty. But the ratification debate in Germany had brought into the open the long-simmering disagreement between France and Germany over Europe's fundamental orientation and aims. The following years would see the two countries move even farther apart in the questions that divided them.

PERSONALITIES AND FOREIGN POLICIES

Franco-German defense relations, in the period between Germany's entry into NATO and the signing of the Elysée Treaty, combined aspects of both cooperation and competition. This was true under both the Fourth and the Fifth Republics, although the two French regimes adopted significantly different approaches toward partnership with Germany.

The Fourth Republic, having been compelled to accept Germany as a military ally, and having in turn imposed certain institutional safeguards on German rearmament, showed surprisingly little reluctance to develop ties of mutual dependence with Germany—provided that these ties served the larger purpose of making Europe, in the long run, a power capable of ending its military dependence on the United States and escaping American economic and cultural domination. This was one of the major motives behind the Fourth Republic's support for creating the Common Market. It was also a motive for the largely unsuccessful Fourth Republic initiatives aimed at integrating West European armaments production. The governments of the Fourth Republic were groping toward the establishment of a sort of continental bloc that would counterbalance "Anglo-Saxon" dominance in a variety of spheres: economic, political, nuclear, and industrial. Lacking confidence in its ability to lead Europe alone, moreover, the Fourth Republic was gradually moving toward acceptance of the idea of partnership with Germany on a basis of equality.

Franco-German cooperation along these lines held considerable attraction for Bonn, because it offered prospects not available in the framework of the Atlantic Alliance. Adenauer's government fully recognized that the American security guarantee was vital to West Germany for the indefinite future. But Germany's relationship to the United States, if only because of America's size and power, could not be one of full equality. The element of dependence would never be far below the surface. In the case of relations with Fourth Republic France, by contrast, the long-term possibilities were much more promising. If it was a given that a divided Germany could never recover its full independence in international affairs, the Rome Treaty at least seemed to point the way toward the next best thing: a powerful Western Europe under shared Franco-German leadership, in partnership with the United States.

It was precisely this element of shared leadership in Europe that de Gaulle torpedoed on his resumption of power. De Gaulle strongly favored Franco-German reconciliation and military cooperation, but on a notably different basis from the Fourth Republic. In de Gaulle's schema, France alone would rise to great-power status and would do so by standing on Germany's shoulders. Germany would be compelled to accept cooperation with France on these revised terms, because the alternative—the political and economic fragmentation of Western Europe—would be even worse from Bonn's perspective than a Franco-German partnership in which France reaped the lion's share of the gains. It is not surprising that German leaders became increasingly discontented with France from 1958 onward, and that the Bundestag was grudging in its acceptance of the Elysée Treaty. At times, Adenauer's strong personal bond with de Gaulle seemed to be the only factor preventing Franco-German relations from deteriorating into acrimony.

Many observers have commented on the importance of the de Gaulle-Adenauer relationship in laying the basis for reconciliation between France and Germany. The profound rapport between the two leaders, flowing from shared political values and religious beliefs as well as similar leadership styles, seemed to cement the Franco-German rapprochement in ways that went beyond mere calculations of national self-interest. In the last years of his chancellorship, Adenauer became increasingly preoccupied with Franco-German relations, to a point that Gilbert Ziebura has labeled "fetishization." Noting the many ways in which French and German foreign policy goals were incompatible or even diametrically opposed, Ziebura concludes that Adenauer's relationship to de Gaulle escapes rational analysis.[24] Ziebura seems to consider Adenauer's solicitousness about his relations with France (especially a Gaullist France whose objectives diverged sharply from those of the German government) to be the product of simplicity and naïveté.

To explain Adenauer's policy toward France, however, it is not necessary to argue that a crafty de Gaulle somehow mesmerized Adenauer into acting against his own country's interests, or that the chancellor failed to grasp de Gaulle's aims. Adenauer's behavior toward de Gaulle followed logically from his overriding priority of integrating the Federal Republic irrevocably into a unified Western Europe. Without close, cooperative ties between Paris and Bonn, there could be no European Community, nor an effective organization of Western military defenses in Europe. A disunited Europe would offer easy prey to Communist expansionism, inviting Soviet pressures and encroachments on Germany. It would present an unattractive partner to the United States, thereby strengthening American tendencies to disengage from Europe. It would greatly increase the risk of German political isolation.

Given Adenauer's priorities, good relations with France were virtually an absolute necessity. In de Gaulle, Adenauer rightly saw a leader who was both willing and (unlike the leaders of the Fourth Republic) institutionally capable of putting the Franco-German reconciliation on a firm, durable footing. This is all that is necessary to account for Adenauer's preoccupation with de Gaulle. Indeed, the very fact that Paris and Bonn were at odds on so many key questions was a major factor driving the German chancellor to seek common ground with the French leader. Given the necessity of maintaining good relations with France, the more troublesome de Gaulle became, the more effort Adenauer was willing to expend to reach some accommodation with him. What choices did Adenauer have, after all? Turning a cold shoulder to Paris would not have made de Gaulle give up his nationalist ambitions, nor sped the process of European unification, nor brought France back into conformity with NATO strategy. On the other hand, it might well have further alienated de Gaulle from NATO, or encouraged him to patch up his relations with Moscow.[25] Contrary to what one might infer from Ziebura's charge of irrationality, Adenauer did not allow his friendship with de Gaulle to interfere with the foreign policy priorities he had established for Germany. Although, from necessity, he followed de Gaulle's lead on European unification, Adenauer consistently did all he could to redirect the French president's initiatives into paths that would reinforce Western unity instead of French independence. In short, whatever Adenauer's personal sentiments toward de Gaulle, his policy choices were those that might have been expected from an unsentimental practitioner of Realpolitik.

There was thus a somewhat ironic reciprocity in Franco-German relations under de Gaulle and Adenauer. Each of the two countries viewed its partner in essentially instrumental terms. For de Gaulle, Germany was important primarily for the weight it could lend to France's international ambitions. For Adenauer, rapprochement with France was important above all to prevent Paris from obstructing Western unity or European integration. Neither de Gaulle nor Adenauer was very successful in turning the Franco-German partnership to his own uses, because neither could offer his partner a sufficient incentive to dissuade him from a foreign policy whose fundamental reference points were the United States and the Soviet Union. Each of the two countries had only secondary significance for the other, in comparison to the importance each attributed to its position in relation to the superpowers.

It is true that near the end of his term as chancellor, Adenauer seems increasingly to have seen the Franco-German partnership as a goal to be pursued for its own sake. This apparent shift was not due to any new offer on de Gaulle's part, but to Adenauer's gnawing fear that the United States was in the process of ending its commitment to West Germany's defense after all. Adenauer was deeply disappointed by American inability to counteract the construction of the Berlin Wall. He worried constantly that Kennedy lacked the necessary resolve to confront Communism. Finally, it may be that de Gaulle's repeated attempts to convince Adenauer of the unreliability of the American security guarantee had at last begun to bear fruit, especially in the context of the Kennedy administration's adoption of flexible response. Perhaps Adenauer, like his defense minister Franz Josef Strauss, had begun to see Franco-German military cooperation as a long-term alternative to a constricting and worrisome dependence on the United States. But with Strauss's resignation from office in December 1962 in the aftermath of the *Spiegel* affair, and Adenauer's retirement less than a year later, those who gave a high priority to relations with France found themselves a minority in the governing coalition in Bonn.

By the time of Adenauer's departure, however, Franco-German rapprochement was no longer the urgent priority it had been a few years earlier. With the Common Market firmly established and the Elysée Treaty ratified, the reconciliation of the once-bitter enemies was an accomplished fact. In the wake of Moscow's retreat and resulting loss of prestige in the Cuban missile affair, moreover, the Soviet threat that had driven Paris and Bonn together during the Berlin crisis seemed to have receded. Finally, the implacable divergence of French and German defense policies left neither side reason to devote much additional effort to a seemingly futile search for common ground.

THE BARREN PARTNERSHIP

When Adenauer stepped down as German chancellor in the fall of 1963, prospects for a mutually satisfactory application of the Elysée Treaty appeared dim. The preamble to the treaty added by the Bundestag during the German ratification debate had made clear the gap between Bonn's goals—to strengthen NATO, promote European integration, and bring Britain into the European Community—and the French government's objectives of restoring French strategic independence, enhancing France's influence in world politics, and holding to a minimum the political and strategic influence of the "Anglo-Saxon" powers on the European continent. The new chancellor, Ludwig Erhard, was strongly pro-American. In succeeding Adenauer he completed a shift in the tone of German foreign policy that had begun at the end of 1962 when Kai-Uwe von Hassel replaced Franz Josef Strauss as defense minister.

The hallmark of German foreign and defense policy under Erhard, von Hassel, and Gerhard Schröder (who had been foreign minister since 1961) was its nearly absolute support for Washington's foreign policy. Like the Adenauer government before it, the Erhard government strongly supported defense cooperation with France. The new leadership, however, was less willing than Adenauer to seek accommodation with de Gaulle on issues where French and German foreign policies were clearly at odds. It was not long before the differences in perspective between de Gaulle and Erhard began to manifest themselves. Two questions in particular were to focus the growing discord between the two governments: the nature of political Europe and the extent of German control-sharing over nuclear weapons.

The first of these questions, the nature of political Europe, was in essence merely the latest installment in the never-ending debate over European unification. For de Gaulle, political Europe had been reduced by mid-1962 to the Paris-Bonn axis represented in the Elysée Treaty. The French leader had no intention of including Britain in Europe, at least not for the time being, and regarded his 1963 veto of the British application for Common Market membership as the end of the matter. Nor was de Gaulle interested in pursuing his earlier proposals for political union of the Six, in view of the hesitations and resistance the Fouchet Plan had encountered from the Netherlands, Belgium, and Italy. His idea was instead to employ Franco-German diplomatic coordination as the core of a European foreign policy that would represent Europe's interests and be free of American domination.

Erhard's European policy ran counter to de Gaulle's in every respect. A few weeks after his initial meeting with de Gaulle in Paris, Erhard delivered a speech before the Bundestag in which he stated that a new initiative on European political unification was "urgently necessary."[26] A few days after this speech, Erhard traveled to London for two days of talks with British political leaders. At the end of the trip, Erhard declared his government's desire to strengthen the ties binding Germany and Britain. Implicit in his remarks was the idea of reviving Britain's Common Market application as soon as might appear feasible. Erhard followed up his trip to London with visits to Rome, the Hague, Brussels, and Luxembourg, in each case with the evident intention of showing Bonn's support for European political unification and its rejection of the idea of an exclusive Franco-German partnership. Meanwhile, Erhard also went out of his way to demonstrate loyalty to the United States. The joint communiqué issued after Erhard's meeting with President Johnson in Washington in June 1964 could hardly have been more provocative to de Gaulle. The communiqué noted the German government's support for U.S. involvement in Vietnam, for American trade policy, and for the proposed NATO multilateral nuclear force—all key points of disagreement between Washington and Paris.[27]

The incompatibility of French and German policies became fully evident at the de Gaulle-Erhard summit in Bonn on July 3–4. De Gaulle opened the conference with a sweeping overview of the world situation and of his vision for Europe's role in world affairs. The French president envisaged a Europe that would reject American foreign policy tutelage and refuse the superpower-imposed partition of Europe into blocs. Western Europe would have its own foreign policy independent of the superpowers and reflecting its own interests. The backbone for such a policy would be France's emerging strategic nuclear force. Although, as de Gaulle noted, France's nuclear armament was a purely national force subject to the exclusive authority of the French president, its deterrent value indirectly protected Germany as well as France. If Paris and Bonn acted together in concert, argued the general, they could dominate European politics. The smaller West European countries would have little choice but to go along with what France and Germany decided.

To the astonishment of both delegations, Erhard did not react at all to de Gaulle's grandiose presentation. Instead, after a moment of uncomprehending silence, he merely suggested that the two sides proceed with the scheduled order of business.[28] Nothing could better have revealed the utter absence of genuine dialogue between the two sides. In the months following this meeting, de Gaulle appeared to lose interest in the bilateral relationship with Germany. Instead he became publicly critical of Erhard's government for lacking a sufficiently "European" orientation.[29]

DISAGREEMENT OVER CONVENTIONAL FORCES

Erhard's government also experienced persistent friction with de Gaulle over the question of conventional military strategy in Europe. The focus of discord concerned the implementation of a "forward defense" strategy by NATO in Central Europe. The concept of forward defense was not new; indeed, it had been adopted as official doctrine by the Alliance at the September 1950 NATO Council meeting in New York. It was at this meeting that Washington had first proposed rearming Germany as a means of strengthening Western defense. The forward defense doctrine was, in fact, chosen with the explicit intention of showing the Germans that NATO regarded Germany as an integral part of Western Europe and would defend it accordingly.[30]

NATO's actual military plans, however, were far less attractive to West Germany than the official doctrine implied. Under the operational plans of the early 1950s, allied forces were to drop back in the first days of a Warsaw Pact attack, using an ordered retreat to buy time for mobilization and the organization of a counterattack. In effect, therefore, Alliance defense began not at the inter-German border but at the Rhine. At the outset of a Warsaw Pact attack, allied forces would abandon nearly all of West Germany, then launch a counteroffensive to restore the territorial status quo ante. This "fallback" strategy insured that any East-West conflict in Central Europe would be fought largely on West German soil, hence at the cost of the West Germans.

Upon joining the Alliance in 1955, therefore, Germany began to seek revisions to NATO's operational plans in Central Europe. Primarily what the Germans wanted was for the Alliance to shift its line of defense eastward, so that the main battle in a NATO-Warsaw Pact conflict would be concentrated within a few tens of kilometers of the inter-German border. The revised version of forward defense would obviously be much more attractive to West Germans, both politically and psychologically, than the fallback plan. Forward defense was preferable for another reason as well: it implied a more rapid rate of military escalation than the fallback strategy. Whereas the fallback strategy was based on the assumption of a drawn-out conventional conflict lasting until massive reinforcements could be brought from the United States, forward defense was based on the premise of an all-or-nothing stand at the inter-German border very early in the conflict. If the NATO forces at the forward line were overwhelmed, the United States would have no choice other than rapid escalation to the strategic nuclear level. No lengthy war would be fought in Germany: either the Warsaw Pact would abandon its aggression, or nuclear strikes directly against the Soviet Union would ensue.

Despite Bonn's persistent efforts, it was not until 1963 that NATO revised its tactical doctrine so that the initial line of defense would be the inter-German border instead of the Rhine.[31] Revision of NATO's tactical concept, however, was far from the end of the problem. For the revised concept to make sense militarily, it would be necessary to redeploy German and allied troops based in West Germany eastward so as to bring actual force dispositions into accordance with it.

This was a problem especially with regard to France. The French ground forces in Germany consisted of two heavy armored divisions with 65,000 troops. These were garrisoned, as they had been during the Occupation, in the southwest corner of Germany near the French border. Also stationed in Germany was a French tactical air corps incorporating some 450 fighter-bombers and equipped with U.S.-owned tactical nuclear warheads.[32] Under NATO military plans of the 1950s, the French ground forces in Germany had been assigned the role of a strategic reserve for NATO. Stationed as they were, hundreds of kilometers from the inter-German border, the two heavy French divisions would have no way of participating in the early stages of a conflict that began with a Warsaw Pact invasion of Germany from the East.

When NATO moved its line of defense eastward, therefore, it was decided that France would relocate its German-based divisions to the vicinity of Straubing in Bavaria, which would place them in close proximity to the German-Czech border. This was the famous "crenel" in NATO troop dispositions whose rejection would later become one of the touchstones of Gaullist dogma. The eastward relocation of the French forces was of great importance to the German government for two reasons. The first was military: locating France's two divisions near the Czech border would increase their military value in any actual battle. As long as they were stationed in southwest Germany, the French forces were practically useless from a German perspective, since the battle for Germany would already be lost before France's troops even came into play.

Second, the German government wanted France to move its forces eastward for political purposes. It had always been one of Bonn's main objectives to prevent any situation that would cause Germany to become isolated within the West. The greater Germany's isolation, the reasoning went, the easier it would be for the Soviet Union to victimize the Germans or to contemplate a military action directed against West Germany alone. Forestalling diplomatic isolation in the West was one of the major reasons for Germany's support of European integration. It was also a reason why Germany sought the forward deployment of troops from as many allied countries as possible. If the armed forces of Germany's allies were deployed along the East-West dividing line, they would be involved automatically in any military aggression initiated by the Warsaw Pact in Central Europe.

By making it evident that there was no way of isolating Germany militarily from its allies, forward deployment of allied troops was seen by Bonn as one of the most effective components of deterrence against Eastern bloc states. Allies with forward-based troops in Germany included Britain and (most importantly) the United States. The redeployment of French troops east-ward would insure that French involvement was automatic as well. Stationing its two divisions near Germany's eastern border would thus be a demonstration of France's firm commitment to aid in defending Germany against military aggression from the east.

Unfortunately for Bonn, its reasons for wanting France to deploy its divisions farther to the east ran precisely counter to the logic of de Gaulle's military policy. The central point of Gaullist diplomacy was to restore to France the strategic independence de Gaulle believed his nation had allowed to erode under the Fourth Republic. A forward deployment of France's divisions in Germany, by insuring that French forces would auto-matically become involved in any armed conflict that began along the East-West border, was antithetical to Gaullist objectives.

There were other practical considerations that also made the idea of an eastward redeployment unpalatable to de Gaulle. Participation in forward defense would require increased coordination of logistics and greater inte-gration of military planning between the French forces in Germany and NATO forces. Given that de Gaulle's ultimate objective was to escape NATO military integration, it was not likely that he would go along with a plan that necessitated an even higher level of military integration of French forces in NATO than currently existed. From a national military viewpoint, moreover, forward deployment of the two French divisions stationed in Germany made little sense. It would merely increase the geographic dispersion of the French army, reducing whatever effectiveness it might otherwise have for the conventional defense of France proper. Finally, financial considerations weighed strongly against redeployment. The existing deployment of the French forces in Germany near the French border enabled Paris to keep the foreign exchange costs of its troop stationing low, because it was able to pay its troops in francs and supply them directly from France with most day-to-day necessities. Moving the two French divisions east would greatly increase the foreign exchange cost to France of deploying troops in Germany. This was an expense hardly to be considered at a time when the French government's resources were already stretched by the costs of its nuclear weapons program.

During the period 1963 to 1965, the German government availed itself of every possible opportunity to press the French for a definite commitment to move their troops eastward.[33] Since the French divisions in Germany were assigned to NATO and (at least formally) governed by NATO planning, the French could not flatly refuse the role assigned to them by the Alliance command. Besides, France was quite content to see NATO move its line of defense eastward, since France itself would benefit directly from the shift if a conflict in Central Europe should occur. The French government had no intention, however, of relocating its own troops. Bonn's repeated attempts to raise the troop deployment question with Paris thus yielded no result except mutual irritation.

THE NUCLEAR CONTROL-SHARING QUESTION

In addition to their disagreement over the deployment of French forces in Germany, de Gaulle and Erhard were at odds on another major strategic question: the extent of German control-sharing over allied nuclear weapons. As noted in Chapter 1, the German government regarded reliable nuclear control-sharing arrangements to be a vital German interest. Under Kennedy, however, the United States had begun introducing measures to restrict control-sharing. The Kennedy administration's priorities were to prevent the accidental or hasty use of nuclear weapons by imposing new procedural constraints on the release of warheads to allied states, and by improving NATO's ability to respond to limited conventional attacks without resort to nuclear warfare.[34]

The changes to U.S. nuclear doctrine by Kennedy and McNamara caused great uneasiness on the part of the West Germans, who feared that the United States had decided to avoid nuclear escalation in a Central European conflict and to sacrifice Germany instead, if necessary.[35] Defense Minister Strauss reacted to the changes in U.S. nuclear policy by insisting that Bonn be given a measure of codetermination over the use of the American nuclear warheads stored in Germany. Two important objectives made the question of nuclear codetermination an urgent one for the German government. First was the primordial goal of exercising some influence over events if NATO and the Warsaw Pact should become involved in a major conflict on German soil. Since nuclear weapons would be crucial to the outcome of such a conflict, Germany would have no say in its own fate unless it exercised some degree of control over the employment of nuclear arms. Bonn's second interest in nuclear codetermination came from its goal of equality of rights among states in the Western Alliance. By the early 1960s it was apparent that all of NATO's major states except West Germany would soon possess strategic nuclear forces of their own. Under such circumstances it became all the more important to German leaders that they be enabled to participate in some form of nuclear codetermination as a symbolic demonstration of equality of rights, even though Germany could not possess its own national nuclear forces.[36]

Convinced that something had to be done to meet German demands for nuclear codetermination, the U.S. State Department offered a proposal in mid-1962 for what it called the Multilateral Force, or MLF. The proposal called for the creation of a fleet of twenty-five surface vessels equipped with a total of two hundred Polaris A-3 nuclear missiles. Participating European states would own and operate the force collectively. Individual ships in the fleet would be manned by crews of several nationalities, such that no single country's personnel would control any given ship. Because the MLF would be supranational yet integrated into NATO, its proponents in the State Department hoped to use it simultaneously to advance European integration, to satisfy German demands for nuclear codetermination, to bind Britain to Europe and Europe to the United States, and to isolate de Gaulle.[37]

The practical difficulties involved in actually implementing something like the MLF, however, were daunting. The cost-effectiveness of the project was very doubtful, since it would absorb a large proportion of the procurement budgets of its European "owners" while making a negligible addition to the total strategic nuclear forces in the Alliance. Consisting entirely of surface ships, the MLF was likely to be vulnerable to preemptive enemy strikes. Worse, the problems of command and control on ships manned by mixed-nationality crews had not been worked out; nor was there ever any resolution of the question of whether the U.S. president would retain a permanent veto over the firing of the MLF's missiles. Finally, the proposed force did nothing to resolve the problem of the independent French and British nuclear forces, since the French clearly had no intention of participating in the MLF and the British were unenthusiastic at best.[38]

The liabilities and unresolved problems associated with the MLF made the other European states also reluctant to embrace it. Repeated trips by U.S. officials to European capitals during 1962 and 1963 to sell the allies on the MLF met with little success. Only Bonn showed much interest, and this was due in large part to a desire to accommodate Washington rather than to interest in the MLF for its own sake. The hesitations and conditions attached to the project by the European allies had led Kennedy, by mid-1963, to all but shelve the idea.

But events intervened to give the MLF new life. Lyndon Johnson, succeeding to the presidency following Kennedy's assassination, came to office believing that his predecessor was fully committed to the plan. A whole new push was mounted by Washington during the first months of 1964 to convince its European allies of the merits of the project. At their summit meeting in June, Johnson and Erhard agreed to try to have an MLF treaty ready for signing by the end of the year. To get around the recalcitrance of the other allies in the ongoing MLF negotiations, U.S. and German representatives began meeting bilaterally to work out an unofficial treaty draft.[39] Matters came to a crux in October, when Erhard suggested publicly that the United States and West Germany might proceed alone on an MLF treaty if other allies could not be persuaded to join in.

It was at this point that the French government intervened with a massive campaign against the project. Earlier, Paris had taken a much more complacent view of the MLF. Indeed, de Gaulle had at one point explicitly assured Adenauer that France understood Bonn's position on the subject and did not object to West German participation in such a force.[40] In view of the later switch in the French position, it appears likely that de Gaulle's initial complaisance was based on the assumption that the MLF had no chance of ever coming into existence. By October 1964, however, the situation had changed: a treaty creating a bilateral U.S.-German nuclear force appeared nearly ready for signature. Such a treaty would lead to far greater German involvement with nuclear weapons than the French government was prepared to accept.

French intervention against the MLF took the form of ominous hints and veiled threats about the consequences if the force were to come into being. Rumors circulated that creation of the MLF would prompt France to quit the Atlantic Alliance, possibly seeking a Franco-Soviet accord directed against Germany in its place.[41] French officials including Prime Minister Pompidou suggested publicly that German participation in the MLF would lead Paris to denounce the Elysée Treaty.[42] Meeting with former Chancellor Adenauer on November 9–10 in Paris, de Gaulle personally underlined the gravity of the situation for Franco-German relations.[43] The pressure from France proved to be more than the Bundestag could withstand. On his return to Bonn on November 11, Adenauer persuaded the CDU parliamentary bloc, despite Erhard's objections, to vote an indefinite delay in Germany's participation in the MLF.

By this point, the project was doomed. President Johnson, faced with strong French and British stands against the MLF, the waning enthusiasm of the Germans, and latent opposition to the project in Congress, decided that the matter did not warrant any further investment of effort and political capital.[44] Instead, he and Defense Secretary McNamara began to consider an alternative means of satisfying Germany's desire for nuclear codetermination.

In mid-1965 McNamara returned to a proposal he had originally made at Athens in May 1962 to create a committee within NATO to discuss nuclear doctrine and operations. The purpose of such a group would be to provide the Allies with regular and detailed information on U.S. strategic nuclear planning, together with insight into the data and reasoning on which it was based. As envisaged by McNamara, the proposed committee would give the Allies a substantive role in nuclear planning, which they had heretofore lacked. After some initial skepticism, the Erhard government became a strong supporter of McNamara's proposal, since it would actually meet most of Germany's demands for a voice in Alliance nuclear strategy. A consultative role in NATO nuclear strategy was not, of course, the same thing as direct control over a strategic nuclear force. Nevertheless, the proposed Nuclear Planning Group (NPG) held the potential to satisfy the German government's most pressing concern, namely, to be well-informed regarding U.S. nuclear doctrines and operational plans and to have a voice in those aspects of nuclear planning that directly affected Germany.

The French government opposed creation of the NPG for precisely the reasons that made the idea attractive to Germany and the other European allies—that it might succeed in making the shift to flexible response more acceptable. If it satisfied European demands for participation in NATO nuclear planning, the NPG would increase France's isolation in the Alliance. From the time that Washington had proposed the adoption of flexible response, Paris had sought to exploit German anxieties over the doctrine to win Bonn's support for the French nuclear force and for closer Franco-German defense cooperation. If the Europeans, especially the Germans, reconciled themselves to flexible response in exchange for the consultative arrangements provided by the NPG, France would find itself alone on questions of nuclear strategy. The French government accordingly did all it could to obstruct the formation of the NPG. In the long run this was a losing battle, however, and de Gaulle's decision to withdraw from allied military bodies might well have been hastened by the recognition that French influence on NATO's strategic planning would drop to a new low once the NPG was in full operation. In fact, de Gaulle announced France's pullout from NATO military structures only weeks after the NATO defense ministers created a working group to implement the NPG proposal.[45]

FRANCE BY ITSELF

After the MLF was shelved, Franco-German relations entered a new phase. As events were soon to show, de Gaulle had finally given up his attempt to create Europe around a Paris-Bonn axis. Erhard, for his part, continued doggedly on the same course as before. Early in 1965, for example, the Erhard government pushed ahead with its long-announced initiative on European political union. The German proposals, which bore a strong resemblance to the defunct Fouchet Plan, foundered when confronted with a complete lack of interest on de Gaulle's part.[46] Meanwhile, the French president had evidently decided that since Bonn would not cooperate in building an independent and self-assertive Europe, France would take action on its own. To do so, however, required that France have its hands free. France remained formally bound by the supranational and integrative structures of the EEC and NATO. Indeed, France's position in Atlantic and European institutions was still not fundamentally different from what it had been under the Fourth Republic despite more than six years of proposals and maneuvers by de Gaulle aimed at increasing France's autonomy within the West. This was now to change.

The years 1965 and 1966 saw de Gaulle move decisively to cut France loose from the formal constraints on its independence embodied by EEC and NATO institutions. This was a two-step process. The first step was to eliminate the challenge to national sovereignty emerging from the EEC Commission, the Common Market's executive body. In March 1965, the Commission had proposed that the European Parliament exercise direct control, independently of the governments of the Six, over receipts from tariffs on industrial and agricultural imports. The Commission made further proposals which aimed to strengthen its own independent powers over EEC financing and to reduce the ability of individual member states to block measures favored by the Commission and by the majority of EEC governments.

De Gaulle's response to the Commission's actions was decisive. When negotiations on future financing arrangements for the Common Market agricultural fund failed to produce an agreement by the prearranged deadline of June 30, 1965, de Gaulle reacted with a virtual boycott of the Community. Paris recalled its permanent representative to the EEC and ordered the French delegation in Brussels not to take part in any of the ongoing negotiations on expanding the implementation of the Rome Treaty. As later events showed, the agricultural financing dispute was more a pretext than the real cause of de Gaulle's resort to an "empty chair" policy.

De Gaulle's primary objective was to reduce decisively the Commission's powers and to establish once and for all the futility of projects that aimed at creating a supranational Europe.[47]

The crisis dragged on for months amid resistance by the other EEC members to de Gaulle's tactics. Once de Gaulle had been elected to a second term as French president in December 1965, however, it was clear that there was nothing to do but accommodate the French position. The foreign ministers of the Six accordingly met in Luxembourg to negotiate terms for France's return to Brussels. The so-called Luxembourg Compromise, reached on January 29, 1966, reduced considerably the Commission's independent powers and prerogatives by obligating it to work closely with the Council of Ministers on all important questions. The question of majority rule in the Council was nominally left unresolved; in practice, if not in principle, this amounted to recognition that no major decision in the EEC could be imposed on France against its will. The compromise solution thus ended for the foreseeable future any possibility of constructing an integrated Europe on supranational principles.

The French Withdrawal from NATO Integration

Hardly was the ink on the Luxembourg Compromise dry when de Gaulle moved to liquidate the other urgent question remaining on his foreign policy agenda—the redefinition of France's status and role in the Western Alliance. In a series of memoranda distributed to France's NATO allies during March 1966, de Gaulle announced his decision to withdraw all French forces and territory from Alliance military structures.[48] As of July 1, 1966, all French personnel were to be withdrawn from allied military commands in Europe, and the assignment of French land and air forces to NATO would be terminated. French staff and students would be withdrawn from the NATO Defense College at the end of the semester. Further, all NATO military bodies and installations were to be removed from French territory; de Gaulle proposed April 1, 1967 as an appropriate date for completion of the move. Finally, all U.S. and Canadian military forces and installations located in France were also to be removed, with April 1, 1967 again suggested as a feasible date for completion of the transfer.

The withdrawal of France's troops from NATO integrated structures meant that the two French divisions stationed in Germany would revert to French national command as of July 1, 1966. In a memorandum to the NATO allies dated March 11, the French government proposed that its forces in Germany could remain there after July 1 under the terms of the

October 1954 Convention on the Presence of Foreign Forces in the Federal Republic of Germany.[49] The German government, however, deeply resented the idea of French troops staying on German soil on the basis of the 1954 convention. Germany's original agreement to integrate its armed forces into the NATO command structure had been conditional on the willingness of the other allied states in Central Europe to do the same. Once France left the NATO military organization, French troops in Germany would no longer be governed by any mutually agreed plan for employing them to defend West Germany in the event of a conflict. By withdrawing from the NATO command structure and from allied military planning, France was in effect withdrawing its commitment to employ its forces in Germany on behalf of West Germany's defense. For many Germans, French troops stationed on German territory without any agreed mission to defend West Germany were equivalent to an army of occupation.

In a note to the French government dated March 29, 1966, the German government pointed out that France's right to station troops in West Germany was linked juridically and politically to the other agreements which paved the way for West Germany's entrance into NATO.[50] In an official statement on April 6, the German government announced its preference that French troops remain in Germany, but insisted that "these forces should . . . assume a strictly defined task in the framework of the common defense of NATO and cooperate with NATO forces in a manner to be agreed."[51] A further memorandum to the French government on May 3 reiterated this view. Paris replied on May 18 with a memorandum that appeared to concede West Germany's right to demand the withdrawal of French troops.[52] However, the French side remained insistent that its troops would no longer be subject to NATO command. In other words, Bonn could either accept French troops on its soil that were not integrated into NATO, or France would begin pulling them out.

The French note exposed the weakness of Bonn's bargaining position. Since de Gaulle was evidently quite willing to remove his troops from Germany, Bonn had no choices except those of accepting the French troops on de Gaulle's terms or else seeing them depart altogether. Ultimately Bonn would decide to accept de Gaulle's terms; but this was not a decision that came easily. Erhard and Schröder were both furious at de Gaulle for pulling out of the integrated command, and neither felt inclined to make concessions to him.

The German military, however, was extremely anxious that the French troops remain. This was not because the French forces in Germany had great military value in themselves. Indeed, if they were not integrated into NATO operational plans, the French forces in Germany were of little use for German defense. Of far greater concern to the German military was the necessity of retaining access to French territory as a strategic and logistical hinterland for the Bundeswehr.[53] According to one report, Germany had 100,000 tons of munitions and equipment stored at various locations in France, and these reserves comprised a considerable fraction of the Bundeswehr's total supplies.[54] The German military feared that failure to resolve the troop stationing issue could lead to a complete rupture of Franco-German military relations, ending Germany's access to storage facilities in France and requiring it to transfer its supplies to less desirable storage sites elsewhere.

Political considerations came into play as well. The troop stationing issue with France arose at a time when the cost of maintaining troops abroad was causing both the United States and Britain to cut back the number of their troops in West Germany; also, Washington was transferring some troop units from Germany to Vietnam. A pullout of French troops, occurring while U.S. and British troop reductions were under way, would give the appearance that Germany was being abandoned by the West. It was necessary to weigh the situation's long-term political implications. Once the French troops were gone, there would be little chance of ever bringing them back. Making a concession to de Gaulle in the short run would preserve the possibility that the French forces could be reintegrated into NATO under a future French government.

In a speech to the Bundestag on May 26, Erhard acknowledged his wish that the French troops remain, but reiterated his view that French forces in Germany must accept a defined mission under NATO command.[55] Thus the Erhard-de Gaulle relationship continued to be a dialogue of the deaf. In the end, the troop stationing dispute ended only after the demise of Erhard's government in November 1966 and its replacement by the CDU-CSU-SPD "grand coalition" government headed by Kurt Georg Kiesinger. Following Kiesinger's accession, it was quickly agreed that the French troops would remain in Germany, and that their legal status would be resolved through a simple exchange of letters between Willy Brandt, the new foreign minister, and French Foreign Minister Maurice Couve de Murville.

Under the exchange of letters, dated December 21, 1966, the German government declared its intention not to call into question the existing emplacement of French forces in West Germany.[56] Any necessary modification in the emplacement of the French forces was to be decided by bilateral agreement of the French and German governments, that is, *not* as a function of NATO planning. These provisions ended once and for all Bonn's hopes for an eastward redeployment of the French divisions.

Despite France's withdrawal from the integrated NATO command, it was never de Gaulle's intention to quit the Atlantic Alliance, which he continued to regard as a vital element of France's security. Indeed, in the very memorandum announcing the French pullout from the NATO command, de Gaulle proposed that talks be initiated between military representatives of France and NATO to arrange the modalities of French cooperation in Alliance defense. What de Gaulle rejected was not participation in a military alliance, but the notion of *automatic* military involvement in case of a European conflict and an integrated defense planning system that did not allow France to develop its own military plans based on its own national interests. If France were to become involved in a European military conflict, it must be as the result of a deliberate decision of the French president at the time of the conflict rather than as a function of the pre-delegation to NATO of authority over French forces.

Needless to say, de Gaulle's viewpoint was hardly satisfactory to either Washington or Bonn. The American government considered the pre-delegation of authority over European forces to be essential. It was impossible to devise effective plans for a European defense involving France without advance assurance that French troops and territory would be committed to a conflict if one occurred. The Germans, meanwhile, considered de Gaulle's conditions to be unsatisfactory above all from a political perspective: for conventional deterrence to be maximally effective, it had to confront potential aggressors with the near-certainty that all of West Germany's allies would be automatically involved in Germany's defense in the event of a conflict. If the French commitment were clearly conditional, it would contribute little to deterrence. In fact, it might even encourage the Soviet Union to think that it could attack Germany without running the risk of French involvement.

In October 1966 the NATO Council took up de Gaulle's offer to develop contingency plans for joint military action between French forces and NATO. The Supreme Allied Commander in Europe, General Lyman Lemnitzer, was authorized to work out a framework agreement with French chief of staff Charles Ailleret on military cooperation between France and NATO. The resulting agreements, signed in August 1967 and known as the Ailleret-Lemnitzer accords, provided a framework within which substantive agreements could later be worked out between France and NATO on air defense, coordinated action of land forces, and logistics.[57] At the heart of the Ailleret-Lemnitzer agreements was the principle of non-automaticity. Any operational plans worked out for French participation in an Alliance military action had to depend on a decision by France's political leadership at the time of the action. No installations or operational plans were acceptable that would involve France automatically in military actions undertaken by other NATO states.

One other question requiring attention concerned the future status of Germany's military supply depots inside France. Shortly after its announced withdrawal from the NATO command structure, the French government had proposed that existing agreements permitting Germany to store military goods in France be renewed. The Franco-German storage arrangements did undergo some important modifications, however. These were in line with the same principles governing other aspects of French military cooperation with the Allies, namely, that French military commitments were not to be automatic. Under the modified agreements, Germany's access to its supply depots in France during a military conflict would require an explicit decision by French political leaders.

Other areas of routine Franco-German military cooperation were essentially unaffected by France's changed role in NATO. For example, French and German troops continued the annual joint exercise in which they transferred German munitions stored in France to and from German vessels standing off the French coast.[58] The regular exchanges of small units and individual soldiers and officers between the French and German armed forces continued without interruption.[59] Also, German armed forces continued to make occasional use of French firing ranges for training purposes. An agreement for the continued use of military exercise areas in France by the German armed forces was signed in June 1966.[60]

THE WEIGHT OF THE POSTWAR ORDER

In surveying the Franco-German strategic relationship from 1960 to 1967, it seems clear that both sides found themselves at a dead end and were compelled to scale down their foreign policy ambitions. Under Adenauer, West Germany had hoped to find in de Gaulle an ally for its foreign policy goals of equal status in the Western alliance, the rollback of Soviet power in Eastern Europe, and supranational integration in Western Europe. De Gaulle proved unwilling to assist in any of these objectives. Of all the major Western countries, de Gaulle's France was the most steadfast in resisting nuclear control-sharing for Germany or a German voice in NATO nuclear strategy. Far from taking a hard line toward Moscow, France led the West in calling for détente. And de Gaulle singlehandedly brought the process of supranational European integration to a halt, thereby blocking Bonn from using the EEC as a vehicle for its national aspirations. Although de Gaulle did seek close political and military cooperation between France and Germany under the Elysée Treaty, he in no way envisaged a partnership of equals. Rather, de Gaulle's plan for partnership basically called on Germany to support France in the latter's effort to hold the balance between East and West. Since French policy seemed targeted much more against American than Soviet power, Bonn had little incentive to go along. Viewed from West Germany's perspective, de Gaulle seemed to be asking Germany to choose between France and the United States. Placed before this choice, the German state inevitably chose loyalty to its primary guarantor.

The result of the estrangement between de Gaulle's France and Erhard's Germany was that both countries found themselves effectively blocked from making fundamental gains in international power. De Gaulle, after removing France from NATO's integrated military command, declared that French foreign policy was now independent; but it was independence without real weight. With German support, France might have been an actor to be reckoned with, both in Alliance politics and in the East-West equation. As it was, France after 1966 was largely irrelevant to politics in both arenas. Within the West, France stood alone in opposition to the policies of its fourteen allies. In East-West relations, an isolated France found that Moscow did not take it seriously as an arbiter; instead, the Soviet government showed that it preferred to deal directly with the United States and West Germany in deciding the terms of détente. Again, a closer bond between Paris and Bonn would have given de Gaulle a stronger hand in his opening to Moscow.

After 1966, moreover, France increasingly lacked the military means to give substance to its political aspirations. Gaullist France concentrated its resources on developing an independent national nuclear arsenal. To be sure, France could hardly do otherwise if it wanted to lay the basis for a great-power role. Over time, however, France's concentration on its nuclear program meant the gradual evisceration of its conventional military capabilities. In later years, France lacked the conventional forces that would have been necessary on a practical basis for it to count as a major actor on the world stage or even in the more limited context of Europe.

The Luxembourg Compromise and France's withdrawal from NATO, taken together, marked a turning point in the Franco-German security relationship. Although the strategic policies of France and Germany had been on divergent paths since the beginning of the Fifth Republic, de Gaulle's moves of 1965-1966 formalized the contradiction between the two countries' goals. In doing so, they helped to lay the groundwork for Germany's fundamental reformulation of its security strategy later in the decade.

NOTES

1. The most comprehensive discussion of the negotiations on European political union is Robert Bloes, Le "Plan Fouchet" et le problème de l'Europe politique (Bruges: Collège d'Europe, 1970). Also useful are Alessandro Silj, Europe's Political Puzzle: A Study of the Fouchet Negotiations and the 1963 Veto (Cambridge, Mass.: Center for International Affairs, Harvard University, 1967), and Suzanne J. Bodenheimer, Political Union: A Microcosm of European Politics, 1960–1966 (Leiden: A. W. Sijthoff, 1967). Couve, Une politique étrangère, pp. 347–84, offers a valuable if partisan firsthand account.

2. De Gaulle, September 5, 1960 press conference, in Major Addresses, pp. 92–93. Note also de Gaulle's broad attack on supranational integration at his press conference of May 15, 1962, in Major Addresses, pp. 175–77.

3. Couve, Une politique étrangère, p. 376.

4. Couve, Une politique étrangère, p. 349.

5. Hoffmann, Decline or Renewal?, p. 295.

6. Couve, Une politique étrangère, pp. 359–60.

7. Couve, Une politique étrangère, p. 360.

8. Schwarz, "Das aussenpolitische Konzept," pp. 122–23.

9. Schwarz, "Das aussenpolitische Konzept," p. 146.

10. See, for example, Adenauer, Erinnerungen, 1959–1963, pp. 136–50 and 194–95, and Blankenhorn, Verständnis, p. 384.

11. Adenauer, Erinnerungen, 1959–1963, p. 168; Couve, Une politique étrangère, p. 253.

12. Couve, Une politique étrangère, pp. 253–54.

13. See Adenauer, Erinnerungen, 1959–1963, pp. 178–81.

14. Irmgard Heinemann, Le Traité franco-allemand du 22 janvier 1963 et sa mise en oeuvre sous le général de Gaulle, 1963–1969 (doctoral thesis, University of Nice, 1977), p. 87.

15. Interview with Schröder in Die Zeit, August 21, 1964.

16. See Johannes Bauer, Die deutsch-französischen Beziehungen, 1963–1969: Aspekte der Entwicklung nach Abschluss des Vertrages vom 22. Januar 1963 (doctoral dissertation, Bonn, 1980), pp. 102–4, and Heinemann, Le Traité franco-allemand, pp. 86–88.

17. See Lois Pattison de Ménil, Who Speaks for Europe? (New York: St. Martin's Press, 1977), pp. 213–17, for the full text of the treaty.

18. De Gaulle's conversations with Erhard at the Franco-German summit meetings of February and July 1964, discussed below, certainly suggest that this was his reasoning.

19. Willis, *France, Germany*, pp. 313–14; Bauer, *Die deutsch-französischen Beziehungen*, pp. 170–75. Adenauer, who for his own part shared many of de Gaulle's doubts about the British application, was far out of step with the mainstream of German opinion on this issue.

20. Bauer, *Die deutsch-französischen Beziehungen*, pp. 164–67.

21. Bauer, *Die deutsch-französischen Beziehungen*, p. 176; Heinemann, *Le Traité franco-allemand*, pp. 124–25; Theodore C. Sorenson, *Kennedy* (New York: Harper and Row, 1965), p. 646.

22. Grosser, *The Western Alliance*, p. 208.

23. See de Ménil, *Who Speaks for Europe?*, p. 125.

24. Gilbert Ziebura, *Die deutsch-französischen Beziehungen seit 1945: Mythen und Realitäten* (Pfullingen: Neske, 1970), pp. 104, 109.

25. Adenauer had a lasting fear of a renewed Franco-Russian entente directed against Germany. Cf. Blankenhorn, *Verständnis*, p. 439, and Schwarz, "Das aussenpolitische Konzept," pp. 112–13.

26. The speech is reprinted in Heinrich Siegler, *Europäische politische Einigung: Dokumentation von Vorschlägen und Stellungnahmen, 1949–1968* (Bonn: Siegler & Co., 1968), pp. 242–45.

27. See *The New York Times*, June 13, 1964.

28. The incident is recounted in Paul Frank, *Entschlüsselte Botschaft* (Stuttgart: Deutsche Verlags-Anstalt, 1981), pp. 95–96. For other discussions of the pivotal July 1964 summit, see Bauer, *Die deutsch-französischen Beziehungen*, pp. 256–57; Heinemann, *Le Traité franco-allemand*, pp. 197–98; and Klaus Hildebrand, "Der provisorische Staat und das Ewige Frankreich: Die deutsch-französischen Beziehungen 1963 bis 1969," in Schwarz, ed., *Adenauer und Frankreich*, pp. 67–68.

29. See, for example, de Gaulle's July 21, 1964 press conference, reprinted in de Gaulle, *Discours et messages*, vol. 4, p. 230.

30. Osgood, *NATO*, pp. 72–73.

31. Wilhelm Grewe, *Rückblenden: Aufzeichnungen eines Augenzeugen deutscher Aussenpolitik von Adenauer bis Schmidt* (Berlin: Propyläen, 1979), p. 687.

32. Harrison, *Reluctant Ally*, p. 153.

33. See, for example, *Le Monde*, August 17, 1963, June 6, 1964, October 21, 1964, and May 5, 1965.

34. See Steinbruner, *Cybernetic Theory*, pp. 202–4, and Schwartz, *NATO's Nuclear Dilemmas*, chapter 6.

35. Grewe, *Rückblenden*, pp. 680–81; also Kelleher, *Germany*, chapters 6 and 7.

36. Grewe, *Rückblenden*, p. 612.

37. Steinbruner, *Cybernetic Theory*, pp. 233, 249–51.

38. Henry A. Kissinger, *The Troubled Partnership* (New York: McGraw-Hill, 1965), pp. 140–59.

39. Steinbruner, *Cybernetic Theory*, pp. 288–90.

40. Grewe, *Rückblenden*, p. 619.

41. See Dieter Mahncke, *Nukleare Mitwirkung: Die Bundesrepublik Deutschland in der atlantischen Allianz, 1954–1970* (Berlin: Walter de Gruyter, 1972), pp. 184–87.

42. See de Ménil, *Who Speaks for Europe?*, pp. 161–62.

43. Heinemann, *Le Traité franco-allemand*, p. 207, and Kelleher, *Germany*, p. 250.

44. Steinbruner, *Cybernetic Theory*, p. 309.

45. On the genesis and activities of the NPG, see Paul Buteux, *The Politics of Nuclear Consultation in NATO, 1965–1980* (Cambridge: Cambridge University Press, 1983). For an evaluation of the NPG's importance and effectiveness from a West German perspective, see Grewe, *Rückblenden*, pp. 629–33. Grewe participated in NPG meetings from 1966–1970 in his capacity as Bonn's permanent representative to NATO.

46. Herbert Müller-Roschach, *Die deutsche Europapolitik, 1949–1977* (Bonn: Europa Union Verlag, 1980), pp. 153–55. The text of the West German proposals appears in Siegler, *Europäische politische Einigung*, pp. 280–87.

47. For a detailed analysis of the 1965 crisis, see Miriam Camps, *European Unification in the Sixties* (London: Oxford University Press, 1967).

48. See Radoux, *France and NATO*, pp. 48–50 and 53–55.

49. The Convention is reprinted in Stares, *Allied Rights*, pp. 103–4.

50. Text reprinted in Assembly of Western European Union, *France and NATO*, Document 375, June 1966, p. 27.

51. Text in Radoux, *France and NATO*, pp. 56–57.

52. Text in Radoux, *France and NATO*, pp. 83–84.

53. Grewe, *Rückblenden*, p. 687.

54. *Frankfurter Allgemeine Zeitung*, April 9, 1966.

55. *Frankfurter Allgemeine Zeitung*, May 26, 1966.

56. The letters are reprinted in *Le Monde*, December 23, 1966, and the *Frankfurter Allgemeine Zeitung*, December 22, 1966.

57. The content of the accords remains confidential. The discussion in this section is based on interviews with French and German military officials and defense analysts.

58. This series included the exercises "Prelude" (October 1964), "Intermezzo" (September 1965), "Allegro" (May 1966), "Presto" (September 1967), and "Crescendo" (May 1968).

59. *Frankfurter Allgemeine Zeitung*, January 22, 1968.

60. *Kölnische Rundschau*, June 23, 1966.

CHAPTER 3

Attempts at Arms Procurement Collaboration, 1955–1964

Relatively little has been said up to this point about cooperation between France and West Germany in weapons development and procurement. This chapter will examine the early history of Franco-German attempts at cooperation in major weapons projects, and will examine how the broader foreign policy objectives of the two sides affected the overall pattern of armaments collaboration. The question of weapons procurement cooperation has been an important one in Franco-German relations for both political and military reasons. It has also been important because of the relationship between technological capabilities and strategic autonomy. No country can aspire to great-power status if it lacks the capability to develop and produce technologically advanced weaponry.

For France in particular, self-reliance in weapons technology seemed indispensable if it wanted the ability to resist U.S. attempts to undercut its foreign policy independence. But to develop and produce all its arms on a national basis would be extremely costly. From the mid-1950s on, French leaders began to think of weapons production partnership with Germany and other European states as a means of maintaining self-sufficiency in advanced weapons technology at a cost that was within France's means. As will be seen below, efforts by Paris to use weapons cooperation with Germany to reinforce its own autonomy from the United States have been a constantly recurring theme of Franco-German relations. For Germans also—or at least, for those made restless by the constraints on their independence imposed by strategic dependence on the United States—the logic of Franco-German weapons collaboration held great appeal.

Because of its obvious importance to Europe's great-power potential, the degree of intra-European weapons collaboration can be viewed as an important indicator of overall West European movement toward strategic self-reliance. As with other areas of Franco-German defense cooperation, however, there has often been a gap between stated objectives and actual accomplishments. Armaments production involves a complex web of issues for the contemporary nation-state. Economic interests, and hence domestic political actors, come into play much more directly in arms procurement decisions than in questions of strategic doctrine or military operations. Economic interests enter into arms procurement choices in several ways. First, leaders may view such choices as important from a technological standpoint. Weapons research has been a major engine of technological advance in many areas including electronics, aeronautics, data processing, new materials, and nuclear fission. Many political leaders in Europe (as in the United States) have believed that a country could not maintain an internationally competitive civilian economy unless it possessed a well-developed and technologically advanced weapons industry. There has accordingly been a strong predilection in both France and West Germany to view arms procurement as an instrument of civilian industrial policy, and to award weapons development and production contracts in ways that would bring technological gains to domestic manufacturers.

Closely associated with the view of arms procurement as industrial policy has been concern among European leaders about the implications of specific procurement decisions for domestic employment. The arms procurement choices of Western governments have been heavily shaped by the desire to provide work to the hundreds of thousands of workers employed by domestic arms producers. This is particularly true in regard to France, where the bulk of the armaments industry has been state-owned since the late 1930s. The state's responsibility for maintaining employment and prosperity in the nationalized weapons industry has strongly influenced French arms procurement policy throughout the post-1945 period. French governments during the Cold War insisted that weapons for the French armed forces be designed and produced by domestic arms makers whenever possible, and were extremely active in promoting exports of French-made weapons abroad.

In West Germany, by contrast, the armaments industry was decimated by the war and by the general prohibition on weapons production imposed from 1945 to 1951. The German weapons industry, which began to revive in the latter 1950s as a result of Germany's rearmament, was mostly privately owned and anxious to keep a low profile politically. In consequence, governments in Bonn were initially less zealous (or at least less consistent) than the French in protecting the interests of domestic arms producers. As employment in the German arms industry grew, however, German governments also began to weigh procurement decisions in terms of their effects on the livelihood of arms industry workers.

Fear of broad-based technological dependence on the United States has been another recurring element in European arms procurement decisions. The Cold War had already made Western Europe heavily dependent on the United States for its security. What if this dependence were compounded by European dependence on the United States for both advanced military technology and related civilian technologies? Many Europeans, especially in France, believed that unchecked technological dependence would make Europe completely subordinate to American political dictates. More abstractly, European leaders feared that so much dependence on the United States could be psychologically debilitating for European publics.

EUROPEAN WEAPONS PROCUREMENT AND U.S. INTERESTS

Pressures emanating from the United States further complicated European procurement decisions. From the early years of the Western alliance, Washington took a major interest in the arms procurement choices of its European partners. In general, the thrust of U.S. policy was to encourage strongly the sale of American armaments and military technology to Europe.[1] This policy had several motives. One consistent U.S. objective was the desire to enhance the military effectiveness of Alliance defenses by standardizing the weapons and equipment used by NATO members. U.S. administrations tended to view American arms sales to Europe as the best method for achieving this aim. Economic considerations also motivated the United States to promote export sales of its arms to Europe. As the primary guarantor of Europe's security, Washington frequently attempted to translate European strategic dependence into sales for American manufacturers and producers. Of course, West European governments strongly resisted any explicit linkage between the American security guarantee and European trade concessions. Even so, Washington had some success (especially with West Germany) in persuading European governments to buy U.S.-made arms as a partial quid pro quo for the cost of the U.S. security commitment. An additional U.S. motive for arms sales to Europe, which the American side understandably downplayed, was Washington's desire to reinforce its leverage over European foreign and defense policies by encouraging West European reliance on the United States for key weapon systems.

European arms procurement policies thus evolved against a backdrop of steady U.S. pressure for West European purchases of American-designed weapons. In some ways, Europeans stood to gain from going along with American preferences. First, U.S. weapon designs were often available to European governments at lower prices than comparable European designs. Thus, it was frequently the case that a European government could purchase the design for a given weapon from an American manufacturer and produce it in Europe under license at a much lower cost than developing a similar weapon on its own. Reliance on U.S. military technology could therefore save money. Second, consistent European use of U.S. weapon designs offered potential military advantages in that it would lead to a more rational and effective allied fighting force than one in which each NATO member designed and produced its weapon systems independently.

In practice, however, reliance on U.S. military technology had limited—and declining—appeal for France and Germany. From the late 1950s onward, in fact, the French government did all it could to avoid buying U.S.-origin weapon systems. West Germany, by contrast, made repeated major purchases of U.S.-designed military aircraft during its first two decades of NATO membership. As will be argued in this chapter, however, these purchases were motivated not so much by considerations of cost-effectiveness or military rationality as by the perceived need to accommodate U.S. wishes and by the fact that German industry was unable to provide high-performance military aircraft on its own.

In fact, despite steady U.S. pressure on behalf of allied weapons standardization, concerns over military rationality usually played a negligible role in the weapons acquisition choices of France and West Germany. Far more important as influences were the attempts by Paris and Bonn to protect the interests of domestic arms manufacturers and to use arms procurement policy as a means of reinforcing broader political objectives. For Paris this meant using weapons cooperation with Germany to strengthen its strategic independence vis-à-vis Washington. For Bonn it meant using weapons procurement to fortify cooperative links between itself and its major allies—the United States, France, and Britain. The contradictions inherent in French and German foreign policy perspectives, as well as the frequently divergent interests of the arms industries of the two sides, placed sharp limits on the achievements of Franco-German arms procurement cooperation throughout the 1950s and 1960s.

INITIAL EFFORTS AT COOPERATION

West European cooperation in arms production first emerged as an important Alliance issue at the 1954 London and Paris conferences, where the conditions for Germany's entry into NATO were decided. Debate initially centered on the French government's proposal for an "armaments pool" to coordinate and control arms production in Western Europe.[2] The French plan, circulated by Premier Pierre Mendès-France in September 1954, would have created a centralized European authority with exclusive responsibility for procuring and allocating military equipment within the Western European Union. The authority would be equipped with a broad range of powers enabling it to control every aspect of weapons acquisition in the WEU member states. Mendès-France's purpose in making this proposal was to create an effective means for controlling German rearmament in lieu of the failed European Defense Community. The French plan found little support, however, in the United States or elsewhere in Western Europe; allied governments were not anxious to create an international agency with the wide-ranging powers advocated by the French. The arms pool idea thus went nowhere, and the French were forced to abandon their last-ditch plan to control Germany's rearmament from Paris.

The armaments co-production question was soon to resurface, however. It did so primarily as a result of France's growing disillusion with NATO during the last years of the Fourth Republic, a development that increasingly led Paris to view armaments cooperation with Germany as an important means for France to attain its national political and industrial goals. French views on Germany as a partner in armaments production thus paralleled France's views toward Germany as a political partner more generally. French bitterness over the lack of support from the United States and NATO in the Suez and Algerian conflicts injected powerful political overtones into the question of weapons procurement. Increasingly, the French government regarded the ability to produce technologically advanced weaponry as the decisive factor determining whether France would be able to maintain its independence and uphold its claim to great-power status. French leaders came to believe that France could control its own destiny only if it possessed the capability to produce all major types of high-technology weaponry, conventional as well as nuclear, independently of the United States.

It was against this background that the governments of the Fourth Republic began discussions with Germany over the possibility of systematic cooperation in arms procurement questions. Burdened with the costs of the war in Algeria, France lacked the funds to keep up with weapons development in the United States and Britain. The more France shared the expense of weapons research and development with Germany, the broader an array of weapons development activities it would be able to afford. Armaments cooperation with Germany, French leaders believed, could thus help France to increase its influence vis-à-vis the United States and Britain.

At the same time that French attitudes on armaments cooperation were coming into focus, the German government's views on armaments production were also evolving. A key event in this evolution was the appointment of Franz Josef Strauss as defense minister in October 1956. Before Strauss's arrival, the German government's policy on arms purchases reflected the views of Economics Minister Ludwig Erhard, the architect of Germany's "economic miracle" and a crusading advocate of free-market principles. In Erhard's view, armaments should be treated as any other manufactured good in a market economy, that is, they should be purchased from whichever source could supply them most cheaply. Why should Germany invest government funds in building up a national armaments industry where none currently existed? To do so, in Erhard's view, would be an inefficient use of resources. Engineers in Germany were scarce, and could not be spared from civilian industries to design weapons. Besides, Erhard contended, Germany could buy all the weapons it needed from its allies, especially the United States, at lower prices than it could hope to produce them itself.[3] Erhard's views were widely shared among German industrial leaders. The perceived role of arms manufacturers in Hitler's Reich had made many industrial firms reluctant to produce military goods. Most industrial leaders regarded weapons production as a public-relations liability.

Strauss put greater emphasis than Erhard on the political implications of an advanced national capability in weapons research and production. Like Adenauer, Strauss was preoccupied with the goal of political equality for Germany within the Alliance. Strauss did not in any way envisage the development of a West German armaments autarky. He did, however, believe that full equality within NATO could be secured only if Germany possessed advanced technological capabilities in at least some areas of weapons production, to use as a bargaining tool in political and military negotiations with its allies.[4]

Strauss also saw advanced weapons research as a vital component of technological progress for the German economy as a whole. Without access to the most advanced military technologies, Strauss believed, German industry would ultimately lose its world competitiveness in key civilian industries. Strauss laid particular stress on the aeronautics sector, which he identified as one of the major arenas of technological and industrial competition among the industrial powers. His long-range goal, according to one close associate, was to see the creation of a European aeronautics industry capable of competing successfully with U.S. aeronautics firms.[5] To the extent that cooperative European arms projects could help West Germany reestablish its technological capabilities in key sectors, Strauss strongly favored them.

Strauss's goals for West German arms procurement, although partially compatible with French objectives, also contained the potential for conflict with Paris. The French government was motivated above all by the desire to counteract "Anglo-Saxon" domination of the Alliance. It sought weapons cooperation with Germany as a way of building a continental counterpoise to the powerful American and British armaments industries. From France's perspective, therefore, procurement choices on any given weapon system increasingly boiled down to two options: production by France alone, or production in cooperation with Germany.

The German government took a far more flexible view of its procurement options. Strauss was interested in using arms procurement as an instrument for building up West Germany's technological capabilities in whatever ways were compatible with its other political and military commitments. Cooperative weapons development with France and other European allies was one possible route to this goal. But there was also the option of German production, under license, of weapons designed in Britain or the United States. Joint development had the advantage of enabling a country to improve its own design and engineering capabilities; licensed production, on the other hand, had the advantage of permitting the licensee to acquire technological know-how quickly and easily. Which option was preferable depended on the particular case.

The Armaments Triangle

The first systematic discussion of the possibilities for Franco-German armaments cooperation came during Strauss's extended consultations with French Defense Minister Maurice Bourgès-Maunoury in January 1957. As a result of these conversations, a bilateral military committee was set up to explore various proposals for joint weapons development.[6] The Gaillard government, coming to power in November 1957, expanded on the existing talks with its proposal for an "armaments triangle" consisting of France, Germany, and Italy, which would completely integrate the research and development efforts of the three countries in advanced weaponry. Strauss endorsed the triangle proposal enthusiastically. During the first months of 1958, meetings among the French, German, and Italian defense ministers examined specific projects where the prospects for cooperation seemed greatest. These included battle tanks, fighter aircraft, transport aircraft, nuclear weapons (see Chapter 1), and basic research in conventional weaponry. France and Germany were the major participants in plans for all of these projects. Italy, preoccupied with internal political and economic difficulties, soon faded to little more than a background presence.

The other NATO allies reacted to the announcement of the armaments triangle in January 1958 with displeasure.[7] The United States reiterated its established position that all questions concerning armaments cooperation should be dealt with in the existing NATO committees on weapons standardization. Other allies including Belgium, Denmark, Norway, and the Netherlands echoed the American position, not liking the creation of a separate, exclusive European organization to address issues of weapons acquisition that were of importance to all members of the Alliance. Britain, meanwhile, viewed the armaments triangle as a threat to its own prospects for arms exports to the Continent.[8]

Viewed in broad perspective, the arms procurement policies of France, Britain, and the United States in the latter 1950s amounted to a competi- tion for control of the West German arms market. The German armed forces were expected eventually to reach a size of several hundred thousand soldiers. All these troops would have to be provided with modern military equipment—but by whom? West Germany's own arms production capa- bilities had shrunk greatly as a result of the general prohibition on the manufacture of military goods imposed by the occupation powers from 1945 to 1951. (Aircraft production had been prohibited until 1955.) To equip its rapidly expanding forces, Germany would need to rely heavily on imports. The extraordinary German economic expansion in the 1950s had put Germany in a position to afford the best equipment its allies could sell it. In short, Germany was shaping up as the world's biggest market for arms manufactured by its NATO allies.

The Starfighter Sale

Germany's equipment needs during the first years of rearmament were temporarily filled by surplus American matériel, largely of wartime vintage, that the United States sold to Germany at low prices or donated outright. One military requirement that could not be satisfied by this method, however, was the Bundeswehr's need for a supersonic fighter aircraft to perform a variety of missions, especially nuclear counterair strikes. In late 1957 Washington had agreed to make American nuclear warheads available to a number of allies, including Germany, under a "double key" control arrangement (see Chapter 1). It was up to the allied governments themselves, however, to procure appropriate aircraft and tactical missiles to serve as delivery vehicles for the U.S.-owned warheads. Bonn's announcement of intent to purchase a large number of nuclear-capable fighter aircraft thus set off an intense scramble among American, British, and French airframe manufacturers.[9] The German order promised to amount to an enormous sum of money. Big as the prospective value of a sale to Germany was, however, even greater stakes were involved for the competing manufacturers. The airplane chosen by Bonn stood a good chance of being accepted by Italy, Belgium, and the Netherlands as their standard fighter plane. The company that sold its fighter to Germany would thus be in a strong position to dominate the European market in military aircraft for many years to come.

By early 1958, the German government had narrowed its choice to an American plane, the F-104 Starfighter manufactured by Lockheed, and a French plane, the Mirage III of Marcel Dassault. Lockheed and Dassault each mounted an all-out campaign in Germany to win the final selection. The French and American governments also joined the fray, lobbying for the sale as intensely as the manufacturers themselves. In October 1958, the German defense ministry announced that it had decided in favor of the F-104. A total of 96 Starfighters would be purchased directly from Lockheed, while 554 more would be produced in Germany under license. A number of considerations influenced the German decision to buy the Starfighter, making it difficult to identify any single factor as decisive. Political pressure from Washington played an important role; choosing the Mirage III would undoubtedly have subjected the Germans to American charges of ingratitude and disloyalty. However, the Starfighter was a more capable aircraft than the Mirage, and was preferred by the German air force.[10] The Starfighter also seemed the best choice in terms of German industrial interests, appearing to offer greater prospects than the Mirage for licensed production in Germany and hence for domestic employment and technological gains.[11]

The German decision illustrated the difficulties faced by the French in trying to use Germany's arms procurement budget in support of their own political aspirations in the Alliance. The German fighter plane purchase had been one of the major subjects of discussion in the French-German-

Italian armaments triangle. In his frequent meetings with Strauss during the first four months of 1958, French Defense Minister Chaban-Delmas had spent much of his time attempting to persuade his German colleague to buy the Mirage. Thus the Starfighter sale had to be reckoned a major setback for the armaments triangle, at least from the French government's point of view. The armaments triangle also registered a major failure in its project to equip the French and German armies with a common main battle tank. The project, under discussion from 1957 to 1963, collapsed when the Germans decided to build a battle tank on their own.[12]

The Transall

Franco-German cooperation on the C-160 Transall, a military transport aircraft, was the principal achievement of the armaments triangle.[13] The Transall originated in a mutual Franco-German requirement for a successor to the Noratlas, a military transport developed and manufactured in the early 1950s by the state-owned French firm Nord-Aviation. Under a 1956 agreement, a consortium of private German companies had produced the Noratlas under license for German forces. From the initial days of the armaments triangle, the idea of jointly developing a new transport aircraft came under discussion. Both France and Germany needed such an aircraft, but their initial military requirements were highly dissimilar. The French government wanted an aircraft suited to France's military commitments in North Africa. This meant a long-range, high-capacity transport optimized for operation in a desert environment. The Germans, by contrast, sought a medium-range, medium-capacity transport designed for Central European weather conditions and with a short takeoff and landing capability.

Despite the divergence in their preferences, both sides had strong motives for seeking a cooperative venture. The French were determined not to buy a U.S.-manufactured transport aircraft, even though Lockheed's C-130A Hercules was available and ideally suited to France's military requirements. Given France's tight financial situation, however, a purely national development program would be extremely difficult to finance. Joint development with Germany offered a more practicable option. For Germany, meanwhile, joint development with France offered an opportunity to maintain employment and production at several airframe companies in northern Germany after work on the Noratlas was finished. The German companies themselves were highly interested in the prospect of collaboration with the French, which would give them the opportunity to play a major role in the design and development of the aircraft.

In December 1958, Strauss and French Armies Minister Guillaumat signed an agreement for the joint development of a military transport aircraft. Participants in the program would be essentially the same firms as those involved in the Noratlas program: Nord-Aviation on the French side, Weser Flugzeugbau and Hamburger Flugzeugbau on the German side. A bilateral managerial structure was established in which French and German interests were equally represented at all levels. At the governmental level, the project was supervised by a bilateral steering committee. The participating companies formed a bilateral technical directorate and, below that, a bilateral management committee. Bilateral technical committees were also formed for each major subassembly. The result of this organizational structure was to render decision making slow and difficult. "Because neither country totally dominated the project," writes Mark Lorell, "every problem, even one as trivial as the types of rivets, screws, and screwdrivers to be used, resulted in a new round of meetings and negotiations."[14] As the Transall program progressed, it was marked by repeated delays and steadily accumulating cost overruns. Since the aircraft itself was a relatively simple design based on established technologies and fitted with proven engines, the program's difficulties can be attributed largely to its burdensome organizational structure. Significantly, the aircraft that ultimately emerged from this process conformed much more closely to French than to German specifications.

In Germany, the mounting delays and cost overruns of the Transall produced a rising tide of criticism in the Bundestag. Moreover, German air force officials were deeply dissatisfied with the aircraft because of its failure to meet their military requirements. As a result, the Bundestag's defense committee came close to cancelling the program in October 1963. But as in the case of the Elysée Treaty, which it had ratified less than six months earlier, the Bundestag was unwilling to risk a head-on confrontation with France. Instead, the defense committee ultimately backed down and approved funding for full-scale production of the aircraft.

An intergovernmental agreement for manufacture of the Transall was signed in July 1964. A total of 160 aircraft were to be produced, 110 for Germany and 50 for France. Despite vigorous efforts by the two countries to find additional buyers for the Transall, none materialized. Since the Lockheed C-130A was superior to the Transall in most performance characteristics, and was available for approximately half the price, the Franco-German aircraft held little attraction for potential customers. The lone export agreement was a South African order for nine Transalls, which came in 1966 after the U.S. government had banned further exports of the C-130A to the apartheid regime.

Leaving aside the cost overruns that plagued the aircraft, as well as its failure to satisfy the military requirements of the German air force, the Transall project can be regarded as a success of sorts. It did ultimately produce a functional transport airplane on the basis of a common Franco-German design. It is clear that both political and industrial considerations contributed to German willingness to follow through with the Transall program despite its shortcomings. In effect, there was a convergence of German political and industrial interests that superseded the Luftwaffe's military requirements.

Politically, the Transall served the function of shoring up Germany's relations with France following the Starfighter decision. Coming only two months after the announced Starfighter purchase, the agreement on joint development of the Transall was clearly intended at least in part as a consolation package to ease French disappointment. In addition, the Transall project was attractive to German industrialists even if not to the German air force. The German aeronautics industry had all but ceased to exist during its decade of forced inactivity, with many of its best engineers having abandoned aeronautics or gone to firms in other countries. At the time when the Transall development agreement was reached, the German air industry lacked the capability to design and produce a transport airplane by itself. At most, it could contribute to the design of such an aircraft in cooperation with a more advanced partner. Thus, awareness of its own limitations made the German air industry willing to accept cooperation on terms that allowed Nord-Aviation to dominate the design of the Transall.

The Institut de Saint-Louis

Aside from the Transall, Franco-German armaments cooperation recorded one other notable success stemming from the armaments triangle discussions. This was a 1958 agreement granting Germany equal participation in the French military research laboratory at Saint-Louis. The Institut de Saint-Louis (ISL) had been created in August 1945 from the remains of the Luftwaffe's Ballistics Institute in Berlin. Approximately forty German scientists, led by the renowned physicist Hubert Schardin, had accepted the French government's offer at the end of the war to provide them with a laboratory where they could pursue their research. The location of the laboratory, in a converted aluminum foundry near the French-German-

Swiss border, enabled the scientists to live in their native Germany even though working for the French government.[15]

Because many of the ISL scientists were among world leaders in various aspects of weapons research, the German government was anxious to regain access to the fruit of their labors. Under a convention signed by Strauss and Chaban-Delmas on March 31, 1958, the French and German governments agreed to share equally in the administration and financing of the ISL. The research findings of Institute scientists were to be made equally available to both governments.[16] In subsequent years, the ISL proved to be one of the most successful projects in Franco-German military cooperation. Its research findings made important contributions to French and German military technology, particularly in the areas of munitions, armor, and antitank missiles. By the 1980s the ISL employed some 450 people, of which approximately 90 were researchers. Its major areas of basic research included air waves and turbulence, lasers, conventional explosives, armor and armor penetration, and intra-atmospheric ballistics.[17]

The central lesson of France and Germany's efforts at armaments cooperation in 1955–1962 was that cooperation was more difficult to achieve than either had originally anticipated. The French were frustrated by their discovery that the Germans did not care much about helping France preserve a viable armaments industry in the face of American and British competition. The German government, meanwhile, was irritated by what it regarded as France's excessively nationalistic approach to armaments questions. In sum, neither France nor Germany was very satisfied with the results of their first sustained effort at armaments collaboration. The overall level of armaments cooperation would only be improved, it appeared, by greater political will on both sides to overcome the inevitable obstacles arising from divergent military, industrial, and foreign policy perspectives. Whether the requisite political will would be forthcoming, however, depended on the larger political shifts taking place in the Alliance as the Adenauer era came to an end in Germany and as de Gaulle moved to consolidate his independent defense strategy for France.

THE EMERGENCE OF INCOMPATIBLE ARMS PROCUREMENT POLICIES

The early 1960s witnessed the entrance of several important new factors into the question of Franco-German armaments cooperation. On the German side, the most important new factor was the creation of the so-called "offset agreements" with the United States and Britain. Arguing that the stationing of 240,000 U.S. troops in West Germany caused a major drain on the American balance of payments, the U.S. government proposed in November 1960 that West Germany make payments to the United States of about $650 million per year to help defray the costs of the American presence. Bonn rejected the proposal, which in its view bore too close a resemblance to the occupation costs West Germany had been forced to pay the victors of the war until 1954.

In the fall of 1961, however, a compromise agreement was reached. Germany would buy armaments and related services (such as maintenance and training support) from the United States in quantities sufficient to offset the foreign exchange drain occasioned by the stationing of U.S. troops in West Germany. The agreement was valid for a two-year period beginning July 1, 1961. In March 1962 Bonn reached an analogous agreement with Britain, which provided for German purchases of British military and civilian goods to offset about 75 percent of Britain's foreign exchange expenditure for British troops in Germany.[18]

Implications of the Offset Accords

American military expenditures in Germany in 1961 and 1962 averaged $670 million per year. Bonn covered this entire amount through purchases of military equipment and related services in the United States. The U.S.-German and Anglo-German offset accords were each renewed several times, finally lapsing in the mid-1970s as it became apparent that they were no longer an appropriate tool for resolving the problem of burden-sharing within the Alliance. Over the entire period of the offset agreements, West German expenditures for U.S. armaments, training, and other services amounted to nearly 26 billion marks. German purchases of British armaments and related goods under the Anglo-German offset accords added up to 3.7 billion marks.[19]

In defining Germany's offset obligations in terms of arms purchases, the initial offset agreements represented a convergence of American and German interests.[20] The Germans needed to make large-scale equipment purchases for the Bundeswehr in any case; buying the equipment from the United States enabled Bonn to fulfill its procurement program and satisfy Washington at the same time. The United States was content with the agreement because it accorded well both with White House concern over the American balance of payments deficit and with McNamara's drive, beginning in 1961, to export more U.S. arms to Europe as a means of achieving weapons standardization in NATO.[21]

The U.S.-German offset agreements constituted a formidable obstacle to Franco-German armaments cooperation. The funds earmarked for purchases of U.S. military goods amounted to a substantial portion of the West German military equipment budget. At their peak between 1962 and 1965, such purchases accounted for nearly a quarter of total West German military equipment expenditures.[22] Of course, West Germany would undoubtedly have bought a good deal of military equipment from the United States even in the absence of the offset agreements. Indeed, decisions made well prior to the offset agreements—above all, the 1958 Starfighter deal—had already committed West Germany to large purchases of military goods and services in the United States for years to come. It does appear, however, that several major German procurement choices of the 1960s were determined at least partly by offset commitments to the United States. In late 1964, for example, Bonn justified its decision to acquire the American-made Bell UH-1D military transport helicopter, rather than the comparable French-manufactured Super-Frélon, on the grounds of its offset obligations.[23] Two similar cases were the October 1968 decision to buy 88 McDonnell-Douglas RF-4E Phantom reconnaissance aircraft, and the March 1971 decision to acquire 175 F-4F Phantom combat jets. Both decisions appear to have resulted more from Germany's offset obligations than from military, technological, or industrial considerations.[24]

The UH-1D and Phantom purchases epitomized the indirect ramifications of the U.S.-German offset agreements for Franco-German weapons cooperation. To cover its offset agreements, Bonn showed a strong tendency to rely on periodic large orders for big-ticket, high-technology weapon systems—especially combat aircraft—that could fulfill its offset requirements at a single stroke. To satisfy its offset obligations with purchases of miscellaneous small weapons and low-technology equipment would have been an arduous, perhaps even impossible task. Purchases of combat aircraft from the United States were also sensible in that aeronautics was the one major category of conventional weaponry where West Germany lacked the industrial capability to meet its own needs.

Unfortunately for Franco-German cooperation, however, combat aircraft was also the weapons category in which France most ardently desired German support. Of all categories of conventional weaponry, combat aircraft involved by far the largest initial investment in development and testing costs—and, by implication, the largest potential savings from economies of scale. To the extent that the U.S.-German offset accords limited Franco-German cooperation in the production of combat aircraft, therefore, they had an even greater impact than their dollar amount would imply.

Implications of French Nuclear Spending

If the U.S.-German offset agreements acted as an obstacle to Franco-German cooperation on the West German side, nuclear ambitions posed an equally imposing constraint on the French side. After de Gaulle's return to power in 1958, the development of an independent national nuclear force quickly emerged as the French government's highest foreign policy priority. It was several years, however, before the financial implications of the French nuclear program became fully evident.

In the late 1950s and early 1960s, Paris had continued to hope for indirect American or British assistance for its nuclear program. Where the United States was concerned, the French government envisaged assistance of two sorts: first, access to technical data like that supplied by the United States to the British nuclear program; second, access to American technology needed for the production of strategic delivery systems. French hopes were not realized on either count. As de Gaulle took his first steps toward detaching France from NATO military integration in 1959, Washington retaliated with steps aimed at undercutting the French nuclear program. For example, France had planned to purchase a U.S.-manufactured inertial guidance system for a surface-to-surface missile it was developing. Although France had already paid for the system, the Eisenhower administration embargoed its export.[25] France was forced, at considerable expense, to develop an inertial guidance system on its own. In March 1962, with a new U.S. administration in office, the French tried again, sending a purchasing mission to Washington with a lengthy shopping list of advanced technologies needed for the development of missiles and nuclear submarines.[26] The United States refused to permit the sale of the desired items.

However, Washington did prove willing to assist the French nuclear program in some important respects. For example, the Kennedy administration allowed the French government to purchase twelve KC-135 tanker aircraft. The tankers, which enabled in-flight refueling of Mirage IV strategic bombers, were a crucial contribution to France's nuclear capabilities. In 1962, the United States also expressed its readiness to make Polaris submarine missiles available to France on terms similar to those offered Britain. On the surface, the U.S. government's willingness to sell strategic delivery systems to France might seem odd in view of its policy statements critical of the French nuclear force. It appears in reality that the U.S.

government was willing to accept France's nuclear program as long as it led to major purchases of U.S.-made equipment. Such purchases would give Washington leverage over French nuclear doctrine and enable American manufacturers to make further gains in the European armaments market. The French, for precisely these reasons, avoided buying American weapon systems that might compromise French nuclear independence. French policy thus left Washington without much incentive to be helpful.[27]

De Gaulle's hopes for nuclear-related cooperation with Britain also came to nothing. Although the possibilities for cooperation in nuclear delivery technology were apparently not discussed between the two sides in detail, strong evidence exists that de Gaulle favored Anglo-French cooperation in the development and manufacture of strategic missiles.[28] The French objective was to develop independence from the United States in the technologies of nuclear weaponry and delivery systems; thus, collaboration with Britain in the development of an Anglo-French strategic missile could serve French goals. But Macmillan's 1962 decision to buy the Polaris from the United States made Britain's nuclear missile program subject to American licensing and technology-transfer regulations, ending any possibility of cooperation on terms acceptable to Paris.

France's inability to secure American technical aid for its nuclear force, or to mount a cooperative program with Britain, was to have important repercussions for its procurement policy regarding conventional armaments. Despite the lack of outside assistance, the Gaullist regime's highest priority remained the development of a national strategic nuclear force independent of the United States in all the key components of warhead and delivery-system technology. The French government was determined to proceed regardless of cost, and alone if necessary.

As it turned out, the cost was enormous. In the period 1960–1964, about 70 percent of France's total military equipment expenditures were devoted to the strategic nuclear force, with only around 30 percent going to conventional forces. In the period 1965–1970, conventional forces received only about 43 percent of total equipment expenditures, with the majority again going to the strategic nuclear forces.[29] Because some expenses indirectly related to the nuclear program were concealed in the budgets of other agencies, moreover, it is likely that the total cost of France's strategic force was substantially higher than the government's direct authorizations for nuclear forces would suggest.[30]

THE FAILURE OF FRANCO-GERMAN ARMAMENTS COLLABORATION

In view of its discord with the United States over strategic questions and its difficulties in gaining access to advanced United States military technology, Paris was increasingly determined to avoid dependence on the United States in all major conventional as well as nuclear technologies. National nuclear independence would be pointless, after all, if it came at the price of increased dependence on the United States for essential conventional weapon systems. With the nuclear weapons program absorbing the lion's share of its military equipment budget, the French government accordingly found itself driven even more than before toward cooperation with other European countries in producing conventional armaments.

Western Europe offered France two partners for cooperation in conventional armaments, Britain and West Germany, who could be taken seriously in terms of financial and technological capabilities. Of the two, Germany was on the whole preferable. Even in the best of times, France's relations with Britain were clouded with a degree of ingrained rivalry and mutual suspicion that discouraged cooperative endeavors. The Polaris debacle and de Gaulle's subsequent veto of Britain's application for Common Market membership had further soured the atmosphere between Paris and London. The Franco-German rapprochement, by contrast, lay at the heart of de Gaulle's program for a European political union. Armaments cooperation would complement the other aspects of the Franco-German understanding. Also, Germany would be both politically and industrially easier for France to dominate in joint armaments ventures than Britain.

On his return to power in 1958, de Gaulle renewed the effort initiated under the Fourth Republic to build a systematic Franco-German partnership in conventional armaments. Indeed, de Gaulle raised the subject of joint weapons production at his very first meeting with Adenauer.[31] The U.S.-German and Anglo-German offset agreements of 1961–1962 were seen by de Gaulle and his aides as a decisive obstacle to Franco-German weapons cooperation. Unless France could somehow counteract the accords, the "Anglo-Saxons"—above all the United States—would become entrenched as the major suppliers of advanced military equipment to the continental members of NATO. Noting that the U.S.-German agreement was valid only for a two-year period ending in mid-1963, the French government focused its efforts on achieving a reorientation of German arms procurement policy to take effect at the expiration of the U.S.-German accord.

The major instrument for accomplishing this reorientation was to be the Elysée Treaty. Although the primary goal of the treaty, for de Gaulle as well as for Adenauer, was to consecrate the reconciliation of the French and German nations, the French government also intended the treaty as a major initiative in the area of weapons collaboration. De Gaulle had proposed early in his discussions with Adenauer on the treaty that it include a section promoting bilateral armaments cooperation.[32] The final treaty text incorporated clauses on armaments cooperation corresponding closely to the French suggestions. In the future, France and Germany were to coordinate closely their arms procurement planning. Bilateral committees would be set up to organize joint programs on a systematic basis. Progress would be monitored and encouraged through regular meetings of the two defense ministers.

The Kennedy administration regarded the Elysée Treaty as a challenge to U.S. domination of the West European arms export market and quickly launched a counteroffensive. Three weeks after the treaty was signed, Deputy Secretary of Defense Roswell Gilpatric arrived in Bonn for talks with Adenauer, Foreign Minister Schröder, and Defense Minister von Hassel. A major part of Gilpatric's mission was apparently to promote German purchases of U.S.-made weapons.[33] At the end of July, McNamara traveled to Bonn for extended talks with von Hassel. At the completion of the talks, it was announced that the German government had agreed to renew the 1961 offset agreement for a second two-year period, and would place orders for about $1.3 billion in U.S.-manufactured armaments by the end of 1964. McNamara and von Hassel had also reached an agreement on the joint development of a new battle tank for use in NATO countries in the 1970s.[34]

The McNamara-von Hassel agreements amounted, in practical terms, to the defeat of France's bid to reorient German arms procurement policy in a direction more favorable to France. Coming so soon after the failure of the Franco-German tank project, Germany's agreement to develop a new battle tank in cooperation with the United States carried particular symbolic weight. The following year marked further advances by the United States in consolidating a Washington-Bonn axis in arms development and procurement. West Germany announced plans to acquire the Bell UH-1D helicopter, which would be produced in Germany under license. In early 1965, the United States and Germany reached yet another major agreement, this time on joint development of an advanced vertical/short takeoff and landing aircraft.[35] The French government nonetheless persisted in pressuring Germany to increase its purchases of arms from

France, even after Adenauer was succeeded as chancellor by the "Atlanti-cist" Ludwig Erhard. De Gaulle raised the question of arms procurement yet again at his July 1964 summit meeting with Erhard, expressing strong disappointment that Germany was not buying more of its armaments from France.[36] Under the circumstances, however, the possibilities for coopera-tion were clearly limited.

An Isolated Success: Short-Range Missiles

The one area in which Franco-German armaments cooperation broke new ground in the years immediately following the signing of the Elysée Treaty was in short-range guided missiles. In February 1963, France and Germany signed an intergovernmental agreement providing for the joint development of a new generation of antitank missiles. The participating firms were Nord-Aviation on the French side and Bölkow-Entwicklungen on the German. In 1964, a further agreement was reached for the joint development of a surface-to-air missile for defense against low-flying air-craft.

The missiles developed through this framework of agreements proved to be technical and commercial successes. Two wire-guided antitank weapons were developed. One (the Milan) was a light, portable missile with a range of 75 to 2,000 meters. The other (the HOT) was a heavier weapon with a range of up to 4,000 meters; it was developed in vehicle-mounted and helicopter-mounted versions. The Roland mobile anti-aircraft missile, effective against aircraft flying at low and very low altitudes, was developed in two versions, a clear-weather version based on optical acquisition and tracking of targets, and an all-weather version with automatic radar-guided target acquisition and tracking. Mass production of the Milan, HOT, and Roland missiles began in the early and mid-1970s. Within a few years the three missiles had established an impressive export record, with sales to more than thirty countries.[37]

The creation of a Franco-German program in guided missiles resulted from a combination of circumstances. On the one hand, the Erhard government sought to make a cooperative gesture toward France in matters of armaments production. Though its overall orientation was strongly Atlanticist, the Erhard government viewed Franco-German reconciliation as an important strategic asset for Germany, and was determined to imple-ment the terms of the Elysée Treaty in good faith, including the clauses on armaments cooperation. Few possibilities for high-profile cooperation were evident, however. The tank project was dead. Prospects for cooperation in military aeronautics, aside from the ongoing Transall program, were dim. On both sides, moreover, the possibilities for cooperation were limited by the prior commitment of procurement funds to other programs: the national nuclear program in the case of France and the offset agreements with the United States and Britain in the case of Germany. The decision to concentrate on short-range missiles was thus determined to a significant extent by a process of elimination.

Collaboration in the development of short-range missiles also grew to some extent out of the Franco-German arrangement governing the Institut de Saint-Louis. Under the 1958 agreement described earlier, Germany and France had equal access to ISL research findings. As it happened, the ISL's research on explosives was directly relevant for the development of short-range missiles.[38] For example, the ISL had developed the hollow-charge explosive which later formed the basis of the Milan and HOT missile warheads. In these circumstances, a joint Franco-German program to make use of the ISL's work followed naturally. Separate national programs in antitank and anti-aircraft missiles, each beginning from the basis of the work done at Saint-Louis, would have been an obvious waste of effort.

The companies involved in the missile program also played an important role in initiating cooperation. The German firm of Bölkow had sought out Nord-Aviation as a possible partner in guided missile manufacture as early as 1956. Franco-German governmental discussions over common tactical requirements for short-range missiles began in 1960, and by 1962 Bölkow and Nord had reached an agreement to cooperate in the development of guided missile systems.[39] Given the degree to which French and German firms were interested in cooperation in this area, it seems quite probable that the two governments would have begun a joint short-range missile development program even in the absence of the Elysée Treaty.

NOTES

1. See Robert Rhodes James, *Standardization and Common Production of Weapons in NATO* (London: Institute for Strategic Studies, 1967).

2. See the account of the armaments pool proposal in Paul Noack, *Das Scheitern der Europäischen Verteidigungsgemeinschaft* (Düsseldorf: Droste, 1977), pp. 151–63.

3. *The New York Times*, January 25, 1956.

4. See Kelleher, *Germany*, pp. 104-5, and Regina H. E. Cowen, *Defense Procurement in the Federal Republic of Germany: Politics and Organization* (Boulder, Colo.: Westview, 1986), pp. 16–17.

5. Schmückle, *Ohne Pauken und Trompeten*, p. 195.

6. *Deutsche Zeitung,* April 27, 1957.

7. See Schmückle, *Ohne Pauken und Trompeten,* p. 236.

8. See, for example, the report in *Le Monde,* January 24, 1958.

9. See Anthony Sampson, *The Arms Bazaar* (New York: Viking, 1977), pp. 124–32. Also of interest is the anecdotal account by Gerd Schmückle (Strauss's press secretary at the time) in *Ohne Pauken und Trompeten,* pp. 216–37.

10. Kelleher, *Germany,* p. 102.

11. See Alfred Mechtersheimer, *Rüstung und Politik in der Bundesrepublik: MRCA Tornado* (Bad Honnef: Osang, 1977), p. 19.

12. For details see the accounts in Dietrich Willikens, "Wehrtechnik Land," in Theodor Benecke and Günther Schöner, eds., *Wehrtechnik für die Verteidigung* (Koblenz: Bernard & Graefe, 1984), pp. 132–34; *Le Monde,* August 17, 1963; and *Der Spiegel,* June 19, 1963, pp. 22–23.

13. This section draws heavily on the history of the Transall project in Mark A. Lorell, *Multinational Development of Large Aircraft* (Santa Monica, Calif.: Rand Corp., 1980), pp. 31–47. See also the relevant comments by Gustav A. Bittner, "Eine positive Bilanz," in Kaiser and Lellouche, *Deutsch-französische Sicherheitspolitik,* pp. 114–16, and by Albert Wahl and Fritz Engelmann, "Wehrtechnik Luft," in Benecke and Schöner, *Wehrtechnik für die Verteidigung,* pp. 180–81.

14. Lorell, *Multinational Development,* pp. 36–37.

15. See Bruno Klinker, "Wehrtechnische Forschung," in Benecke and Schöner, *Wehrtechnik für die Verteidigung,* p. 103, and Pierre Thévenin, "L'Institut de Saint-Louis," *L'Armement,* June 1984, p. 47.

16. *Le Monde,* April 2, 1958 and October 8, 1958.

17. Thévenin, "L'Institut de Saint-Louis," pp. 47, 50–51.

18. Gregory F. Treverton, *The Dollar Drain and American Forces in Germany* (Athens, Ohio: Ohio University Press, 1978), pp. 32–34.

19. Hans-Günter Bode, *Rüstung in der Bundesrepublik Deutschland* (Regensburg: Walhalla und Praetoria Verlag, 1978), p. 9.

20. Peter Schlotter, *Rüstungspolitik in der Bundesrepublik: Die Beispiele Starfighter und Phantom* (Frankfurt am Main: Campus Verlag, 1975), pp. 128–29.

21. See John Stanley and Maurice Pearton, *The International Trade in Arms* (New York: Praeger, 1972), pp. 87–89.

22. See Horst Mendershausen, *Troop Stationing in Germany: Value and Cost* (Santa Monica, Calif.: Rand Corp., 1968), p. 132.

23. *Rheinischer Post* (Düsseldorf), September 30, 1964.

24. Cowen, *Defense Procurement,* pp. 158–63. Compare also Schlotter, *Rüstungspolitik,* pp. 133–34.

25. Comments by Pierre Usunier in Institut Charles-de-Gaulle, *L'aventure de la bombe,* p. 159. See also the list of similar examples mentioned in Robert Gilpin, *France in the Age of the Scientific State* (Princeton: Princeton University Press, 1968), pp. 53–54.

26. John Newhouse, *De Gaulle and the Anglo-Saxons* (New York: Viking, 1970), p. 156. Compare also Kohl, *French Nuclear Diplomacy*, p. 217.

27. Newhouse, *De Gaulle*, pp. 157, 163, 224–25.

28. See the discussion in Kohl, *French Nuclear Diplomacy*, pp. 323–30.

29. *Le Monde*, December 5, 1969.

30. See Kohl, *French Nuclear Diplomacy*, pp. 196–98; compare also Ruehl, *La politique militaire de la Ve République*, pp. 263–97.

31. Adenauer, *Erinnerungen, 1955–1959*, p. 433.

32. Adenauer, *Erinnerungen, 1959–1963*, p. 179.

33. *Kölnische Rundschau*, February 14, 1963.

34. This overly ambitious project, dubbed the MBT-70, encountered major technical difficulties and was scrapped in 1972.

35. Known as the AVS, the aircraft was abandoned in 1968 because of incompatible U.S. and German military requirements as well as insuperable technical problems. See Mechtersheimer, *Rüstung und Politik*, pp. 28–35.

36. *Sunday Telegraph* (London), August 2, 1964.

37. Bittner, "Eine positive Bilanz," pp. 122–23.

38. Klinker, "Wehrtechnische Forschung," p. 106.

39. Bittner, "Eine positive Bilanz," p. 121.

CHAPTER 4

The Reformulation of Security Strategy, 1967–1973

During the mid-1960s, changing conditions in world politics began to lead West German political leaders toward a fundamental reappraisal of Germany's foreign policy.[1] It appeared clear that Germany's position in the international system had suffered grave setbacks in the first half of the 1960s. In the Adenauer era, Bonn's foreign policy had aimed at three goals: equality of rights for Germany as a sovereign state, integration of Germany into the West, and eventual reunification. These were interlocking objectives, each of which depended for its meaning and its realization on the other objectives. The integration of Germany into the West, for example, was valued by Adenauer both as an end in itself and as a means for Germany to attain acceptance and equality of rights as a sovereign state in international politics. Acceptance within the West was in turn a precondition for reunification, which could be achieved on terms acceptable to West Germany only with the active support of the Western Allies.

By late 1966, when Kurt Kiesinger became chancellor, it was apparent that the assumptions on which Adenauer's foreign policy had rested were in question, and that Germany's overall foreign policy goals needed to be reevaluated. Prospects for obtaining equality of rights (Gleichberechtigung) within the Alliance had been damaged considerably by the developments of preceding years. Germany's strategy for attaining Gleichberechtigung had, in practice, centered on the principles of nuclear control-sharing and European integration. Both of these principles had been irreparably undermined by the events of the 1960s. Despite Bonn's unyielding insistence from 1956 onward that Germany not be subject to discrimination within the Alliance on nuclear questions, a two-class system of nuclear and non-nuclear powers had emerged after all, and Germany had been relegated definitively to the less-privileged class. The rise of independent French and British nuclear arsenals, the demise of the MLF, and U.S. sponsorship of the Nonproliferation Treaty were cumulative setbacks for Germany in its quest for a non-discriminatory Alliance policy on access to nuclear weapons. The cause of European unity had also suffered several grave blows, most of them emanating from Paris. These included de Gaulle's veto of British membership in the Common Market, the 1965 agricultural financing crisis, and the Luxembourg Compromise weakening the supranational powers of EEC institutions. Unity within the Western Alliance as a whole had been shaken by France's withdrawal from the NATO integrated defense system.

Finally, German reunification was nowhere on the horizon. Adenauer's foreign policy strategy had seen reunification as the eventual product of Western strength and unity vis-à-vis the Eastern bloc. The unstinting support of a strong Western alliance, Adenauer had believed, would enable West Germany ultimately to attain reunification on terms that would preserve its ties to the West, its sovereign rights, and its liberal political institutions. As in the case of Adenauer's other foreign policy goals, however, reunification appeared in 1966 to be farther from attainment than ever before. The end of the U.S. nuclear monopoly and Washington's resulting adoption of flexible response had put an end to any possibility that a policy of Western firmness would pave the way to reunification. The tacit American acceptance of the Berlin Wall showed Bonn that German reunification was a lower priority for the United States than peaceful coexistence with the Soviet Union. Indeed, the accelerating momentum of détente after 1962 appeared increasingly likely to lead the Western powers to sacrifice Bonn's claims in exchange for a reduction of tension and instability in Europe.

In short, the events of the first half of the 1960s had greatly altered the structure of external incentives and sanctions confronting West German foreign policy. To begin with, U.S. adoption of flexible response represented a quantum erosion in the terms of the American security guarantee to Germany. With the adoption of flexible response, Germans could no longer have much faith in the possibility of a successful defense against Warsaw Pact forces. Any large-scale attack from the East would lead to intolerable levels of destruction in Germany, because the United States would delay escalation to the strategic nuclear level as long as possible—and would perhaps not escalate to the use of nuclear weapons at all.

Second, it was increasingly apparent that West Germany could aspire to a far greater degree of international status and influence in the non-military dimensions of world affairs than in its military dimensions. In Adenauer's long-range program, the achievement of *Gleichberechtigung* within the West had been intended as the first step toward the full recovery of Germany's international standing, which together with reunification would be the end products of a final peace settlement in Europe. But the gradual hardening of a two-class system of nuclear and non-nuclear states in the Alliance had established that full equality of rights, even within the West, lay beyond Germany's grasp. In the economic and other non-military dimensions of international affairs, Germany was a nation like other nations, at liberty to shape its external relationships and exert its influence as it chose. But Germany was not free to convert its financial and industrial capabilities into a commensurate military capability, because that would have required autonomous control over nuclear weapons.

The degree to which Germany could achieve foreign policy autonomy thus depended in part on the level of East-West tensions in Europe. When East-West hostility was great, Germany's underlying dependence on its nuclear-equipped allies would be more evident, reducing Germany's own independence and influence in world affairs. If East-West relations were relaxed, on the other hand, influence would derive more from non-military sources of power, and Germany's weight in the international system would be accordingly greater. Germany therefore had a particular stake in détente, since its own leverage and autonomy in the international system varied directly with the degree of inter-bloc tension in Europe.

To these incentives for détente was added a final one: the United States, Britain, and France had all been moving toward détente since the beginning of the decade. Even the Berlin and Cuban crises had only temporarily interrupted the search for an end to the Cold War and some form of modus vivendi with the Soviet Union. As the Western desire for détente intensified, Bonn realized that refusal to join in the search for accommodation would not stop the movement toward détente but would only succeed in isolating Germany from its partners.[2]

In the changing strategic environment, therefore, the pursuit of détente became an increasingly central aspect of Germany's security policy. Détente also became part of official NATO policy with the approval of the Report on the Future Tasks of the Alliance (Harmel Report) at the NATO Ministers' meeting of December 1967. The result of a year-long study, the Harmel Report grew out of the recognition by West European governments that the United States would give priority in some circumstances to agreement with the Soviet Union against the wishes of its allies, and that the increasing U.S. preoccupation with extra-European questions (e.g., Vietnam) cast doubt on the long-term future of the U.S. commitment to Europe.[3] The Harmel Report declared that the search for détente was one of the "two main functions" of the Atlantic Alliance, the other being "to maintain adequate military strength and political solidarity to deter aggression and other forms of pressure and to defend the territory of member countries if aggression should occur." In a key section, the Report stated: "Military security and a policy of détente are not contradictory but complementary. . . . The way to peace and stability in Europe rests in particular on the use of the Alliance constructively in the interest of détente."[4] The Harmel Report was a milestone in NATO's evolution. By making the search for détente an official goal of the Alliance, it in effect gave West Germany the formal go-ahead to seek its own terms for coexistence with the Soviet regime.

FRANCE'S DECREASING IMPORTANCE TO GERMANY

The profound changes in West Germany's external strategic environment also transformed the stakes of its defense relationship with France. In Adenauer's time, cooperation with France had been the key to two of Germany's main strategic objectives: European integration and *Gleichberechtigung*. But as events seemed to make these objectives increasingly unattainable, France became less valuable to Germany as a strategic partner. With regard to European integration, many Germans had viewed participation in a supranational Europe as a way of regaining indirectly the sovereign prerogatives to which Germany as a national actor could not aspire. But by torpedoing supranational Europe and substituting for it *l'Europe des patries*, de Gaulle had made the process of European integration less strategically valuable to Germany. As a result, it became less important for Germany to obtain France's cooperation in the political construction of Europe.

In the military sphere, analogous considerations applied. By ending any automatic commitment to the defense of Germany, France became much less important to Germany in terms of both deterrence and military operations. De Gaulle had asserted to Erhard that the French strategic force was advantageous to Germany because its deterrent value indirectly protected German as well as French territory.[5] From the German perspective, however, France's nuclear force served no constructive purpose. Nearly all

German political and military officials regarded the military significance and the deterrent value of French nuclear forces as negligible.[6] After all, until the late 1960s the French strategic force consisted only of fifty Mirage IV bombers equipped with one warhead each. A program to construct eighteen solid-fuel intermediate-range missiles and base them in the Plateau d'Albion was not completed until 1973, and it was 1971 before the first of a handful of nuclear missile submarines became operational.[7] If anything, German leaders viewed the French nuclear force as a *nuisance* to German security, since its vulnerability might make it a tempting object for a preemptive Soviet strike in a situation of high U.S.-Soviet tension. French conventional forces, meanwhile, added little to deterrence from Bonn's point of view; they would come into play only at the point where West Germany was already overrun by Warsaw Pact forces. Furthermore, France's withdrawal from military integration meant that French territory was lost to NATO as an assured logistical hinterland, which undermined the credibility of NATO military plans.

Chancellor Kiesinger and Foreign Minister Willy Brandt came to office strongly determined to improve relations with France from the low point of the Erhard years. Kiesinger and Brandt were both sympathetic to de Gaulle and both placed a high value on the Franco-German relationship. During the period of their coalition government, both went to great lengths to preserve cordial ties with Paris. In practice, this largely meant downplaying the fact that French and German policies were sharply at odds regarding both Atlantic relations and European integration. The one vital issue where the opposition of views between Paris and Bonn could not simply be ignored was the matter of British membership in the European Community. Under Kiesinger and Brandt the German government's commitment to British membership was, if anything, even stronger than in the Erhard years. De Gaulle's continuing rejection of British membership did not remove the question from the Franco-German agenda; it merely insured that the topic would resurface anew at every bilateral summit.

The Kiesinger government's goodwill toward de Gaulle also could do nothing to change the fact that by the late 1960s France had effectively deprived itself of its formerly central role in Germany's defense and security. France remained important, but no longer because Bonn needed French cooperation to attain its major foreign policy goals. Instead, France now derived its importance to Germany largely from its role as a potential threat to German security which had to be contained and neutralized where possible.[8] France posed a problem for German foreign policy in two major respects. First, and most immediately, Germans worried that the French might make a deal with the Soviet Union at German expense, for example, by extending diplomatic recognition to East Germany in exchange for privileged trade relations with the Soviet bloc. Second, Gaullist foreign policy loomed as a potentially important obstacle to arms control and disarmament in Europe. France's rejection of both the Test Ban Treaty and the Nonproliferation Treaty boded ill for any superpower-sponsored negotiations. If French obstructionism prevented agreement by the superpowers on major arms control measures in Europe, the failure to agree would come first and foremost at Germany's expense.

From the French perspective, meanwhile, the strategic context had also been transformed. Having removed itself from the integrated structures of NATO, reasserted French independence in foreign and defense policy, and decisively slowed the pace of supranational integration in the EEC, France had its hands free at last. No longer formally shackled to the "bloc system," France was at liberty to mediate between East and West, between North and South, between Germany and the Soviet Union. But in liberating itself from responsibilities within the West, France had also dissipated most of the influence it might once have been able to exert over German foreign policy. Isolated politically within the Alliance, France carried too little diplomatic weight to be able to deliver German concessions in exchange for Soviet blandishments. As events were to demonstrate, the French were useful to Moscow less as arbiters of an East-West settlement than as an instrument that could be exploited to create internal divisions within the West.

FRENCH AND GERMAN PERSPECTIVES ON DÉTENTE

As the emphasis in East-West relations shifted from confrontation to negotiation, détente and arms control became key issues in Franco-German defense relations. Predictably, Paris and Bonn did not fully agree on how to pursue détente. Under Adenauer and Erhard, an essential tactic of German foreign policy had been *never to foreclose options* on any key question regarding the postwar order, in hopes that Germany could someday overcome the provisional settlement imposed on it by the Occupation and the Cold War. Thus, the key elements of Bonn's policy toward Eastern Europe were its refusal to recognize East Germany as a separate state, its claim to speak for all Germans, its insistence on special ties between West Berlin and West Germany, and its unwillingness to accept the Oder-Neisse line formally as Poland's western boundary. Beginning in 1961, Schröder as German foreign minister had begun the task of restoring West Germany's relationships with the states of Eastern Europe, primarily by opening trade missions in several East European capitals. These steps, however, were motivated as much by the desire to pressure East Germany into a more pliant attitude toward Bonn as by the search for East-West détente.

De Gaulle, meanwhile, aspired to a privileged relationship with Moscow which, together with France's special ties to Germany, would make France the arbiter of a European settlement. The French approach to détente was to deal directly with Moscow, since all the key elements of a European settlement—loosening of the Eastern bloc, resolution of the German question, and eventual construction of a peaceful Europe "from the Atlantic to the Urals"—could come about only with Moscow's active participation, not against its opposition. On the German question, however, de Gaulle was fundamentally much closer to Bonn than to Moscow. The Soviet Union demanded the recognition of East Germany as a sovereign, independent state. De Gaulle, by contrast, had repeatedly made clear his view that German reunification must be part of any durable peace settlement in Europe.[9] Moscow and de Gaulle did however agree that Germany must rule out all irredentist ambitions as a precondition for a genuine European détente. It was for this reason that de Gaulle had been urging Bonn since 1959 to recognize the Oder-Neisse boundary.

De Gaulle's approach to détente, which appeared more accommodating than the line adopted by Bonn, initally evoked a more positive response from Moscow. An exchange of visits by the Soviet and French foreign ministers—Gromyko in April 1965 and Couve de Murville in October 1965—laid the groundwork for an announcement, in January 1966, that de Gaulle would visit Moscow the following June. The planning for de Gaulle's trip to Moscow thus took place amid France's announced withdrawal from the NATO command and the expulsion of NATO military installations and organizations from French territory. In Bonn, anxiety over the French president's next move ran high. What would de Gaulle do once in Moscow? In his eagerness to establish himself as the Soviet Union's privileged partner in the West, would he give away positions regarded by Bonn as vital to its own interests?

The actual events of de Gaulle's trip assuaged most of Germany's worries. Though triumphal, de Gaulle's tour of the Soviet Union did not herald any fundamental change in Franco-Soviet relations. Far from making common cause with Moscow against Bonn, de Gaulle used his meetings with Soviet leaders to advocate Bonn's point of view. The only agreements reached were on secondary matters such as scientific and cultural ties, trade relations, and more frequent diplomatic contacts. The results of Soviet Premier Kosygin's return visit to Paris in December 1966 were along much the same lines.[10]

As it turned out, de Gaulle's Moscow trip was the high point of French détente policy in the 1960s. What de Gaulle's talks with Soviet leaders had demonstrated, more than anything else, was the limited nature of France's diplomatic influence. De Gaulle had liberated France from the formal constraints on its foreign policy independence, but doing so did not change the fact that France was only a medium power in a superpower-dominated world. Soviet leaders would gladly have accepted unilateral concessions by de Gaulle on questions of European security, had de Gaulle been willing to make them; but they did not take France seriously enough to negotiate with de Gaulle in earnest on a European settlement. De Gaulle, in turn, was not about to give the Soviets something for nothing. Once the Franco-Soviet dialogue got past the stage of atmospherics and symbolic cooperation, therefore, it had nowhere to go.

In the meantime, West Germany's own détente policy, aimed primarily at improving relations with East European capitals, had run into difficulties. After an early success—the establishment of diplomatic ties with Romania in January 1967—the Kiesinger government found its way blocked by Soviet pressure on the other East European states not to follow the Romanian example. Obviously uneasy at the prospect of a diminished hold on its satellites, Moscow intended to keep the reins of détente firmly in its own grasp. The Soviet government's determination to reassert control over developments in Eastern Europe was brought home with full force by its military intervention in Czechoslovakia in August 1968. The Soviet invasion put an end to both the French and the German projects for détente, even if only temporarily.

THE CHANGING BALANCE OF POWER IN EUROPE

As the decade of the 1960s drew to a close, it was evident that the underlying power relationships in Western Europe were undergoing a substantial shift. As World War II receded farther into the past, German leaders demonstrated growing self-assurance and a greater determination to stand up for Germany's own preferred policies even if doing so subjected Bonn to criticism from its allies. In October 1969, Willy Brandt was elected chancellor in West Germany—the first Social Democrat to hold the office in the history of the Federal Republic. Brandt's government differed from all its predecessors in its willingness to accept formally some aspects of the

Cold War international order in exchange for the restoration of political, economic, and cultural contacts with the Eastern bloc countries. Under Brandt, Germany moved swiftly and decisively to establish a substantive détente with Moscow.

Germany's New Policy in the East

Following intensive and largely secret bilateral negotiations during the first half of 1970, the German and Soviet governments reached agreement on a treaty, signed at Moscow in August, which provided the underpinning for the Brandt government's subsequent *Ostpolitik*. Under the terms of the Moscow Treaty, West Germany and the Soviet Union both renounced the threat or use of force to alter the existing situation in Europe. Both sides also affirmed that peace in Europe could be maintained only if no one called into question existing boundaries. In November of the same year, Germany reached an agreement with Poland (the Warsaw Treaty) in which the two sides recognized the Oder-Neisse line as Poland's western boundary, affirmed the present and future inviolability of their existing borders, and renounced all territorial claims each other. Like the Moscow Treaty, the Warsaw Treaty included a mutual renunciation of the threat or use of force to settle disputes.

Brandt's government drew a linkage between German ratification of the Moscow Treaty and the conclusion of an agreement on Berlin by the four occupation powers, whose shared responsibility for the city remained officially in force as a legacy of World War II. Negotiations on a Berlin accord had been under way since early in 1970, but hesitations on the part of both superpowers had caused the talks to stagnate.[11] Not wanting to endanger the agreement it had worked out with Bonn, the Soviet leadership finally resolved itself to significant concessions. In September 1971, Moscow and the three Western powers reached an agreement in which the Soviet Union guaranteed unhindered passage between West Germany and West Berlin and accepted the continuation of the Federal Republic's special ties to West Berlin.

The Moscow and Warsaw Treaties, together with the Four Power Agreement on Berlin, laid the basis for a direct agreement between East and West Germany. The treaty between the two Germanys, signed in November 1972, pledged the two sides to the development of normal, good-neighborly relations on the basis of equality and the renunciation of force. The signatories affirmed the inviolability of their common border and agreed to respect each other's sovereignty in internal and external affairs. Additional protocols were to be worked out regarding various practical and humanitarian issues in inter-German relations. The final major elements of *Ostpolitik* came in December 1973 when the German government signed a treaty, similar in content to the Warsaw agreement, with Czechoslovakia. In the same month, West Germany established diplomatic relations with Hungary and Bulgaria.

The network of agreements reached between West Germany and the Eastern bloc states in 1970–1973 added up to a fundamental restructuring of the options and instruments of West German foreign policy. Bonn's new policy toward Eastern Europe was founded on acceptance of the major features of the existing European order and the renunciation of military force as a means of altering it. This definitive shift in the instrumentality of West German diplomacy was, in fact, among the most far-reaching implications of *Ostpolitik*. Adenauer's "policy of strength" toward the Eastern bloc had rested on an implicit threat of resort to force by the Western allies. By the time of Brandt's accession to the chancellorship, it was evident that the policy of strength was a dead end for German foreign policy. Not only had the policy lacked credibility for some years already, but adherence to it had magnified Germany's dependence on its allies. *Ostpolitik* was an attempt to deemphasize military power as an instrument of diplomacy in Europe and to replace it with the leverage offered by expanded economic and cultural ties. Bonn sought thereby to transform East-West politics from a game in which it was a weak and dependent player to one in which it held many of the trumps. Even if economic incentives could exert only marginal leverage over the Soviet Union, they nonetheless represented an improvement over a policy of strength that was entirely futile.

The *Ostpolitik* agreements were also significant for their impact on Germany's relations with its Western allies. Bonn's new ties with the Eastern bloc states liberated it from much of its previous dependence on allied states for mediation between itself and the East. West Germany's admission (together with East Germany) to the United Nations in 1973 gave it new standing in international politics. Most importantly, the 1972 treaty between the two Germanys provided Bonn with the means to strengthen inter-German ties on its own, independently of its Western partners.

Reactions in France

The French government observed the course of German *Ostpolitik* with thinly disguised anxiety. In public, President Georges Pompidou applauded the fact that Bonn had finally undertaken the policy of détente long recommended to it by de Gaulle. Indeed, the Brandt government's acceptance of the Oder-Neisse border and its renunciation-of-force agreements were precisely in line with what de Gaulle had advised; as such, Pompidou could hardly oppose Brandt's program. Pompidou's private misgivings over *Ostpolitik* were, however, considerable.[12] They were also widely shared within the French political elite.[13] Several aspects of Brandt's foreign policy were especially worrisome to the French government. One was Bonn's independence in its negotiations with Moscow, and the fact that the German government did not always keep Paris fully apprised of the progress of its talks with the Soviets. Another was the fact that it was Germany rather than France which seemed to be emerging as the Soviet Union's privileged partner in Western Europe. Above all, there was anxiety in France that West Germany's improving relations with Eastern Europe might pave the way to a reduced German commitment toward the West. The French worried that West Germany was drifting toward neutrality, possibly in exchange for a deal with the Soviet Union on German reunification.[14]

The French government's anxieties about German *Ostpolitik* reflected its sensation of having lost control over developments in its external environment. As de Gaulle had recognized, French strategic autonomy depended heavily on the continued cohesion of the Atlantic Alliance. The U.S. defense commitment to Western Europe, Germany's military integration into NATO, and the presence of U.S. troops in Germany had created a strategic shelter within which France could safely pursue an independent foreign policy course. Over time, French leaders had come to regard this strategic shelter as a more permanent fixture of European politics than it actually was. They were unprepared for the speed and success of Brandt's accommodation with the East. *Ostpolitik* abruptly and brutally exposed the fragility of France's strategic posture. By providing Bonn with the means of pursuing détente on its own, *Ostpolitik* reduced France to little more than a bystander as basic changes to Europe's political structure took place. Under the circumstances, Paris could hardly help but be anxious over each new German understanding with the Soviets or the East Germans.

Disagreement over Arms Control

The success of West Germany's *Ostpolitik* also gave rise to a divergence of views between Paris and Bonn regarding arms control and disarmament in Europe. In abandoning Adenauer's policy of strength toward the Soviet

Union and East Germany, Bonn irrevocably altered the course of West German foreign policy. To achieve the benefits of a European détente, the Brandt government had cashed in nearly all the bargaining chips it held for dealing with the East. Under Brandt, Germany had signed the Nuclear Nonproliferation Treaty.[15] It had concluded renunciation-of-force agreements with Moscow, Warsaw, Prague, and East Berlin. It had formally accepted the Oder-Neisse line. Above all, it had ended its attempt to isolate East Germany internationally, extended de facto diplomatic recognition to East Berlin, and in so doing conceded an indefinite postponement of German reunification. In exchange, the Federal Republic had secured reliable access to West Berlin, Soviet acceptance of special ties between West Berlin and West Germany, the restoration of contact between the people of the two Germanys, and trade and diplomatic ties between West Germany and the countries of Eastern Europe.

The trouble with these arrangements was that Bonn's concessions in the bargain were, in a practical sense, irreversible, whereas most of its gains from détente could still be jeopardized by the renewal of East-West tensions. West Germany's stake in détente was thus very great indeed. After 1972, the consolidation of détente quickly emerged as a central objective of Bonn's foreign policy. The means available for pursuing détente consisted primarily of negotiating on arms control, disarmament, military confidence-building measures, and the like. From Bonn's perspective, therefore, the promotion of East-West arms control and disarmament negotiations became increasingly an end in itself. What mattered most was to keep the negotiation process alive, even if progress came slowly. Ideally, of course, Bonn hoped that Washington would give West European security concerns the same priority as it gave to its own. More important than weighing down superpower negotiations with burdensome European demands, however, was to provide support and encouragement for U.S.-Soviet arms talks so that the superpowers would be less likely to retreat into a renewal of the Cold War.

The French view of superpower arms control was substantially more skeptical than Bonn's. The Pompidou government's increasing awareness of French vulnerability was reflected in apprehension about any substantial changes to existing European security arrangements that might arise as a result of détente. Paris showed especial distrust toward arms control and disarmament negotiations conducted between the superpowers or formulated in terms of the East-West military balance. In the case of the U.S.-Soviet negotiations on a strategic arms limitation treaty (SALT), both Pompidou and Defense Minister Debré cautioned lest the talks lead to a superpower "condominium" over Europe. Only after it became clear that the SALT agreement of 1972 would in no way implicate France's own nuclear forces or restrict French freedom of action did Paris issue a cautious endorsement of the accord.[16] French sensitivity to security cooperation between the superpowers came to the fore again following the U.S.-Soviet agreement on the prevention of nuclear war, signed by Nixon and Brezhnev in Washington in June 1973. The accord pledged the two sides to "enter into urgent consultations" immediately if events appeared to involve the risk of a nuclear war between them or between either of them and a third party. Pompidou viewed the agreement with great uneasiness, perceiving it as decoupling the United States from Europe's defense.[17] Michel Jobert, the French foreign minister, made no secret of his own hostility to the accord.[18]

Pompidou's government reserved its harshest criticism, however, for the negotiations between NATO and the Warsaw Pact on mutual reductions in the troops and equipment deployed in Central Europe.[19] Paris objected to the concept of mutual and balanced force reductions (MBFR) on several grounds. Because the MBFR talks were structured in terms of existing alliances, argued the French, they would perpetuate the division of Europe and reinforce superpower dominance over the continent's security. Since the superpowers would naturally put their own interests ahead of those of their allies, any agreement in the superpower-controlled MBFR framework was likely to compromise France's security, either by consolidating super-power hegemony in Europe or by allowing the United States to reduce its defense commitment to Europe under the guise of mutual disarmament. Above all, the French feared that an MBFR agreement might result in substantial withdrawals of American troops from West Germany, creating a power vacuum in Central Europe and potentially putting France on the front line of any East-West conflict in Europe.[20] Such a development would not only undermine France's security, but would greatly constrict French strategic autonomy, pushing the country back into explicit defense dependence on its allies. Pompidou and Defense Minister Debré implicitly acknowledged the relationship between the U.S. commitment to Europe and French defense independence in their repeated statements emphasizing the importance of an undiminished U.S. troop presence in Europe.[21]

Their differing perspectives on the value and implications of arms control put Paris and Bonn sharply at odds over MBFR. The Brandt government was NATO's strongest proponent of East-West negotiations on force reductions in Europe. In Bonn's view, MBFR provided the necessary multilateral framework through which its bilateral accords with Moscow and the individual East European governments could be consolidated. A reduction of U.S. troops in Europe was seen as inevitable in any case, but MBFR offered an opportunity to establish the principle that such reductions should be matched by proportional cuts in Warsaw Pact forces. In addition, MBFR—together with the Conference on Security and Cooperation in Europe (CSCE), which opened at Helsinki in mid-1973—was seen as providing the basis for a new, cooperative European security system founded on a stable and mutually agreed balance of forces in Central Europe.[22]

The French government's criticisms of MBFR, and its refusal to have anything to do with the MBFR negotiations, thus posed a substantial obstacle to Bonn's own effort to lay the basis for a new security system in Europe. German officials tried repeatedly in the late 1960s and early 1970s to talk Paris into a more positive view of MBFR, but to no avail. Like their disagreement over Alliance military strategy, their divergent views on arms control solidified over time into a fact of life for Paris and Bonn.

Germany's foreign policy reorientation under Brandt dealt a major blow to France's lingering great-power aspirations. Until the successes of *Ostpolitik*, the French government could continue to hope that Bonn's hostility toward the Soviet Union and its dissatisfaction with U.S. support for German objectives would eventually lead it to join Paris in creating a self-reliant, French-led Europe that would begin to shake off superpower domination. Germany, however, blocked on all sides from attaining political *Gleichberechtigung*, finally decided to renounce its fading hopes for restored international power in exchange for more tangible and immediate gains: an easing of Soviet political pressures and the liberty to engage in economic and cultural exchanges with Eastern Europe. Through the various agreements stemming from *Ostpolitik*, the Federal Republic formally sacrificed the option of resort to military force—a crucial component of great-power status—and accepted the diminished political role accorded to it by the Cold War international order.

Germany's Eastern policy was a blow to France's international ambitions in that it definitively removed German support for any policy of strategic self-assertion by Western Europe. After 1972, Germany was *doubly* indentured: to the United States for its military security, and to the Soviet Union for the continuation of détente in Europe. Bonn was accordingly less available than ever for French initiatives aimed at enhancing European autonomy. West Germany's dependence on continued détente meant that it supported superpower arms control almost unconditionally. French leaders, by contrast, could see few if any advantages flowing from a U.S.-Soviet dialogue about European security arrangements, believing that any resulting agreements would almost certainly come at Europe's expense. Lacking any realistic hope of gaining German assistance for its own strategic aspirations, Pompidou's France found itself locked solidly into the splendid but largely impotent pose bequeathed to it by General de Gaulle.

GERMANY AND THE PROBLEM OF FRENCH NUCLEAR STRATEGY

As noted in Chapter 2, France's withdrawal from the NATO integrated command system did not put an end to military cooperation between France and its allies. That such cooperation should take place was simple common sense: any effective plan to defend France against a Warsaw Pact offensive would require the closest possible coordination between French and allied military actions. During the Pompidou years there was significant progress in repairing the breach between NATO and French military planning. French and allied field commanders developed a series of operational agreements to coordinate the actions of the French First Army with those of NATO forces in Central Europe in the event that a major defensive action became necessary. These arrangements, known as the Valentin-Ferber accords, provided for a variety of scenarios. Under some contingencies, the French First Army would remain close to its bases in northeastern France and southeastern Germany; under other contingencies, the First Army would move farther eastward into Germany. In no circumstances would French forces move all the way east to the front lines of NATO defense, which would have been incompatible with the reserve status accorded to French forces by the Ailleret-Lemnitzer framework.[23]

Of course, the new cooperation was not the same as if France had remained a member of the integrated command. For one thing, there was no ironclad assurance that French forces would join in NATO military actions if a conflict should occur. More generally, France remained outside many key areas of allied military cooperation including joint force planning, discussions of nuclear doctrine in the Nuclear Planning Group, and major NATO troop exercises. Perhaps most importantly from the German point of view, there was also still no guarantee that French territory would be available for allied troop transport and resupply purposes in the event of a European war. Nevertheless, the Valentin-Ferber accords represented a substantial improvement over the situation that had existed in 1967.

In the meantime, however, French nuclear doctrine was evolving in a direction that undermined the rationale for military cooperation between

France and its allies. Because its nuclear arsenal was so small in relation to the Soviet Union's, France could not incorporate counterforce tactics or differentiated escalation options into its nuclear planning. Rather, French nuclear deterrence necessarily rested on a strategy of massive retaliation. Although France could not hope to defeat an aggressor (i.e., the Soviet Union) in a nuclear exchange, it did claim the ability to inflict damage on an aggressor's homeland sufficient to outweigh any gains the aggressor might hope to achieve in attacking France's vital interests.[24]

In the latter 1960s Paris gradually modified the missions of France's conventional forces to reflect the centrality of strategic deterrence in French defense policy. This evolution went hand in hand with the government's development of theater nuclear weapons. As in the case of strategic nuclear arms, the initial decision to produce theater nuclear weapons did not derive from a prior strategic rationale. In both cases the justification was diffuse, incorporating an amalgam of political, technological, and military considerations. If the superpowers were investing heavily in nuclear weapons, reasoned the French, and if nuclear weapons were the *sine qua non* of modern military power as well as the key to a wide array of important technological capabilities, then France too must acquire nuclear arms.[25] If the superpowers were developing tactical as well as strategic nuclear weapons, then France should develop tactical nuclear weapons also. It was French policy not to allow the superpowers to hold an uncontested monopoly in any major weapons category.[26] On the basis of such a rationale, Paris went ahead with the development and production of tactical nuclear warheads. The first French tactical nuclear weapons were deployed on fighter aircraft in 1972.[27]

As part of the overall subordination of France's armed forces to the mission of strategic deterrence, the French land army was also to be equipped with tactical nuclear weapons. The army's role, as developed by French strategists in the late 1960s and laid down in the 1972 White Book on Defense, was to carry out the "national deterrent maneuver." The concept of the national deterrent maneuver was based on abandonment of the idea of a direct military defense of France. On the grounds that a military defense against Soviet forces would be futile yet inordinately destructive, French military planners rejected any notion of an extended conventional battle on French soil. Instead, French forces were assigned the far more limited mission of "testing" enemy intentions.[28] French troops would engage the adversary, first with conventional and then with tactical nuclear weapons, to demonstrate France's determination to defend its vital interests. Resort to tactical nuclear weapons would constitute a final warning to the opponent to cease his aggression. If the adversary persisted beyond this point, France would use its strategic nuclear arms to strike directly at the opponent's homeland.

The idea that France's armed forces (with the exception of certain elite units intended for overseas intervention) existed primarily to carry out France's national deterrent maneuver was difficult to reconcile with planning for military action alongside NATO forces in a Central European conflict. The heart of the problem lay in the question of when to resort to nuclear arms. Since introducing tactical nuclear weapons into a conflict would qualitatively alter the nature of the battle, agreement between France and NATO on when to use nuclear weapons in a European conflict was essential for effective operational planning. The French government's view, however, was that the decision on when and how to employ its nuclear arms (whether tactical or strategic) must be France's alone, and could not be shared with other states.

The Pluton Question

The difficulties for Alliance military planning posed by the French stance became increasingly evident as France moved forward with the production of theater nuclear weapons. The major tactical nuclear arm to equip French ground forces was the Pluton surface-to-surface missile, with a range of up to 120 kilometers. The missile was tightly integrated into the organization of the French army. In fact, *all* French plans for military action by the First Army—whether alone or alongside NATO forces—involved rapid escalation to the tactical nuclear level, even if resort to nuclear arms was preceded by a brief period of conventional battle.[29] Thus, if a joint military action involving NATO forces and the French First Army were to take place as provided for in the Valentin-Ferber agreements, artillery regiments equipped with Pluton missiles would move eastward into Germany with the First Army. The farther east the French divisions moved, the deeper into Germany the Plutons would move with it. Indeed, in no case would the First Army move eastward as part of an allied military action *without* its Plutons.

The French government planned to equip several artillery regiments in the First Army with Pluton missiles. Two such regiments were assigned to the French forces in Germany.[30] It soon became clear, however, that if France deployed Plutons on German soil, Bonn would demand a voice in French nuclear planning comparable to the influence it exercised over American and British tactical nuclear forces via the Nuclear Planning

Group.[31] Paris, viewing such a development as an unwelcome complication for French nuclear planning as well as an infringement on France's strategic independence and a large step toward reintegration into the NATO command structure, chose to skirt the issue by stationing all the Pluton missiles and warheads on French territory.

Deploying the Pluton in France, however, did nothing to resolve the problems the missile posed for West Germany. For one thing, the Germans were worried by the Pluton's limited range. Even if fired from a forward position inside West Germany, the Pluton would land and explode within West Germany's borders. This fact alone made Bonn very keen for a consultative role in French targeting plans for the weapon.

Even more important than the Pluton's limited range, in the view of some Germans, was the fact that French theater nuclear weapons held the potential for gravely disrupting Alliance defense plans. The problem lay in the differences between French and NATO forces in missions and capabilities. France's plans for conventional military action, which were intended to test enemy intentions rather than to defeat a large-scale conventional attack, provided for resort to tactical nuclear weapons very soon after the First Army went into action.[32] NATO plans, by contrast, intended a more sustained effort at conventional defense before resort to nuclear weapons. In other words, once France joined with its allies in a coordinated military action in Europe, it was to be expected that French escalation to the tactical nuclear level was imminent; from the perspective of NATO (and especially West Germany), such use might be tragically premature.

The Pluton question was to prove irresolvable, at least under the conditions prevailing in the 1970s. In the mid-1970s the German side raised the Pluton question again. The German defense minister, Georg Leber, indicated in June 1975 that conversations with Paris over the stationing of the Pluton had begun and that the German side had made specific proposals.[33] Later the same month, Chancellor Helmut Schmidt said that official negotiations on the Pluton had not yet taken place but that "we have already discussed it informally and will do so again in the future."[34] The government of French President Giscard d'Estaing, however, quickly made clear that discussions with Bonn on the Pluton would be limited to explication of France's tactical nuclear doctrine, and would not lead to any alteration of existing policy or any German voice in French nuclear planning.[35]

Whatever Franco-German discussions of the Pluton might subsequently have taken place, they evidently yielded no progress on the question. For the French side, allowing the Germans a voice in the operational plans governing use of the Pluton would infringe on the central principle of Gaullist defense policy, namely, that France must make no commitments that would amount to a prior constraint on its freedom of action and decision. Given the Pluton's role as the centerpiece of French military planning in Central Europe, it is difficult to see how Paris could have given Bonn a voice in French nuclear planning without revising its entire strategic doctrine to accord with NATO's. In addition, it was clear by 1975 that both the Gaullists and the opposition parties in the National Assembly viewed the Pluton question as a pivotal element of French defense independence and would strongly resist any attempt by Giscard's government to accommodate the Germans on the issue.[36] In short, it had gradually become evident that the Pluton question was simply another manifestation of the basic contradiction between France's policy of strategic independence and Germany's desire for a unified Atlantic defense system. As such, no genuine resolution of the problem was possible without a fundamental change in either French or German policy.

The overall pattern of French military policy under Pompidou confirmed and extended de Gaulle's policy of strategic independence. To be sure, there was a certain amount of tension between two underlying concepts of France's strategic role: one which emphasized military effectiveness (and hence favored the maximum possible coordination of French forces with those of NATO), and one which sought the maximum possible strategic autonomy for France. The relaxation of political tensions between France and the rest of NATO after de Gaulle's departure permitted a gradual increase in military cooperation between the two sides. At the same time, however, the gradual subordination of France's armed forces to its nuclear deterrence doctrine imposed limits on the coordination of French and allied military operations.

The question of bilateral strategic cooperation between France and West Germany remained essentially dormant throughout the 1970s, with neither side showing much interest in reviving the matter. The one bilateral issue which *did* arise, the Pluton question, proved impossible to resolve. As such, it was both a symptom of the existing Franco-German stalemate and a caveat for those who might have been tempted to try to end it.

LIMITED COOPERATION IN MILITARY AERONAUTICS

Despite the incompatibility of their overall strategic policies, France and Germany did continue to seek areas of potential collaboration in the development and production of armaments. One major Franco-German project evolved during the early 1970s: a training and close air support aircraft known as the Alpha-Jet. The project had its origins in 1967 and 1968, when talks between the French and German air forces had revealed mutual interest in the idea of developing a comprehensive joint pilot training program. The heart of the program was to be a Franco-German pilot training school, which would be established in southern France. The school would be equipped with a new light trainer jet that France and Germany would develop and produce together. The concept answered the needs of both air forces. The French air force urgently required a successor to its Fouga-Magister trainers, in service since the early 1950s. For the German air force, meanwhile, the project offered it a means to realize its long-term goal of moving its pilot training from the United States to Europe.

The notion of training West German pilots in France was not a new one. In fact, the idea had originally been discussed in the late 1950s, when the rebuilding of the German air force was just beginning.[37] Because of limited flying space, extensive pilot training inside the Federal Republic was impossible. The German air force would have to do most of its pilot training abroad; the only question was where. At one point, France and Germany had come close to agreeing on the training of German pilots in Corsica. But when Bonn chose the F-104 Starfighter over the Mirage in 1958, the plan collapsed. In 1963, Germany signed an agreement to train all its Starfighter pilots in the United States, and a Luftwaffe flying school was established at Sheppard Air Force Base in Texas.

The idea of moving its pilot training program to southern France appealed to the German air force for several reasons. Maintaining a flying school in distant Texas was an enormous drain on the Luftwaffe's budget. Training in France would be much more economical, because it would reduce transportation expenses and because equipment and facilities would be shared with the French air force. A program in France would also have the advantage of familiarizing pilots with European weather conditions from the outset of their training. Under existing arrangements, German pilots required extensive supplementary training in European skies after completing their program in Texas.[38]

The Kiesinger government readily assented to the proposal for joint Franco-German pilot training, because the idea accorded closely with the government's own political objectives. One of Kiesinger's main foreign policy goals, as noted earlier, was to restore a positive atmosphere to Franco-German relations after the acrimony of the Erhard period. The

French government (as the West Germans knew) was especially anxious for cooperation in the aeronautics sector. Bonn's 1968 decision to develop the Tornado combat aircraft in collaboration with Britain and Italy had been a considerable disappointment to Paris, because it meant exclusion from the most important European military aircraft project of the era. France also resented Germany's repeated acquisitions of American aircraft, such as the purchase of RF-4E Phantoms announced in October 1968, at the expense of French aircraft. If the Kiesinger government wanted to persuade France of its goodwill toward Franco-German defense cooperation, therefore, nothing would serve better than a gesture of support for the French military aeronautics industry.

The concept of joint pilot training also represented an effort by both Paris and Bonn to influence the shape of France's future relationship to NATO. For France, a joint pilot training center could serve Gaullist objectives in three ways. First, like so many other joint weapons ventures with Germany, it would amount to an indirect German subsidy for France's policy of independence vis-à-vis the United States. Second, it would symbolically draw West Germany into military cooperation with France on France's terms, helping to end the acute political isolation in the Alliance which France had suffered since 1967. Finally, French officials hoped to use the joint pilot program as a way of breaking what they viewed as an American cultural and ideological stranglehold on the German officer corps.[39] For West Germany, on the other hand, the joint training proposal held out the possibility of reestablishing active military cooperation with France and thereby countering France's apparent drift toward complete detachment from Alliance defense plans. Germany was still looking for ways to compensate for the loss of military planning coordination caused by France's withdrawal from the NATO command structure. Thus the joint pilot training proposal, which had started out as an equipment and budget planning measure by the French and German air force staffs, soon turned into a maneuver by the French and German governments to try to increase their political leverage over each other.

Even though the pilot training proposal corresponded to the wishes of both the German air force staff and the German government (albeit for different reasons), the idea had to be abandoned in mid-1971. For one thing, the German air force, unlike the French, had no pressing requirement for a new trainer; its own Texas-based Cessna T-37 and Northrop T-38 trainers would be usable through the mid-1980s. For another, the expensive training of pilots in the United States counted toward West Germany's offset obligations, and made up a sizeable fraction of Germany's total purchases of U.S. military goods and services. If training were moved to France, Bonn would presumably come under U.S. pressure to make up the resulting deficit through additional large purchases of American military equipment. Finally, there were indications that moving Germany's pilot training from the United States to France would provoke a fiercely hostile reaction from Washington.

Having backed down on the joint training proposal, Bonn felt all the more obligated to honor its agreement on co-production of the trainer aircraft itself, so as not to risk further alienation of the French. Although the German air force did not need a new trainer jet, it did have a requirement for a new close air support aircraft to replace its aging Fiat G-91s. Bonn accordingly proposed that the Alpha-Jet be built in two versions: a simple, inexpensive trainer version for the French air force, and a close air support version for Germany. The French were amenable to the suggested compromise. The one major point of disagreement concerned the engine to be used in the aircraft. The French side proposed that the Larzac 02 engine, produced by the nationalized French aircraft engine maker Snecma, be developed into a more powerful version (the Larzac 04) which could then be used in the Alpha-Jet. But the Germans, noting that the expected performance characteristics of the Larzac 04 were roughly the same as those of the already-existing J-85 engine manufactured by General Electric, argued in favor of equipping the Alpha-Jet with the American engine, thereby eliminating the costs and probable delays involved in developing a new engine. This proposal was flatly rejected by the French, who did not want U.S. weapons transfer restrictions interfering with export of the Alpha-Jet to potential customers such as South Africa. Finally the two sides reached a compromise, in which France agreed to pay for the development of the Larzac 04 and West Germany agreed to equip its own Alpha-Jets with the French rather than the American engine.[40]

A governmental agreement on the joint development and production of the Alpha-Jet was signed in March 1972. The leading French aircraft design company, Dassault-Bréguet, was the primary contractor for the airframe; Dornier was the major German subcontractor. Production work on the Snecma-developed engine was shared with the German engine firms MTU and KHD. The Alpha-Jet's maiden flight took place in October 1973, and delivery of the aircraft to the French and German armed forces began in September 1978. France ordered 200 of the aircraft in its trainer version. West Germany originally ordered 200 units of the close air support version but was forced by budgetary constraints to reduce its order to 175, the last of which was delivered in 1983. As of 1985, eight other countries had ordered a total of about 150 Alpha-Jets, with the majority of orders for the trainer version.

The Alpha-Jet was unusual among weapon co-production programs in that development and production proceeded according to schedule and within the cost agreements laid down at the beginning of the program. The project's exceptional efficiency was largely attributable to its streamlined management arrangements. In contrast to the Transall, the Alpha-Jet was not managed by a multilateral joint management company. Instead, one company (in this case Dassault) was designated as the "pilot" firm, and as such exercised final authority on design and management decisions.

Although the Alpha-Jet program was a success from a managerial point of view, it was not one in terms of the jet's performance as a close air support aircraft. Dassault's domination of the project meant that the final product resembled much more closely the simple, easily exportable trainer desired by the French than the high-performance attack aircraft required by the Germans. The close air support version of the Alpha-Jet was slower than the G-91 it replaced. Its avionics were rudimentary: the aircraft was not equipped with an autopilot, an inertial platform, or even a radar.[41] The aircraft's poor performance characteristics made it an object of bitter criticism within the German air force.[42] That the German government never seriously considered withdrawing from the project, even though the aircraft was poorly suited to Germany's military needs, reflected Bonn's continuing sense of political vulnerability in its relations with Paris as the 1970s began.

THE VEXING ARMS EXPORT PROBLEM

By the end of the 1960s, the implications of France's arms procurement policy were becoming increasingly clear. The cornerstone of French arma- ments policy was to retain national self-sufficiency in all major conven- tional military technologies. The costs of technological independence could be reduced in two ways: by sharing development costs with other European countries via joint projects, and by weapons exports.

In the late 1950s and early 1960s, the French government had sought to organize arms development and procurement on the Continent in a way that would help relieve the financial burdens caused by France's nuclear weapons program. This was the impulse underlying the French-German- Italian armaments triangle of the late 1950s and, on a more limited basis, the armaments cooperation clauses of the Elysée Treaty. Over time, how- ever, it became increasingly clear that France could not look to cooperation within Europe as a reliable way of protecting its independence in weapons technology against the United States. The situation became even less promising after France's partial break with NATO in 1966, which angered the other Europeans and resulted in intensified U.S. efforts to isolate France within the Alliance.

The cumulative impact of this situation was to draw France increasingly toward an armaments strategy centered on exports. The role of exports in helping to sustain a weapons production capability is well known. Exporting finished weapons helps smooth out disruptions to employment and production in the armaments sector caused by the cyclical nature of national procurement orders. The longer production runs created by exports permit greater realization of economies of scale. The sale of weapons production licenses to foreign governments allows states to recoup part of their investment in the development of the licensed weapon; surcharges added to the export price of finished weapons or components serve a similar function.[43]

Throughout the Cold War era, the French government had strongly encouraged exports of French-manufactured weapon systems. Indeed, a variety of official and quasi-official agencies existed for the exclusive purpose of facilitating exports of French armaments, including those produced by private firms like Dassault as well as those of the nationalized sector.[44] For France to be able to export weapon systems successfully, however, it was necessary that weapons not include components manufactured or licensed by American firms. U.S.-origin components were subject to end-use restrictions, and could therefore not be exported to states to which the United States refused arms exports. For this reason the French government consistently excluded U.S. content from armaments produced in France, even if the result was to make a weapon system much more expensive than it might have been. The French government's insistence on developing its own engine for the Alpha-Jet was a case in point. The exclusion of American components, because it increased the development costs of weapon systems like the Alpha-Jet, made exports all the more imperative. Dependence on weapons exports was thus self-reinforcing.

France's policy of aggressively exporting arms applied as much to co-produced weapon systems as to nationally produced ones. Like weapons with U.S.-origin content, however, co-produced armaments faced a possible problem in the form of end-use restrictions by partner countries involved in the joint projects. The question of arms exports posed a special problem in the case of cooperative projects with Germany. Acutely conscious of international and domestic sensitivities regarding German weapons exports, and wary of potential backlash, West German governments sought to keep as low a profile on armaments sales as possible.

Two laws passed in 1961, the War Weapons Control Act and the Foreign Trade Act, constituted the legal framework for West German arms export policy. The laws mandated governmental supervision of all manufacture, acquisition, and transport of armaments in West Germany. No export of weapons from West Germany was permitted without official authorization. The War Weapons Control Act specified in addition that authorization for the transfer of weapons to foreign states was to be denied if there was a possibility that the weapons would be used in a war of aggression, or if the transfer would be in conflict with West Germany's international legal commitments.[45]

The West German government established specific administrative guidelines on weapons exports in June 1971.[46] The guidelines permitted essentially unrestricted arms exports to NATO states, except that the re-export of German arms by allies to areas outside the Alliance was to take place only with Bonn's permission. The guidelines imposed heavy constraints, on the other hand, on arms exports to non-NATO states. Weapons exports to Communist states were completely prohibited. Also prohibited were weapons exports to areas of tension (*Spannungsgebiete*), as well as exports that might cause "disturbance to the peaceful coexistence of nations or a substantial disturbance to the external relations of the Federal Republic of Germany." In general, weapons exports to countries outside NATO were to be approved only in exceptional cases, and when there were particular political grounds for the approval.

In comparison with the arms export policies of France or Britain, the German guidelines were highly restrictive. In fact, the guidelines were altogether incompatible with France's arms production strategy, which depended on selling arms to virtually any country that could pay for them. Many of France's best export prospects were precisely those countries, such as South Africa and the hard-line Arab states, which West Germans found most objectionable as arms clients on political and moral grounds.

The difference between French and German export policies had the potential to rupture arms co-production between the two countries completely. All Franco-German co-production projects were organized according to the "single-source" principle: that is, each component of a co-produced weapon system was manufactured at only one site. The only redundancy in co-production projects was that France and Germany normally each had a production line of its own for final assembly of the weapon system. Single-source manufacture was necessary to keep production costs within affordable bounds. For each participant in a co-production project to manufacture all the weapon's components itself—or even most of them—would more than cancel any benefits to be realized from cooperation.

Franco-German weapons co-production under the single-source principle posed a dilemma for the German government. Because weapons manufactured jointly with France contained approximately one-half German content, French exports of these weapons to politically sensitive regions could lead to painful repercussions. The 1966 sale of Transalls to South Africa, for example, produced both domestic uproar and international censure of West Germany by black African states.

Before 1971, the question of exporting co-produced arms was not addressed by the French and German governments in any systematic way. Up to that point, the question had only arisen in connection with the Transall episode; other jointly developed weapons were not yet available for export. Problems were visible on the horizon, however. France had high hopes for the export prospects of several of its ongoing projects with Germany: the Alpha-Jet, the Milan, the HOT, and the Roland. If the German government insisted on adhering strictly to its 1971 guidelines, the two countries would be at odds on exports to many of the most promising markets.

Before committing itself fully to the Alpha-Jet, therefore, the French government demanded a fundamental resolution of the differences in French and German policy relating to export of co-produced weapons. On the West German side, the problem fell into the lap of Helmut Schmidt, who was defense minister under Brandt from 1969 to 1972. Schmidt, according to one close associate, realized that it was an either/or situation: if Germany tried to control France's exports of joint Franco-German weapons in any binding way, the result would be an end to armaments cooperation.[47] Believing that cooperation with France was indispensable to German foreign policy, Schmidt concluded that West Germany had no alternative but to accede to France's demands.

Negotiations led to an agreement, which was signed by Schmidt in December 1971 and by French Defense Minister Debré the following February. The agreement stated that neither France nor Germany could veto the other's export of jointly produced weapon systems to third countries, and that neither could withhold components required by the other to assemble units designated for export. The agreement also specified that France and Germany would, in the case of jointly produced arms, apply their national laws concerning arms exports in a spirit of cooperation. Each side was entitled, in exceptional cases, to raise objections to an export planned by the other, and it was agreed that the other side would not carry out the objectionable export before it had been discussed thoroughly in bilateral consultations. The agreement applied specifically to the Alpha-Jet, Transall, Milan, HOT, Roland, and RATAC weapon systems.[48]

Although the Schmidt-Debré agreement resolved the policy dispute between the two sides, there was some doubt as to whether the arrangement was consistent with West German law. The transfer of weapons components to France for weapon systems that were later exported outside the NATO area seemed in potential violation of the War Weapons Control Act, which forbade exports of military goods that might be used in an offensive war or exports that conflicted with West Germany's international legal commitments. The German government circumvented the problem by resort to a legal fiction. It adopted the position that weapons components or subassemblies produced in Germany, if they were later integrated into a weapon system elsewhere, ceased to be defined as German-origin goods; instead, the entire weapon system was regarded for legal purposes as having originated in the country of final assembly.

Although the German government thus found a satisfactory basis for weapons cooperation with France, France's aggressive export policy continued to pose potential problems for Bonn with regard to domestic and international opinion. According to German defense ministry officials, West German objections to exports of co-produced weapons were frequently a subject of discussion at meetings of the French and German defense ministers in the years following the Schmidt-Debré agreement. Depending on the particular case, West German objections were based on military-strategic considerations, on grounds of undesirable technology transfer, or on political-moral grounds. In several instances, according to officials, the German government succeeded in dissuading Paris from a proposed export by making a plausible case that the intended sale would compromise French security. In cases where German objections were mainly political or moral in nature, on the other hand, they tended to carry little weight with the French, who then went ahead with the sales.[49] West German uneasiness over such instances was a further damper on enthusiasm in both Paris and Bonn regarding Franco-German armaments cooperation.

NOTES

1. See Karl Kaiser, *German Foreign Policy in Transition* (London: Oxford University Press, 1968).

2. Helga Haftendorn, *Sicherheit und Entspannung: Zur Aussenpolitik der Bundesrepublik Deutschland, 1955–1982* (Baden-Baden: Nomos, 1983), pp. 191, 278.

3. Haftendorn, *Sicherheit und Entspannung*, pp. 207–8.

4. The Harmel Report is reprinted in *North Atlantic Treaty Organization: Facts and Figures* (Brussels: NATO Information Service, 1984), pp. 289–91.

5. Interestingly, this assertion was at odds with the arguments of the "Gaullist" school of French deterrence theory represented by strategists such as Pierre Gallois and Lucien Poirier, who insisted on the strategic discontinuity of nuclear deterrence at the French border.

6. This conclusion is based on interviews with former German political and military officials.

7. Harrison, *Reluctant Ally*, pp. 121–22.

8. Cf. Hildebrand, "Der provisorische Staat," pp. 75–76.

9. See, for example, de Gaulle's press conference of February 4, 1965. *Discours et messages*, vol. 4, pp. 337–42.

10. *Discours et messages*, vol. 4, pp. 360–64.

11. See Roger Morgan, *The United States and West Germany, 1945–1973* (London: Oxford University Press, 1974), pp. 214–17.

12. Eric Roussel, *Georges Pompidou* (Paris: J. C. Lattès, 1984), pp. 407–8.

13. For an overview of French attitudes on this question, see Andreas Wilkens, *Der unstete Nachbar: Frankreich, die deutsche Ostpolitik und die Berliner Vier-Mächte-Verhandlungen 1969–1974* (Munich: R. Oldenbourg, 1990).

14. Simonian, *The Privileged Partnership*, pp. 180–84.

15. Brandt signed the treaty on November 28, 1969, as one of his first major decisions as chancellor. Ratification of the treaty by the Bundestag, however, did not follow until May 1975.

16. David S. Yost, *France's Deterrent Posture and Security in Europe*, Adelphi Papers 194 and 195 (London: IISS, Winter 1984/85), Part II, pp. 50–51.

17. Henry A. Kissinger, *Years of Upheaval* (Boston: Little, Brown and Co., 1982), p. 167.

18. See, for example, Jobert's remarks to the WEU Assembly, reprinted in *Le Monde*, November 23, 1973. Also compare Jobert, *L'autre regard* (Paris: Grasset, 1976), pp. 304–5.

19. See Yost, *France's Deterrent Posture*, Part II, pp. 42–46.

20. Willy Brandt reports Pompidou's anxieties in *People and Politics: The Years 1960–1975* (Boston: Little, Brown and Co., 1978), p. 259.

21. For a list of such statements see Jean Klein, "France, NATO, and European Security," *International Security*, Winter 1977, p. 32.

22. Haftendorn, *Sicherheit und Entspannung*, pp. 539 and 606–7.

23. See François Valentin, "L'arête étroite," *Défense nationale*, May 1983, pp. 48–52. The French forces stationed in Germany were the 1st and 3rd armored divisions, which together comprised the First Army's Second Corps. In the late 1970s these two divisions were regrouped into three smaller divisions (the 1st, 3rd

and 5th) as part of a larger reorganization which reduced the size of the French army by 20,000 troops. The total manpower of the French forces in Germany was reduced by about 10,000 to a new total of 49,000.

24. France, Ministry of Defense, *Livre blanc sur la défense nationale* (1972), p. 12.

25. See François Valentin, *Une politique de défense pour la France* (Paris: Calmann-Lévy, 1980), p. 57.

26. Jacques Chirac, "Au sujet des armes nucléaires tactiques françaises," *Défense nationale*, May 1975, p. 11, and interviews with French defense officials. This remained French policy in later years as well: see, for example, the interview with French President Mitterrand in *Le Nouvel Observateur*, December 18, 1987, p. 25.

27. Yost, *France's Deterrent Posture*, Part I, pp. 48–49.

28. France, *Livre blanc sur la défense nationale* (1972), pp. 9, 20–21; see also Valentin, *Une politique de défense*, p. 89, and Lucien Poirier, *Des stratégies nucléaires* (Paris: Hachette, 1977), pp. 316–32.

29. It would be "an illusion," wrote General Valentin, to think that the First Army could fight for several days without resort to tactical nuclear weapons. Valentin, *Une politique de défense*, p. 99.

30. Yost, *France's Deterrent Posture*, Part I, p. 49.

31. See the reports in *The Economist*, February 19, 1972, and the *International Herald Tribune*, March 25, 1972; also the interview with former Defense Minister Michel Debré in *Le Nouvel Observateur*, July 28, 1975, pp. 18–19.

32. Valentin, *Une politique de défense*, pp. 90–91.

33. *Le Monde*, June 7, 1975.

34. *Le Monde*, June 28, 1975.

35. See the interview with French Foreign Minister Jean Sauvagnargues in *Le Nouvel Observateur*, July 21, 1975, pp. 16–17.

36. See, for example, *Le Monde*, June 25, 1975, and *Le Figaro*, July 7, 1975.

37. *The New York Times*, February 12, 1958.

38. *Le Monde*, January 21, 1970, and *Aerospace International*, May-June 1971, p. 38.

39. Interview with former French armaments official.

40. Wahl and Engelmann, "Wehrtechnik Luft," pp. 182–83.

41. Wahl and Engelmann, "Wehrtechnik Luft," p. 184, and Mechtersheimer, *Rüstung und Politik*, p. 132.

42. Mechtersheimer, *Rüstung und Politik*, pp. 132–33.

43. On the political economy of arms exports, see Stanley and Pearton, *International Trade in Arms*, chapter 6.

44. Stanley and Pearton, *International Trade in Arms*, pp. 94–95. For a comprehensive history and analysis of French arms exports, see Edward A. Kolodziej, *Making and Marketing Arms: The French Experience and Its Implications for the International System* (Princeton: Princeton University Press, 1987). Also note Jean

Klein, "France and the Arms Trade," in Cindy Cannizzo, ed., *The Gun Merchants: Politics and Policies of the Major Arms Suppliers* (New York: Pergamon, 1980), pp. 127–66; Jean-François Dubos, *Ventes d'armes: Une politique* (Paris: Gallimard, 1974); and Claude Carlier, *L'aéronautique française, 1945–1975* (Paris: Lavauzelle, 1983), chapter 5.

45. See the discussion in Mike Dillon, "Arms Transfers and the Federal Republic of Germany," in Cannizzo, *The Gun Merchants*, pp. 101–26.

46. The text is reprinted in *Die Neue Gesellschaft*, April 1982, pp. 369–70.

47. Interview material.

48. Information supplied by West German Ministry of Defense. Although the agreement was officially secret, information about its existence and contents soon appeared in press articles. See, for example, the *International Herald Tribune*, September 16, 1972. The RATAC was a battlefield radar developed in France and jointly produced by the companies LMT in France and SEL in Germany.

49. Interviews with current and former German defense ministry officials.

———————————————————

CHAPTER 5

The Forging of the Paris-Bonn Axis, 1974-1983

Franco-German cooperation under French President Valéry Giscard d'Estaing and German Chancellor Helmut Schmidt contrasted sharply with the uneasy relations of the Brandt-Pompidou era. During the two years before their arrival to power in May 1974, Schmidt and Giscard had come to know and value each other as finance ministers in their respective governments. As national leaders, their easy rapport was soon reflected in a closer and more effective working partnership than had ever been achieved by their immediate predecessors.

During the initial years of the Schmidt-Giscard period, the most notable thing about defense and security questions was that they were largely absent from the Franco-German agenda. Defense issues receded into the background for a number of reasons. First, they were displaced to some extent by the urgent economic matters arising from the 1973 oil price increases. During the second half of 1974, Franco-German consultation and coordination focused on combating inflation and forestalling protectionism; during 1975, the main problem was restoring economic growth after the deflationary measures of the preceding year.[1] Other preoccupations included the rise in raw materials prices and the problem of secure access to energy supplies.

Second, after all the tensions and upheavals of the previous decade, intra-Alliance relations seemed finally to have stabilized. France's peculiar status in NATO had come, over time, to be accepted on all sides. The Declaration on Atlantic Relations approved by the NATO Council at Ottawa in June 1974 stated that the independent French and British nuclear forces were a positive contribution to Alliance deterrence. With the Ottawa declaration the United States thus formally reconciled itself to France's independent strategic policy. Meanwhile, pressures in the United States to withdraw troops from Europe had abated, allowing French anxieties over German neutralization to subside. The successes of détente had brought an improved feeling of security to Western Europe, yet had proved sufficiently modest that there seemed little imminent danger of a dissolution of the Atlantic Alliance. The Final Act of the Conference on Security and Cooperation in Europe (CSCE), signed at Helsinki in August 1975, represented to some extent the institutionalization of détente in Europe. The act incorporated a statement of principles on relations among the thirty-five signatories, as well as various military confidence-building measures and declarations on economic, scientific, and humanitarian cooperation. With its provisions for later follow-up conferences, the Final Act laid the basis for future incremental improvements to the structure of détente. From the perspective of France and Germany, therefore, the mid-1970s were a relatively calm period in Alliance politics. Each of the two countries had found its own way to make the division of Europe bearable: France, through Gaullism and the rhetoric of independence; Germany, through Ostpolitik and the restoration of inter-German relations.

Finally, it was also true that neither Paris nor Bonn saw much occasion for new Franco-German initiatives in military or strategic questions. Events since the signing of the Elysée Treaty had demonstrated again and again the irreconcilability of French and German strategic concepts. Schmidt himself was a strong supporter of close relations with France, but saw foreign and economic policies—not defense policy—as the areas in which Paris and Bonn could gain most from increased cooperation. Giscard, for his part, showed little interest in building closer bilateral defense ties to Germany. His limited efforts to change France's strategic orientation were aimed at improving France's military relations with NATO as a whole. Giscard's refusal to give Germany a voice in French tactical nuclear planning underlined the narrow limits to bilateral defense cooperation. Indeed, Giscard appeared immune to the hypothetical attractions of a self-reliant European defense system. On several occasions, in fact, he explicitly ruled out the possibility of moving toward a European defense system on the grounds that such a project was not feasible under existing conditions.[2]

The changes Giscard did make to French defense policy were quite modest in both inspiration and implications. On first coming to office, Giscard had seemed to raise the possibility of a major overhaul of French strategic doctrine. At his first press conference, in July 1974, he announced that he would undertake a thorough study of French defense policy in the light of changes in the world since 1960.[3] In October, however, a series of crippling strikes in France demonstrated the limits of Giscard's domestic authority. Meanwhile, the Gaullist bloc in the National Assembly (on which Giscard's governing majority depended) made clear its vehement opposition to any modification in the basic elements of French defense policy. By November 1974, Schmidt had reportedly concluded that Giscard lacked a sufficient popular base in France to undertake any real departure from de Gaulle's foreign policy legacy.[4] This evaluation was corroborated by Giscard himself in a televised speech on March 25, 1975, in which he indicated that French defense policy would continue to hew to the principles of independence and non-automaticity laid down by de Gaulle.[5]

The precise thrust of Giscard's defense policy became clearer in an important address he delivered on June 1, 1976 to the Institut des Hautes Etudes de Défense Nationale. In the speech, the French president spoke of the need for French forces to be organized so as to be able to "give battle." He also dismissed the notion that France could stand aside from an armed conflict in Central Europe, noting that Europe formed a single strategic zone of which France was unavoidably a part.[6] Giscard's speech coincided with the publication of an article by General Guy Méry, chief of staff of the French armed forces, which developed similar themes. Méry used the term "enlarged sanctuarization" to describe the extent of French nuclear deterrence, and evoked the possibility that French forces could participate in the forward battle (bataille de l'avant) of an East-West conflict in Central Europe.[7]

The simultaneous emphasis by Giscard and his armed forces chief of staff on the notion of battle, together with their unwelcome reminders that geography made France part of Europe, instantly brought down a deluge of critical commentary from Gaullists as well as from French Socialist and Communist leaders, who accused Giscard of plotting to return France to military integration in NATO.[8] The virulence of the attacks stemmed largely from Giscard's "Atlanticist" reputation and the suspicions that attached to him for that reason. Examination of Giscard and Méry's June 1976 statements on defense policy reveals little indication of an attempted shift away from the prevailing Gaullist orthodoxy. Indeed, there appears to be nothing in the statements by either man which departed in any significant way from existing French military doctrine. For example, Giscard's characterization of Europe as a single strategic zone echoed the observation in the 1972 White Book on Defense that "our geographic and strategic position on the edge of the European continent is such that we are necessarily part of the continental situation."[9] And if Méry referred to enlarged sanctuarization, the 1972 White Book noted that "[although] deterrence is reserved to our vital interests, their limit is necessarily vague. . . . France exists in a web of interests which go beyond her borders. She is not isolated."[10] As for the notion that France might participate in the *bataille de l'avant*, the context of Méry's remarks makes it clear that he was merely referring to the existing role of the French First Army as NATO's counterattack reserve, and in no way advocating that French forces take up a position on NATO's front line.

The only real nuance introduced by Giscard and Méry into French defense policy, in fact, was a slight increase in spending on conventional arms relative to nuclear forces. This shift derived, moreover, from considerations other than a desire to bring France back into harmony with NATO strategy. Specifically, the renewed emphasis on conventional forces was imposed by the increasingly desperate crisis of morale confronting the French armed services.[11] During the period 1965–1975, the French military budget declined from 4.5 to 2.9 percent of gross national product.[12] Following the domestic upheavals of 1968, French policymakers had sharply reduced military equipment spending in favor of increased social welfare expenditures.[13] As a result, the acquisition of many important conventional weapon systems was slowed or cancelled.[14] The overall quality of equipment for French forces seriously deteriorated as existing matériel became obsolete and was not replaced. Pay and benefits for French soldiers increasingly lagged behind those for other occupations. Living conditions within the military were bad enough to inspire organized protests in 1973–1975.

The problem of poor material conditions was compounded by incomprehension among officers and soldiers regarding French defense doctrine. The idea that the armed forces existed not to defend France, but merely to "test" enemy intentions before proceeding to the nuclear bombing of Soviet population centers, was a source of tremendous discontent in the French military. By the mid-1970s, therefore, it had become imperative to improve the equipment and material condition of France's conventional forces and to reassure French soldiers that their role in national defense was a meaningful one. This was the crucial factor behind Giscard's talk of "giving battle" and his effort to increase the proportion of the defense budget going to conventional capabilities.

Two other considerations also played a role in Giscard's focus on improving French conventional forces. First was the need to maintain adequate conventional capabilities to respond to limited aggressions against France or its overseas territories.[15] Second was the psychological importance of not allowing the gap between French and German conventional capabilities to grow too large. The Franco-German rapprochement continued to require a certain degree of self-assurance on the part of the French. Too great a differential in French and German conventional capabilities held the danger of rekindling French insecurities, to the detriment of all areas of Franco-German relations.[16] The reasoning behind Giscard's attention to conventional forces thus boiled down to nothing more than the entirely Gaullist motive of assuring France the full panoply of military assets necessary for an independent foreign policy.

THE CARTER ADMINISTRATION AND ALLIANCE RELATIONS

With the inauguration of Jimmy Carter as the new U.S. president in January 1977, the Schmidt-Giscard partnership began to undergo a significant evolution. From this point on, Franco-German relations would be strongly affected by the frictions in U.S.-European ties caused by Carter's policies and above all by the tremendous discord between Schmidt and the Carter White House.

The personal relationship between Carter and Schmidt had gotten off on a bad footing even before Carter became president, when Schmidt incautiously revealed his hope that Gerald Ford would win the election. Within weeks of the inauguration, major disagreements between Washington and Bonn were already apparent on East-West relations, nuclear technology export policy, and economic coordination within the West. To these disagreements were soon added frictions over Alliance military policy and the U.S. negotiating position on SALT II. In varying degrees, these disagreements translated into a joint effort by Schmidt and Giscard to insulate Western Europe from the impact of Carter's policies.

The first area of intensified security consultation between the two Europeans came in reaction to Carter's human rights policy. During his first weeks in office Carter had emphasized through both words and actions his support for dissenters in the Soviet Union. The U.S. president wrote a letter to the dissident Soviet physicist Andrei Sakharov, and received the exiled dissident Vladimir Bukovsky at the White House. Schmidt viewed Carter's actions on this question with great consternation. Given Soviet sensitivity to U.S. pressures on its internal politics, he worried that Carter's public reproaches to Moscow on human rights could undermine the entire foundation of East-West détente.[17] Giscard shared Schmidt's anxieties, and the two leaders devised a coordinated plan to dampen Washington's human rights offensive.

This involved a certain division of labor. Schmidt, in view of Germany's history and political vulnerability on human rights issues, felt unable to speak out directly against Carter's policy. It was left to Giscard, therefore, to criticize publicly Carter's human rights stance in a July 1977 *Newsweek* interview, underlining the fact that he spoke for Schmidt as well as for himself.[18] Simultaneously, the German government issued a more conciliatory statement emphasizing that Bonn and Paris were in total agreement with Washington on the "moral principles" of the human rights question, even if not necessarily on the details of how best to achieve progress on the matter.[19] It was precisely for this type of foreign policy maneuver—opposing the Carter administration while not making Germany culpable in world opinion—that Schmidt now found his partnership with Giscard especially useful.

A second area where Franco-German cooperation increased in reaction to Carter's foreign policy involved strategic arms control. Soon after coming to office, Carter had decided that the outline of a second U.S.-Soviet strategic accord, agreed between Ford and Brezhnev at Vladivostok in 1974, was unsatisfactory and that the negotiations should start over again on the basis of a completely new U.S. proposal for "deep cuts" in the superpower strategic arsenals.[20] Carter's moves were thoroughly unsettling to the German government, which feared that the abrupt American shift could derail the SALT negotiations and thereby have a damaging effect on the overall evolution of détente. As in the case of human rights, Schmidt and Giscard's shared concern for détente in Europe led to the adoption of a common position. After the superpowers finally reached agreement on the SALT II treaty in June 1979, the French and German leaders issued a joint declaration calling on the United States to ratify the agreement.[21] The joint endorsement, coming in spite of the fact that neither the Germans nor the French were very satisfied with the actual content of the SALT II treaty, demonstrated how deeply Schmidt and Giscard feared a U.S. abjuration of détente.[22]

Despite the renewed introduction of security questions into Franco-German consultations from 1977 onward, economic cooperation continued to occupy center stage in the Schmidt-Giscard tandem. The major focus of consultation between the two leaders during 1978 and 1979, in fact, was the effort to create a European Monetary System as a means of stabilizing intra-European exchange rates. The stimulus for Franco-German cooperation in monetary policy lay in the intensifying discord between Schmidt's

government and the Carter administration over coordination of macroe-
conomic policy among the Western industrial states. The disagreement had
begun when Carter, almost immediately upon taking office, began pressing
an unwilling Germany to join the United States in expansionary measures
to promote worldwide economic growth. By early 1978 the continuing
crisis of the dollar, the need to deflect American pressure on Germany to
reflate, and growing doubts about the Carter administration's willingness
and ability to stabilize either the dollar or the U.S. economy, prompted
Schmidt to take the lead in pushing for European monetary union.[23]
Schmidt brought his ideas to Giscard, and the two worked out a joint
proposal which was then introduced for consideration in the European
Community. During the ensuing Community negotiations on monetary
union, collaboration between Schmidt and Giscard provided the key
mechanism for overcoming intra-Community disagreements over specific
aspects of the proposal.[24] As difficulties arose they were resolved in each
case by prior agreement between Paris and Bonn, with the other EC
members essentially following the Franco-German lead. Creation of the
European Monetary System, which entered into operation in March 1979,
was the single most important achievement of Franco-German cooperation during the Schmidt-Giscard era.

It is worth noting that, up to approximately the end of 1979, the
Schmidt-Giscard alliance was almost purely tactical. For all their intimate
conversations and consultations, neither Schmidt nor Giscard aimed at a
Franco-German political union of the sort envisaged by de Gaulle and
Adenauer. Rather, each essentially sought a buttress for his own foreign
policy objectives. In Schmidt's case, buttressing was useful above all when
he wanted to take a position that ran contrary to that adopted by Washington. It was axiomatic for Schmidt that Germany could not take any
major initiatives in European or Alliance politics by itself: to do so would
excite suspicion and resistance from all sides—the United States, France,
Britain, and the Netherlands, not to mention the Soviet Union. If Bonn
wanted to take action independently of Washington, it would need a
partner within the Alliance to do so. Giscard, for his part, also stood to
gain from foreign policy coordination with Bonn, understanding that
France's policy would carry much more weight if it were framed as a
common Franco-German position than as France's policy alone. Thus, the
Paris-Bonn "axis" amounted to little more than a pragmatic coordination
of policies on specific issues where both sides stood to gain from a common
stance. Except in the area of monetary union, Schmidt and Giscard did not

attempt to formalize Franco-German policy coordination or to place it in a constraining structural framework.

THE SEARCH FOR A CLOSER PARTNERSHIP

In 1980, however, the Schmidt-Giscard alliance began to evolve in a new direction. A number of factors had entered the picture which seemed to raise grave questions about the future of the Western Alliance. First of all was the American reaction to the Soviet invasion of Afghanistan in December 1979. American disappointment with the results of détente had been visible since 1975. Under Carter, the tone of Washington's pronouncements toward Moscow had steadily sharpened. In the aftermath of the events in Afghanistan, it appeared that the United States was prepared to dispense with détente altogether. January 1980 was punctuated by a series of White House announcements of sanctions to be taken in response to Afghanistan, including postponement of the ratification debate on the SALT II treaty, an embargo on U.S. grain shipments to the Soviet Union, cancellation of sales of high-technology goods, and an American boycott of the summer Olympic games in Moscow. The Carter administration pressured the West Europeans to fall in step with the measures it had announced.

Most West European capitals differed from Washington in their assessment of the Soviet action and of the necessary Western response. To the German government it was clear that Carter's sanctions would not compel a Soviet withdrawal from Afghanistan, and that they were motivated chiefly by an election-year desire to accommodate the anti-Soviet mood of U.S. public opinion.[25] For the Europeans, whose stake in détente was so much greater than that of the United States, there seemed little sense in taking measures that would alter nothing in Central Asia but might well jeopardize détente in Europe. This was true above all for the West Germans, who had the most to lose. The German government drew a distinction between Soviet actions in Europe and Soviet actions elsewhere in the world. The maintenance of secure access to West Berlin and the continuation of human contacts with East Germany were, for Bonn, a near-absolute priority. As long as the Soviet Union did not challenge the framework of European détente as established through the Ostpolitik treaties of the early 1970s, the Four Power Agreement on Berlin, and the Helsinki Final Act, Bonn was not about to do so either.

In the face of heavy U.S. pressures to join in sanctions against Moscow, the German government needed French support more than ever. Paris, for its part, agreed with Bonn in wanting to preserve European détente despite Afghanistan. At their Paris summit meeting early in February 1980, Schmidt and Giscard issued a six-point declaration regarding the international situation. The statement condemned the Soviet invasion of Afghanistan and noted that Soviet actions had made détente more difficult and uncertain. By declaring that "détente could not withstand another blow of this kind," however, the statement implicitly reassured Moscow that Paris and Bonn would stand by their existing policy of détente as long as the Soviet Union launched no additional military adventures.

The February 1980 Franco-German summit marked the beginning of Schmidt's search for a more substantive security partnership with Paris than had existed up to that point. Previously Schmidt and Giscard had made little effort to harmonize policy in the area of military strategy, where their national perspectives were not easily reconciled. Now, however, Schmidt began to show interest in a more structured security relationship with France. In an after-dinner speech at the summit, the chancellor gave a poignant account of his gradual evolution from Anglophile to Americanophile to Francophile, at the end professing his deep personal friendship for Giscard and expressing the hope that it would be lifelong.[26] The speech was a revealing indicator of the transformation taking place in Schmidt's thinking regarding the need for a closer Franco-German defense partnership.

Even if Giscard were willing to go along, however, there remained the problem of incompatible French and German defense strategies. What could the two sides do to emphasize their solidarity in the face of new challenges to détente and world peace? The six-point declaration on Afghanistan was significant but not enough. Schmidt's solution was to turn to armaments production, the one area of defense relations where the French would readily agree to closer bilateral ties. The chosen symbol of cooperation was a third-generation main battle tank. Discussions on the possibility of jointly constructing an advanced battle tank had been under way between France and Germany for several years (see Chapter 6). Although agreement on the specific details of the project had not been reached, the two leaders now made a political decision to press ahead with the tank as a high-profile demonstration of Franco-German defense partnership. On the evening of February 5, in the presence of television cameras and with Schmidt and Giscard looking on, the French and German defense ministers signed an agreement pledging their countries to develop and produce an advanced battle tank together during the 1980s.

In the months following the February 1980 summit, Schmidt came to value the Franco-German partnership ever more as his doubts about U.S. reliability increased. Schmidt's worries stemmed from a combination of circumstances. For one thing, under Carter's stewardship the United States seemed to be declining rapidly in power. Perhaps the most telling series of events was the extraordinary display of American impotence and ineptitude surrounding the Iranian revolution. The storming of the U.S. embassy in Teheran in November 1979 and the seizure of sixty-three embassy personnel as hostages focused world attention on Washington's inability to respond effectively to the crisis. The hostage-taking in itself might not have been an affair of such import had it not been for the fact that the incident could evidently hold American foreign policy hostage as well. The degree to which the hostage crisis came to preoccupy American diplomacy—for example, in the unceasing U.S. efforts to enlist the West Europeans in sanctions against the Iranian regime—could not help but raise questions in the minds of European leaders about whether the United States was losing its superpower status in world affairs. The continuing crisis of the dollar demonstrated Washington's unwillingness to behave responsibly in its external economic relations, while the new round of huge oil price increases (themselves a response to the fall in the dollar's value) and the emerging Third World debt crisis highlighted the sharp decline in Washington's ability to manage the world economy.[27]

A second factor driving Schmidt toward a closer military partnership with France was the cumulative impact of actions by the Carter administration which cast doubt on America's reliability as an ally. The first such incident occurred in August 1977 when reports concerning the contents of Presidential Review Memorandum 10, an internal White House document, appeared in the press.[28] The memorandum reportedly proposed making the Weser and Lech rivers NATO's major line of defense. Such a change would have meant returning to a version of the allied fallback strategy of the 1950s, conceding one-third of West German territory at the outset of a Warsaw Pact attack. Although U.S. Defense Secretary Harold Brown announced that he would oppose any changes to the existing NATO forward defense strategy, European leaders, above all Schmidt, were infuriated that such changes had been contemplated at all, and were appalled by the American government's insensitivity to European concerns.

The Carter administration's unreliability was also evident in its handling of the neutron bomb issue.[29] Production of the warhead, which was to be deployed with U.S. troops in Western Europe, had become politically controversial on both sides of the Atlantic during the summer and fall of

1977. Schmidt faced strong opposition to the neutron bomb within his own party as well as from German public opinion. It was only at considerable political cost that he maneuvered his government into accepting a formula negotiated with Washington for deployment of the neutron weapon in West Germany. Carter's abrupt decision in March 1978 to cancel production of the weapon, without explanation or apology to Schmidt, did much to undermine the chancellor's trust in the Carter administration.[30]

Far more serious than either of these incidents, however, was the question of Soviet intermediate-range nuclear weapons and the Western response to their deployment. Schmidt had long been concerned by the new military threat to Western Europe posed by Soviet deployments of the Backfire bomber and the mobile, multi-warhead SS-20 missile. The chancellor worried lest the superpowers reach an agreement that would control strategic nuclear arms but do nothing about the upgrading of Soviet nuclear weapon systems targeted against Western Europe. Schmidt had voiced his concerns to President Ford in 1975, and obtained Ford's express promise that limits on the Backfire and SS-20 would be part of any SALT II treaty. But Ford was not reelected, and despite repeated appeals to the new administration on the question, Schmidt gradually became convinced that Carter did not intend to abide by his predecessor's pledge.[31]

In a famous October 1977 speech to the International Institute for Strategic Studies in London, Schmidt made public his unease over the growing East-West imbalance in theater nuclear arms. The publicity generated by Schmidt's speech stimulated Washington to undertake a major reevalution during 1978 of its policy regarding Soviet theater nuclear weapons.[32] Further consultations within NATO during 1979 led to adoption of the two-track decision on theater nuclear modernization, approved by the NATO Council at Brussels in December of that year.[33] The essence of the decision was that NATO would deploy new medium-range nuclear forces in Europe—108 Pershing II missiles and 464 cruise missiles—unless negotiations with the Soviet Union yielded acceptable limits on Soviet theater nuclear weapons. Schmidt, who believed it absolutely essential that NATO respond to Moscow's theater nuclear buildup, strongly supported the two-track decision. Nevertheless, the decision came as a tremendous disappointment to him.[34] The Carter administration's procrastination in coming to grips with the Soviet deployments had permitted Moscow several more years of unhindered buildup in Backfires and SS-20s. The delay had all but eliminated the chance that negotiations would yield a solution quickly, and greatly increased the possibility that no solution would be reached at all.

A final factor driving Schmidt to seek closer security ties with France was the labor unrest in Poland leading to formation of the independent trade union Solidarity in the autumn of 1980. The events in Poland raised the possibility of a new Soviet military intervention in Eastern Europe, which, if it should occur, would probably mean the end of détente in Europe despite every effort by Paris and Bonn to preserve it. For this reason the German government was greatly (if quietly) dismayed by Washington's overt moral support for the Polish workers, which Bonn perceived as a further provocation to Soviet intervention.

As 1980 progressed, therefore, Schmidt became convinced as never before of the need for a fundamentally new departure in Franco-German defense cooperation. The existing pattern of Alliance relations was becoming ever less tolerable. Though growing weaker economically, the United States was becoming more confrontational in its attitudes toward the Soviet Union. While showing itself again and again to be an unreliable ally to the Europeans, Carter's Washington was constantly demanding that the Europeans sacrifice their own interests in demonstrations of loyalty to the United States.

For Schmidt, therefore, it became increasingly urgent to find a way of enhancing West European solidarity as a means of enabling the Germans to assert their own interests more successfully vis-à-vis Washington and to insulate themselves better from the erratic lurches of U.S. policy. The chancellor's existing ties with Giscard, however useful, were inadequate for this purpose. The issue-by-issue character of the Schmidt-Giscard axis meant that French support for the German position might be absent precisely when it was most needed. Because it did not extend to military strategy, the Paris-Bonn partnership did nothing to lessen Bonn's strategic dependence on the United States.

There is no evidence that Schmidt at any point during his chancellorship conceived of defense relations with France as an alternative to German membership in NATO. Rather, it appears that he viewed closer defense ties to France primarily as a means of rendering Germany's defense dependence on the United States less traumatic. A more structured Franco-German defense partnership would allow Bonn to stand up for its own interests vis-à-vis Washington on strategic and security questions without risking isolation in the West. Also, by focusing public attention on defense efforts being taken by the Europeans themselves, a Franco-German military initiative might palliate the distress visible in West Germany following each fresh demonstration of American unreliability.

The question of closer defense ties was a major topic of discussion between Schmidt and Giscard during 1980, and by the end of the year Giscard had agreed in principle to the idea of a new Franco-German initiative in defense cooperation.[35] The two leaders had addressed the idea only in general terms, however; France's presidential election was coming up in the spring of 1981, and Giscard wanted to postpone any action that might involve controversial changes to French defense policy. Schmidt, believing that Giscard would gain reelection easily, was content to wait until his French partner was in a stronger position to address the issue. As it turned out, however, Giscard was defeated by the Socialist candidate, François Mitterrand, in the second round of balloting for the French presidency in May 1981. The election of Mitterrand, together with the rise of a mass peace movement in Germany, were to transform the initiative for closer Franco-German defense ties into something much different from what Schmidt intended.

THE SHIFT IN FRANCE'S SECURITY PERSPECTIVE

By eroding Schmidt's faith in American reliability, the Carter administration had restored the question of bilateral strategic coordination to the agenda of Franco-German relations for the first time since 1964. But while the possibility of closer strategic ties between Paris and Bonn was clearly on Schmidt's mind, François Mitterrand came to office with a notably different set of concerns. The most striking of these was undoubtedly his attitude toward Moscow. Before becoming president, Mitterrand had been sharply critical of Giscard's Soviet policy. He assailed Giscard for meeting with Brezhnev in Warsaw and for being overly complacent about the Soviet SS-20 deployments.[36] It was indicative of Mitterrand's outlook that the first point on his 110–point election platform of January 1981 was a demand that Soviet troops withdraw from Afghanistan.

Once in office, Mitterrand moved quickly away from the cautious and accommodative approach to Moscow favored by his predecessor. For example, whereas Giscard had declined to take a public position on the NATO two-track decision (although supporting it privately), Mitterrand warned loudly and repeatedly against Soviet "overarmament" in Europe and insisted that an equilibrium of forces be restored, preferably through a negotiated solution but if necessary through new allied missile deployments.[37] Foreign Minister Claude Cheysson expressed the new government's view in blunt terms. The Soviet SS-20 deployments, he declared, represent an alteration of the nuclear equilibrium. . . . We think that it is necessary to negotiate as soon as possible with the Soviets to do away with [the SS-20s]. . . . If they refuse, then it is necessary to . . . respond at the same level of theater nuclear arms, which is why France entirely approves the decision taken by its Atlantic allies for the American Pershing and cruise missiles.[38]

Mitterrand's government also suspended the semiannual consultations between the French and Soviet foreign ministers that had been instituted by Giscard and Brezhnev. Cheysson affirmed that no "normalization" of Franco-Soviet relations was possible so long as Soviet troops continued to occupy Afghanistan.[39]

The altered tone of France's Soviet policy under Mitterrand had several causes. One reason was undoubtedly a desire to reassure the Reagan administration that the inclusion of four Communist ministers in the newly formed French government did not signify any drift away from the Western Alliance. Also, supporting the U.S. position on East-West relations would make it easier for the French Socialists to win American tolerance for their ambitious program of domestic political and economic restructuring.

A more fundamental factor in the harder French attitude toward Moscow, however, was the changing geopolitical landscape in Europe. Under de Gaulle, a basic objective of French diplomacy had been to overcome the superpower division of Europe and gradually to dissolve the superpower-dominated military blocs, thus enabling the countries of Europe to regain control over their own individual fates. In practice, carrying out this objective had usually meant opposing perceived American hegemonic strivings in Europe while promoting a détente with Moscow that would erode the monolithism of the Soviet bloc.

By the second half of the 1970s the situation had changed considerably. On the one hand, détente had done little to loosen up the Soviet bloc or to modify the premises of Soviet foreign policy. Moscow's military buildup in Europe, both conventional and nuclear, continued without pause. Under Carter, meanwhile, the strength and resolve of the United States appeared to melt away, leaving nothing in its place that could balance the Soviet Union's growing military capabilities. For France, therefore, a logical reaction should have been to throw its weight more on the side of Washington so as to counterbalance Moscow's gains in the European balance.

Changing external conditions did not, however, lead immediately to a reorientation of French diplomacy. Over the years, de Gaulle's associates and self-appointed heirs had come to identify Gaullism with the practices rather than the objectives of the general's foreign policy. During the Giscard era, Gaullist orthodoxy had insisted on a solicitous approach to Moscow even as the original reasons for such an orientation disappeared. Mitterrand, who in contrast to Giscard was not answerable to the guardians of Gaullism, could respond more readily to the accumulating changes in France's strategic environment. Convinced of the need to preserve a superpower equilibrium in Europe, Mitterrand was accordingly more critical of Moscow than his predecessor as well as more inclined to align France behind measures to strengthen NATO.

France's shift to a firmer line vis-à-vis Moscow gave rise to a number of tensions in its relations with Bonn. One area of tension concerned the West's reaction to the declaration of martial law in Poland in December 1981 and the suppression of the independent Polish labor movement. Paris joined the United States in loudly denouncing the Polish government's actions. Bonn, by contrast, seemed conspicuously willing to accept the suppression of the Polish labor movement as the price of continued détente in Europe. The German attitude produced bitter reactions in the French press, with some commentators even hinting at parallels between Bonn's mild reaction to the imposition of martial law and earlier historical instances of Russo-German conspiracy against the Polish nation.[40] It should be noted, however, that Paris was no more willing than Bonn to go along with U.S. demands for economic sanctions against the Polish regime. Even if France's rhetoric on Poland resembled Washington's, therefore, in terms of practical measures Paris and Bonn stood together in opposing the American position.[41]

A second and far more significant area of tension between Paris and Bonn concerned their attitudes toward the NATO two-track decision of December 1979. Superficially, Mitterrand and Schmidt were in complete agreement: each took the view that a negotiated reduction in Soviet SS-20s would be preferable to carrying out the second track of the 1979 decision, namely, the deployment of the Pershing II and cruise missiles. Beneath the appearance of harmony, however, were two quite different perspectives.

For his part, Schmidt was becoming increasingly restive over the Reagan administration's obvious lack of will to initiate negotiations with Moscow on intermediate nuclear forces (INF).[42] Schmidt's domestic difficulties were compounded by the abrupt emergence in 1981 of a large West German peace movement opposed to the planned NATO missile deployments. The peace movement's sudden appearance was a consequence of several factors. In part it was a delayed reaction to the nuclear debate of the late 1970s, which began with the public discussion of the neutron bomb and was greatly stimulated by the Soviet SS-20 deployments and the discussion over appropriate Western responses. The nuclear debate had made many Germans aware for the first time of the implications of NATO's flexible response strategy and fearful that renewed superpower tensions could actually lead to nuclear war in Europe. In this context, Reagan's strident rhetoric toward the Soviet Union and his administration's massive increase in defense spending, which to some Germans had the air of war preparations, added up to an explosive mixture.[43]

On October 10, 1981, more than 250,000 demonstrators rallied in Bonn to denounce the planned INF deployments. Confronted with the obvious unpopularity of the two-track decision, and afraid of losing voters to the anti-establishment Green party, members of the SPD parliamentary delegation began to distance themselves from the deployment half of the two-track decision.[44] Faced with desertion in his own ranks, Schmidt urgently needed progress toward a negotiated solution on INF that would make deployment of the Pershing and cruise missiles in Germany unnecessary. With the Reagan administration clearly less than anxious to conclude an agreement with Moscow, Schmidt would have liked nothing more than for Paris to close ranks with him in applying pressure on Washington for action.

It was therefore to the chancellor's chagrin that he found his Socialist counterparts in Paris more sympathetic to Reagan's viewpoint on INF than to his own. Like the Reagan administration, Mitterrand's government tended to equate carrying out the two-track decision with the idea of carrying out its provisions for Pershing II and cruise missile deployment. Schmidt and Mitterrand therefore found themselves pulling in different directions on the INF issue. The French were anxious above all that the West respond strongly to the Soviet theater nuclear buildup, which to them meant a NATO counterdeployment. Schmidt, by contrast, could not help but push for a negotiated solution as his own party drifted toward repudiation of the deployment decision.

A New Consultative Framework

Extremely disquieted by the German peace movement and worried about its potential influence on Schmidt's government, Paris began to cast about for some way of increasing its influence over German security perspectives. At France's suggestion, the two governments opened discussions in November 1981 on the possibilities for closer coordination of foreign policy. Paris proposed that the two sides should in future consult more closely on policy toward the Eastern bloc.[45] This transparent effort to get Bonn to take a harder line toward Moscow had little appeal for the Schmidt government. When an agreement was announced at the Franco-German summit of February 24–25, 1982, therefore, it was formulated in broader terms. The summit communiqué stated that the two leaders had decided that "their two countries will further tighten the coordination of their foreign policies" and that they would "conduct a deepened exchange of views . . . on security questions."[46]

It took several months for the measures announced in the February 1982 communiqué to take shape. At the initiative of German Foreign Minister Hans-Dietrich Genscher, it was agreed that the foreign and defense ministers of France and Germany would meet in June to decide on the format and content of the new consultations.[47] Before the meeting could take place, however, the governing coalition in Bonn entered a period of prolonged crisis brought on by disagreements over economic and defense policy. In September the Free Democrats switched their support to the Christian Democrats, bringing down the Schmidt government. Helmut Kohl, parliamentary leader of the CDU, was elected chancellor on October 1; Genscher retained the foreign ministry portfolio as part of the deal for the FDP's support.

The change of government had an electrifying effect on Franco-German defense relations. The new defense minister, Manfred Wörner of the CDU, was fluent in French and highly knowledgeable about French strategic doctrine. Wörner brought with him Lothar Ruehl, an expert on French defense policy, who was named to the post of undersecretary in the ministry. Not surprisingly, French defense officials quickly developed a much warmer rapport with Wörner than with his predecessor Hans Apel, a professed pacifist who spoke no French and who had done little to support the now moribund Franco German tank project. The French felt greatly reassured by the new German government's views on nuclear arms questions. For one thing, Kohl's governing coalition had a far more resolute attitude toward INF deployment than did the SPD-dominated coalition it replaced. Kohl also delighted the French by explicitly rejecting the inclusion of French nuclear forces in U.S.-Soviet arms control negotiations.[48]

Three days after becoming chancellor, Kohl traveled to Paris for the express purpose of confirming his desire to go forward with the Franco-German initiative announced by Mitterrand and Schmidt in February. As a strong supporter of NATO, Kohl could only have welcomed the opportunity offered by the initiative to bring France back into closer cooperation with Alliance strategic perspectives.

At the Franco-German summit on October 21–22, the two sides established a structure for the new defense and security consultations. It was decided that the foreign and defense ministers of the two countries would meet together informally before each semiannual Franco-German summit meeting. These meetings would provide overall political direction for the consultations. Detailed policy issues, meanwhile, would be addressed by a Franco-German Commission on Security and Defense consisting of high-level military and civilian officials.[49] The commission's task would be to coordinate all areas of bilateral security and defense cooperation, both within and between the two governments. Two features of the commission were especially significant. First, since its membership consisted of top-ranking officials from the foreign and defense ministries, the commission would have the authority to make policy decisions and to enforce them within the ministries involved. A second important feature of the commission was its small size. With only ten to twelve members altogether, the group could meet flexibly and informally.

Underneath the commission, permanent working groups were established in three areas: armaments cooperation, military cooperation, and politico-strategic affairs. Like the commission, the working groups were kept small, with about five persons on each side. Membership in the working groups and the commission overlapped heavily, so as to facilitate the coordination of activities among the different bodies. The commission was to meet three to four times a year beginning in late 1982; the working groups were to meet even more frequently.

The discussions in the three working groups addressed a broad range of French and German concerns. The French, for their part, showed a particularly intense interest in the working group on armaments cooperation. As noted in Chapters 3 and 4, Paris had been seeking systematic cooperation with Germany in armaments production since the 1950s. At the time that the armaments working group was created, in late 1982, several factors had lent new urgency to France's desire for an arms production partnership with Germany. First, the failure of the Mitterrand government's initially expansionany economic policy had led to the imposition of progressively stronger austerity measures, beginning with restrictions on government spending late in 1981 and culminating in the severe austerity package of March 1983. The foreseeable constraints on military spending gave additional impetus to the search for partners in conventional weapons development. Second, the collapse of the Franco-German battle tank project by early 1982 underlined the need to place armaments cooperation with Germany in a structural framework. The existing ad hoc approach to weapon co-production was clearly ineffectual and too vulnerable to political disruption on the German side.

Third, the French were acutely worried about American competition in arms exports markets. The Reagan administration had reversed Carter's policy of relative restraint in arms exports. Combined with the massive increase in military equipment spending under Reagan, Washington's newly aggressive arms export policy promised to make the United States a much stronger competitor for arms sales. Paris confronted a double threat: that American arms makers would capture Third World markets formerly dominated by France, and that the United States would further tighten its grip on the European market, greatly weakening France's ability to sustain its own conventional arms industry. It was thus more important than ever, in the French view, to build closer ties to Germany across the full range of conventional weapon systems as a way of preventing France's arms industry from becoming isolated within Europe. Although the armaments working group addressed a large number of potential weapons projects, the group concentrated its efforts initially on reaching an agreement for joint construction of a combat helicopter.

The second working group, which focused on military cooperation, began by attempting to inventory all existing Franco-German military cooperation agreements and treaties.[50] This had not been done before, and was no small task. The group also examined the possibilities for improving mutual logistical support and for adding new Franco-German troop exercises to those that already took place on a regular basis. These tasks acquired new interest in 1983, following French establishment of a *Force d'action rapide* (FAR) capable of rapid military intervention in Central Europe. The working group on military cooperation was charged with exploring hypotheses for the possible employment of the FAR in Central Europe, as well as determining the German logistical support necessary in such a case. The group was also responsible for arranging appropriate joint maneuvers between the *Force d'action rapide* and German military units.

The third working group, dealing with politico-strategic affairs, provided the main forum by which the French hoped to influence German attitudes regarding the Soviet Union and the East-West military balance. The group focused initially on such topics as the planned NATO INF deployments, the Soviet menace to Europe, the buildup of Soviet missiles aimed at Europe, Soviet espionage activities and support for terrorist organizations, and Soviet efforts to influence European public opinion.[51] The French also used this working group as a channel for providing the German government with insight into the motives and objectives of French defense policy. For example, Paris briefed Bonn in advance on the rationale behind its 1984–1988 military plan, which provided for a major reorganization of the French armed forces and substantial reductions in French military personnel. The Mitterrand team hoped that such an approach would promote German confidence in France's intentions and its reliability as an ally.

The initial meetings of the Franco-German Commission on Security and Defense and its three subgroups took place in an atmosphere of satisfied anticipation. The easy rapport between the Kohl and Mitterrand governments, and their harmony of views on such matters as INF deployment and the Soviet threat to Europe, gave both sides much to hope for from the new consultative structure. Given the full agenda of the commission and its subgroups, neither side could readily have anticipated that within two years the talks would be at a virtual dead end.

INNOVATION AND AMBIGUITY IN MILITARY TIES

In defense policy as in foreign policy, Mitterrand's government differed noticeably from its predecessor. A number of changes to French defense policy early in Mitterrand's presidency had important implications for Franco-German defense cooperation. In October 1981, the Mitterrand government reached a decision to produce a new missile, the Hadès, as an eventual replacement for the Pluton tactical nuclear missile. The Hadès had already been under development during the Giscard years, when it was said to have a range of 250–300 kilometers.[52] The Hadès decision was further elaborated in October 1982, when Mitterrand announced that the missile's exact range would be 350 kilometers.[53] The announcement was highly significant because it meant that the missile could reach targets in East Germany or Czechoslovakia from launch sites in eastern France. Meanwhile, the French government also announced that all tactical nuclear weapons would be removed from the control of field commanders and placed under the direct command of the armed forces chief of staff. The new command structure was to be in place by the time of the first Hadès deployments in 1992.

A second important change was the French government's decision to create a 47,000–man rapid deployment force (the FAR), for special military missions in Europe and overseas. The FAR was to include five divisions, specifically the 4th air-mobile division, the 6th light armored division, the 9th marine infantry division, the 11th parachute division, and the 27th mountain division. Of these, only the 4th air-mobile division represented an entirely new entity. The 6th light armored division was to be assembled largely from smaller existing units, while the parachute, mountain, and marine infantry divisions had already been in existence for years.

The objective in grouping these five specialized divisions into a single organizational structure was to give the French government a multipurpose instrument capable of carrying out diverse assignments. Of special significance, in terms of Central European defense, was the new 4th air-mobile division. Growing out of several years' reflection by French military planners and the Socialist Party's Defense Committee, the division was intended to provide a highly mobile striking force able to interdict a Warsaw Pact tank breakthrough anywhere along the Central European front. Incorporating some 240 helicopters (80 transport, 120 antitank, and 40 observation helicopters), the 6,400–troop division would be able to respond quickly and flexibly to developments in a Central European conflict.[54]

French planners also envisaged possible joint actions by the 4th air-mobile division and the 6th light armored division. The latter, mounted entirely on wheeled vehicles, could move much more quickly than a traditional heavy armored division built around tracked vehicles. Like the air-mobile division, the new light armored division was to be amply equipped with antitank arms, thus providing an additional weapon against enemy tank breakthroughs. The 6th light armored division could be employed by itself or together with the 4th air-mobile division and infantry from other FAR units.

The planned changes in the French military posture had important implications for France's defense cooperation with NATO. Viewed in some ways, the alterations could be seen as a major gain for Alliance solidarity. For one thing, the planned "denuclearization" of the First Army provided a potential resolution to the intractable contradictions between French and NATO doctrines on the use of tactical nuclear weapons. Once deprived of its tactical nuclear missiles, the First Army would be able to participate in a battle alongside NATO troops without its engagement necessarily implying imminent resort to nuclear arms. The same was true of the FAR, which was designed strictly for conventional military actions and hence did not bring with its use any inevitable escalation to the nuclear threshold.

Second, creation of the FAR would give France the means to participate on the front line of Alliance defense, a point which the Mitterrand government emphasized heavily in its public statements regarding the force.[55] Unlike the heavy armored divisions of the French forces in southwest Germany, which were restricted by their limited mobility to the second line of Alliance defenses, the FAR was supposed to move quickly enough to meet any Central European contingency. Indeed, the whole point of the 4th air-mobile division was its role as a "lightning force" able to mobilize in twelve hours and take up a position anywhere up to several hundred kilometers from its base position in northeastern France. The 6th light armored division, although it could not move as quickly as the air-mobile force, was also intended to be capable of reaching a front-line position in an unfolding Central European conflict.

While the Mitterrand government's changes to the French military force posture created important new possibilities for France-NATO military cooperation, the changes also introduced new ambiguity into the extent of France's commitment to European defense. Indeed, the changes could even be interpreted as an effort by the Mitterrand government to *reduce* its defense commitment to Germany. To see why, it is necessary to note that the existing agreements between NATO and the French First Army enormously constrained the French president's options in a crisis situation. In fact, the existing network of plans and agreements allowed the French leadership only one meaningful decision: whether to engage the First Army or not. Once the First Army was committed to a conflict, it would go into action along a trajectory planned with the Allies in advance. Resort to Pluton tactical nuclear weapons would follow more or less ineluctably, since all hypotheses for the use of the First Army were based on the premise of rapid escalation to the tactical nuclear level (see Chapter 4).

Common to all the changes in France's defense posture under Mitterrand was the goal of giving French leaders a broader range of military options in the event of a European conflict.[56] The *Force d'action rapide*, whose forces were airborne or on wheeled vehicles, was intended to be capable of intervening wherever it was needed. With its ability to react quickly to developments in a Central European conflict, it would enable the French president to escape the straitjacket of the joint France-NATO plans for the First Army.

It was for similar reasons that the Hadès missile had been designed with a range long enough that it could overshoot West Germany even if fired from French territory. In fact, in 1982 Mitterrand's government had instructed the engineers developing the Hadès to increase the missile's range so that it would be able to do so.[57] The French motive, once again, was to increase the government's military options. By replacing the Pluton with a longer-range tactical missile, Paris evidently hoped to escape Germany's persistent demands for a consultative role in French tactical nuclear doctrine and targeting. The Germans had begun demanding such a role early in the 1970s, and had become more rather than less insistent over time. Clearly, as long as France's military plans called for it to employ nuclear weapons on West German territory (whether in terms of launch sites or of targets), Bonn would not back down from its demand. But if the Pluton's replacement, Hadès, had a long enough range that the missile need not be launched from West Germany or land in West Germany, Paris would be in a much better position to continue refusing Bonn a role in French theater nuclear planning.

Finally, the decision to withdraw all tactical nuclear weapons from French battle units and place them under the direct control of the national leadership was also designed to enhance the French president's options. The altered command structure would greatly increase his control over the scale and timing of a French nuclear strike. It would also provide him a vital option he had previously lacked, namely, to participate in a military defense of Europe while avoiding resort to nuclear weapons altogether.

The net significance of the Mitterrand government's defense policy was thus tantalizingly ambiguous, at least as far as the Germans were concerned. On the one hand, creation of the FAR and the denuclearization of the First Army created important new possibilities for France to contribute to Europe's defense. France's new military organization would permit it to engage its troops, whether the FAR or the First Army, in a European defense mission without necessarily entailing unwanted nuclear consequences. On the other hand, the increase in France's battlefield options also increased, by definition, Bonn's uncertainties regarding the extent and reliability of France's engagement of forces in a European conflict. For this reason German officials regarded the changes in the French force structure with a good deal of veiled suspicion.

Not surprisingly, therefore, Bonn soon began using the Franco-German defense consultation groups as a forum for attempting to pin down the conditions of employment of the FAR in West Germany. For example, the German government identified some points along the inter-German border where NATO force dispositions were weakest and proposed that plans be worked out for deploying the FAR at one or another such point in times of crisis. This approach, of course, was antithetical to the French government's original objective in creating a rapid deployment force. Planning for the use of the FAR in Germany was thus a source of significant irritation on both sides. Some degree of advance planning for employment of the FAR was necessary because (as French officials conceded) the force would require allied logistical support and air cover if it were put into action well forward of the First Army.[58] In addition, any plan to project the FAR toward the northern end of the inter-German border would require close advance coordination with NATO, because doing so would cause the FAR's lines of communication and support to cross those of NATO forces.

As for the Hadès, the fact that it could overshoot West Germany did not in any way lessen Bonn's insistence on consultations with Paris on French theater nuclear planning. After all, the Hadès would not fully replace the Pluton for at least a decade. Since the Hadès could be targeted at less than full range, moreover, Bonn still had grounds for worry regarding how and under what conditions French tactical nuclear missiles would be employed. In addition, as West German officials pointed out to their French counterparts, East Germany was also part of Germany, and Bonn was every bit as concerned to be consulted regarding allied use of nuclear warheads east of the inter-German border as west of it.[59]

A second reason for German skepticism regarding the changes to French defense forces was the perceived erosion of France's overall conventional capabilities. Several points were relevant in this regard. First, the FAR did not represent an addition to France's conventional forces but a reorganization of them. As mentioned above, three of the FAR's five divisions existed before 1981. Equipment for the other two divisions, meanwhile, was provided largely at the expense of the First Army. The 6th light armored division, for example, was given 60 of the First Army's 96 AMX-10RC armored reconnaissance vehicles, while the new 4th air-mobile division was assigned no less than 134 of the First Army's 174 helicopters, including 44 of its 60 antitank helicopters.[60] Second, only *parts* of the FAR, not the whole force, came into question for participation in a Central European military action. Limits on French transport capabilities ruled out engagement of the entire 47,000–man force at one time.[61] Third, employment of the FAR in a Central European conflict would tax French resources and logistical capabilities sufficiently that simultaneous engagement of the First Army in such a conflict was virtually out of the question. To a considerable extent, in other words, the FAR amounted to a substitute for the First Army.[62] What some German officials therefore feared was that they were being offered a force of two or three divisions with perhaps 25,000 troops as France's contribution to European defense in place of the 112,000–man First Army.[63]

Accompanying the FAR's creation was an overall reorganization of the French army in which two armored divisions were to be dissolved and their equipment distributed among the remaining armored divisions.[64] At the same time, the land army was to be reduced by 22,000 men in addition to the 20,000–troop reduction that had taken place under Giscard. Was the FAR in fact just a smokescreen to disguise the rapid decline of France's

conventional military capabilities? Paris attempted to dispel German worries by announcing that the French troops in Germany would be reinforced
with an additional one hundred battle tanks.[65] The announcement carried
little weight, since the added tanks did not represent additional capabilities
but were merely existing equipment reassigned to the French forces in
Germany from other French units.

Certainly the doctrinal debate surrounding the announcement of the
FAR provided some grounds for German anxiety. Lucien Poirier, the
influential nuclear theorist, saw in the FAR an instrument for resolving
the long-standing contradiction between the First Army's role of nuclear
trip-wire and France's desire to join its allies in the military defense of
Europe.[66] France could earmark the FAR for conventional missions in
Europe, argued Poirier, while the First Army should be limited more
rigorously than before to its function of "testing" enemy intentions. In
other words, the First Army would no longer play the role of NATO's
counterattack reserve, but would be used strictly for triggering the use of
French nuclear weapons.

For the French government to follow Poirier's recommendation would
presumably have meant discarding all existing plans for joint action by the
First Army and NATO forces, a possibility that would hardly have cheered
the Germans. Subsequent statements by Defense Minister Hernu and
Armed Forces Chief of Staff Lacaze indicated that no clear line would be
drawn between the missions of the FAR and those of the First Army.[67]
Nevertheless, it remained unclear how the First Army's mission would
ultimately be affected by the removal of its tactical nuclear weapons to a
separate command and by the existence of the FAR.

Despite the various grounds for uneasiness about the Mitterrand government's military reorganization, Bonn's overall evaluation of the FAR was
positive.[68] Many German military officers and government officials regarded
the new French force as symbolically important because it gave France the
means, heretofore lacking, to participate in the front lines of European
defense, even if only on a small scale. Given that Germany's security strategy
centered more on deterrence than on defense per se, the possibility of a small
French presence in the early stages of a European conflict was seen as worth
more than a larger French involvement at a later point.

THE DEBATE OVER CONVENTIONAL DETERRENCE

Ironically, the new possibilities for Franco-German military cooperation
created by Hernu's reorganization of French forces disguised the fact that

French and German strategic concepts were perhaps farther apart in the early 1980s than at any previous point in the history of the Alliance.

On coming to power, the Mitterrand government confronted a potential decline in the credibility of France's nuclear forces vis-à-vis the Soviet Union. It was questionable, for example, whether French strategic bombers could penetrate improved Soviet air defenses. More accurate Soviet missiles raised the possibility of a successful first strike against France's land-based strategic missiles and nuclear command installations. If the Soviets eventually made breakthroughs in antisubmarine warfare or ballistic missile defense, the deterrent value of French nuclear systems would be seriously in doubt.

These considerations led the Mitterrand government to embark on an extensive nuclear force modernization program, taking action on a number of measures already under study during the Giscard era. Early in Mitterrand's presidency it was announced that a sixth nuclear missile submarine, armed with M-4 multiple-warhead missiles, would enter service in 1985. Construction would also begin on a seventh submarine, the first of a completely new generation designed for improved survivability in coming decades. In addition, development of a mobile land-based nuclear missile (later named the S-45) was to continue. In unveiling the 1983 military budget, Defense Minister Hernu gave clear priority to nuclear forces: spending on nuclear arms was to rise by 14.4 percent in current francs compared to an overall military spending increase of 10 percent.[69] Further nuclear modernization measures were announced in the 1984–1988 military plan published in April 1983.[70] These included a program, scheduled for completion in the mid-1990s, to retrofit four of the five existing nuclear missile submarines with M-4 missiles. In addition, eighteen Mirage IV strategic bombers would be fitted with medium-range air-launched nuclear missiles, giving them the capability to strike strategic targets from standoff positions.

The French tactical arsenal was to be modernized as well. The planned replacement of the Pluton with the longer-range Hadès missile has already been mentioned. Other modernization programs included an order for thirty-eight Mirage 2000–N tactical aircraft equipped with air-launched nuclear missiles. Super Etendard fighter aircraft based on France's two aircraft carriers were also to be outfitted with air-launched nuclear missiles. Finally, development of a neutron warhead for possible deployment on the Hadès was to continue.

The decision to maintain the credibility and survivability of French nuclear weapon systems thus implied continued heavy expenditures on nuclear forces for many years to come. The proportion of French equipment expenditures devoted to nuclear forces increased to 32.6 percent in 1985 from 30 percent in 1981.[71] Of all the various nuclear programs, the most important was probably the M-4 refit program. In 1983, France's five strategic missile submarines carried a total of eighty warheads. By the mid-1990s the refitting program, coupled with the planned entry into service of two more strategic submarines, was expected to increase France's submarine-launched ballistic missile warheads to a total of 592.[72]

During the same time that Paris was giving its priority to nuclear force modernization, however, Bonn was beginning to move toward a revised concept of deterrence that put the emphasis on conventional forces. The gradual modification of Germany's deterrence concept had several sources. First, there was increased pressure from the United States on its NATO allies for improved conventional capabilities and changes to Alliance strategy that would raise the nuclear threshold. The early 1980s were a period of ferment in American tactical concepts, stimulated in part by advances in conventional weapons technology and in part by a long-term shift away from faith in the desirability of a deterrence strategy based on nuclear escalation. Concepts introduced and promoted by U.S. military planners in the early 1980s included deep strike, Airland Battle, Airland Battle 2000, and Follow-on Forces Attack.[73] What these various concepts had in common was the principle of extending battlefield depth with new weapon technologies that enabled strikes at military targets up to several hundred kilometers behind the opponent's front line.

One such concept, Follow-on Forces Attack, was developed by General Bernard Rogers (who became Supreme Allied Commander in Europe, or SACEUR, in 1979) and his staff.[74] Also known as the Rogers Plan, Follow-on Forces Attack envisaged the use of high-precision conventional weapons to carry out deep strike and interdiction missions against an adversary's logistical infrastructure, lines of communication, and second-line forces, thus cutting off supplies and reinforcements from his front-line forces. The objective of Follow-on Forces Attack was to increase NATO's ability to withstand a Warsaw Pact conventional attack without resort to nuclear weapons. Rogers promoted the concept unceasingly during his tenure as SACEUR. Pressure on the European allies to improve their conventional forces came as well from a 1983 study by a distinguished European-American group of scholars and former government officials.[75] The study strongly urged greater Alliance reliance on advanced non-nuclear technologies in order to reduce NATO's dependence on early resort to nuclear weapons in a conflict.

As these developments were taking place, a series of statements by former U.S. defense and foreign policy officials served to undermine the credibility of American nuclear assurances to Europe. One widely noted statement came from Henry Kissinger in September 1979 at a NATO conference in Brussels. In view of America's growing vulnerability to a Soviet strategic nuclear attack, said the former secretary of state, it was "absurd . . . to base the strategy of the West on the credibility of the threat of mutual suicide." Under the new circumstances, he declared, "our European allies should not keep asking us to multiply strategic assurances that we cannot possibly mean, or, if we do mean, we should not want to execute because if we execute them, we risk the destruction of civilization."[76] Kissinger's remarks were echoed a few years later by Robert McNamara, secretary of defense from 1961 to 1968 and the architect of flexible response, who revealed that "in long conversations with successive Presidents—Kennedy and Johnson—I recommended, without qualification, that they never initiate, under any circumstances, the use of nuclear weapons. I believe they accepted my recommendation."[77] McNamara was also one of four distinguished former U.S. officials who published an article in 1982 calling for NATO to move toward a "no first use" policy on nuclear weapons. Such a move, the authors emphasized, would require that Alliance conventional forces in Europe, including U.S. forces, be strengthened[78]

Bonn thus faced a diverse range of pressures from the United States for the strengthening of conventional deterrence and reduced reliance on nuclear weapons to deter a Warsaw Pact attack in Central Europe. Added to these pressures was an energetic domestic debate in Germany on the morality and desirability of nuclear deterrence and the possibility of replacing it with some other form of security strategy. The public discussion stimulated by the peace movement, together with popular doubts regarding American reliability and skepticism about Reagan's intentions, stimulated a proliferation of "alternative defense" schemes. These ranged from slight modifications of existing NATO strategy to proposals for complete unilateral disarmament and non-violent resistance.[79]

The combined effect of the factors listed above had led, by 1983, to visible strains in West Germany's defense consensus. On the one hand, there was a certain amount of agreement among the established political parties on the necessity of raising the nuclear threshold.[80] Views were far from unanimous, however, on the means by which this was to be accomplished. For his part, Defense Minister Wörner favored the enhancement of conventional deep strike capabilities along the lines espoused by General

Rogers.[81] Most segments of the opposition Social Democrats, by contrast, were strongly opposed to increasing conventional capabilities and advocated intensified arms control efforts as the best method of reducing dependence on nuclear escalation. At its April 1982 party conference, the SPD commissioned a working group that included many of the party's leading officials and defense experts to examine the possibilities for a non-nuclear defense strategy. The group's report, published in July 1983, called among other things for the creation and gradual expansion of a nuclear-free corridor in Central Europe.[82] The most dramatic development in SPD defense policy came at the special party congress in November 1983 in Cologne, where an overwhelming majority of the delegates voted against the planned deployments of Pershing II and cruise missiles in Germany.

West Germany's gradual drift away from its earlier defense consensus toward a new consensus on raising the nuclear threshold (whether through increased emphasis on conventional deterrence, on arms control, or both) widened still further the existing gulf between French and German strategic concepts. The Mitterrand government's long-term commitment to upgrading France's nuclear capabilities promised that French conventional forces would remain underfunded for the foreseeable future, and that Paris would continue to reject negotiated limits on its own nuclear forces. The French government's 1984–1988 military plan, which revealed the extent of Mitterrand's nuclear modernization program, thus produced visible dismay in Bonn.[83]

In addition, the French government adopted an extremely hostile stance toward the idea of conventionalizing deterrence in Europe. In a November 1982 speech, Defense Minister Hernu lashed out at "certain American officials" who, he said, were developing "new theories" which suddenly attempted to "emphasize conventional armaments and to forget nuclear deterrence or relegate it to a secondary position." Hernu rejected such an approach because "to want to raise the nuclear threshold excessively is to renounce deterrence and open the door to war." Even if the proponents of conventional defense did not represent official U.S. policy, Hernu emphasized, their views had the potential to encourage "tendencies emerging here or there in favor of a unilateral denuclearization of Europe or an isolationist withdrawal into the American sanctuary."[84]

During the first part of the 1980s, Paris and Bonn thus found themselves moving farther apart than ever in terms of the substantive priorities of their defense strategies. Despite the symbolic value of the new French *Force d'action rapide* and the efforts devoted by the two governments to maximizing their cooperation in the areas of defense and security, the common ground between French and German security concepts appeared to be shrinking rather than expanding.

NOTES

1. Simonian, *The Privileged Partnership*, pp. 247–50.

2. Examples include Giscard's press luncheon on May 21, 1975 (see *Le Point*, May 26, 1975); his televised interview of November 12, 1975 on Antenne 2 (see *Les Déclarations du Président de la République sur la politique de défense et la politique militaire, juin 1974–décembre 1976* [Premier ministre, Service d'Information et de Diffusion], p. 29); and his remarks at the Elysée Palace on July 14, 1976 (quoted in *Le Monde*, July 16, 1976).

3. *Le Monde*, July 27, 1974.

4. *The New York Times*, November 26, 1974.

5. *Le Monde*, March 27, 1975.

6. Valéry Giscard d'Estaing, "Allocution," *Défense nationale*, July 1976, pp. 16–17.

7. Guy Méry, "Une armée pour quoi faire et comment?" *Défense nationale*, June 1976, pp. 15–17.

8. *Le Monde*, June 3 and June 11, 1976. For systematic critiques of the Giscard speech and the Méry article, see the essay by Lucien Poirier in *Le Monde Diplomatique*, July 1976; also Pierre M. Gallois, "French Defense Planning—The Future in the Past," *International Security*, Fall 1976, pp. 15–31, and *Le renoncement* (Paris: Plon, 1977).

9. France, *Livre blanc sur la défense nationale* (1972), p. 6.

10. France, *Livre blanc sur la défense nationale* (1972), p. 8.

11. See Pascal Krop, *Les Socialistes et l'armée* (Paris: Presses Universitaires de France, 1983), pp. 71–78, and Commission du Bilan, *La France en mai 1981*, vol. 5: *L'Etat et les citoyens* (Paris: La Documentation Française, 1981), pp. 41–42.

12. *La France en mai 1981*, vol. 5, p. 41.

13. Kolodziej, *Making and Marketing Arms*, pp. 83–84.

14. See David S. Yost, "French Defense Budgeting: Executive Dominance and Resource Constraints," *Orbis*, Fall 1979, pp. 579–608.

15. Giscard emphasized this point in his televised interviews of November 12, 1975 on Antenne 2 and May 5, 1976 on TF1. See *Les Déclarations du Président*, pp. 61, 70.

16. Giscard made this point repeatedly in his statements on French defense policy, including his television interview of November 12, 1975 (cited in *Les Déclarations du Président*, p. 62), his interview with *Le Figaro* published November 12, 1975, and his televised interview of May 5, 1976 (cited in *Le Monde*, May 7, 1976). General Méry made the same argument in "Une armée pour quoi faire," p. 19.

17. Helmut Schmidt, *Menschen und Mächte* (Berlin: Siedler, 1987), pp. 84, 222.

18. *Newsweek*, July 25, 1977, pp. 45–48.

19. *Frankfurter Allgemeine Zeitung*, July 21, 1977.

20. See Strobe Talbott, *Endgame: The Inside Story of SALT II* (New York: Harper and Row, 1979), chapter 3.

21. See the *Frankfurter Allgemeine Zeitung*, October 3, 1979.

22. Schmidt bitterly regretted that the accord did not place limits on Soviet intermediate-range nuclear forces. In France, meanwhile, strategic analysts and press commentators were virtually unanimous in harshly criticizing the accord, which was seen as favoring the Soviet Union and compromising Europe's security (see Yost, *France's Deterrent Posture*, Part II, pp. 51–52).

23. Peter Ludlow, *The Making of the European Monetary System* (London: Butterworth Scientific, 1982), pp. 63–64.

24. Simonian, *The Privileged Partnership*, pp. 282–86.

25. Schmidt, *Menschen und Mächte*, pp. 243–50.

26. Kurt Becker, "Die 'Bonne Entente'—Zweiergespann für Europa," *Die Zeit*, July 4, 1980.

27. On European perceptions of a rapid decline in U.S. power, see Fritz Stern, "Germany in a Semi-Gaullist Europe," *Foreign Affairs*, Spring 1980, pp. 868–72. Compare also Edward A. Kolodziej, "Europe: The Partial Partner," *International Security*, Winter 1980/81, pp. 104–31.

28. On this incident see Schwartz, *NATO's Nuclear Dilemmas*, pp. 213–14.

29. For a detailed history see Sherri L. Wasserman, *The Neutron Bomb Controversy* (New York: Praeger, 1983).

30. See Schmidt's account of the incident as reported in Valéry Giscard d'Estaing, *Le pouvoir et la vie* (Paris: Compagnie 12, 1988), pp. 133–34.

31. Schmidt, *Menschen und Mächte*, pp. 210, 225–30.

32. See Schwartz, *NATO's Nuclear Dilemmas*, chapter 7.

33. See Helga Haftendorn, *Sicherheit und Stabilität: Aussenbeziehungen der Bundesrepublik zwischen Ölkrise und NATO-Doppelbeschluss* (Munich: Deutscher Taschenbuch Verlag, 1986), pp. 106–24.

34. Interview with a former Schmidt aide.

35. Giscard revealed the agreement in an interview published in the February 8, 1982 editions of *Paris-Match* and *Der Stern* (cited in *Le Monde*, December 4–5, 1983). See also Helmut Schmidt, "Der General und seine Erben," *Die Zeit*, May 8, 1987, pp. 8–9.

36. *Le Monde*, July 3, 1980.

37. Mitterrand made these points on many occasions, the first of which was a July 1981 interview with the German popular weekly *Der Stern* (quoted in Josef Joffe, *The Limited Partnership* [Cambridge, Mass.: Ballinger, 1987], p. 36). Other instances included Mitterrand's September 24, 1981 press conference (text in *Le Monde*, September 26, 1981), his televised interview on TF1 of December 9, 1981, and his May 14, 1982 speech to the Übersee Club of Hamburg.

38. Quoted in *Le Monde*, July 5–6, 1981.

39. Walter Schütze, "Von de Gaulle zu Mitterrand—Die Entwicklung der französischen Entspannungspolitik," in Deutsche Gesellschaft für Friedens- und Konfliktforschung, ed., *DGFK Jahrbuch 1982/83* (Baden-Baden: Nomos, 1983), p. 99.

40. See, for example, Bernard Brigouleix in *Le Monde*, December 20–21, 1981, and the front-page editorial in *Le Monde*, January 1, 1982.

41. See Simonian, *The Privileged Partnership*, pp. 309–11.

42. U.S.-Soviet negotiations on INF finally opened in Geneva on November 30, 1981, in large part because of Schmidt's prodding of both Reagan and Brezhnev.

43. On the genesis of the West German peace movement and the roles of the NATO two-track decision and of U.S. policy pronouncements in fostering its growth, see Karl Kaiser, "RFA: Un défi au consensus," in Pierre Lellouche, ed., *Pacifisme et dissuasion* (Paris: IFRI, 1983), pp. 59–72, and K.-Peter Stratmann, "A German View," in Hans Sjöberg, ed., *European Security and the Atlantic Alliance* (Stockholm: Swedish National Defense Research Institute, 1984), pp. 41–50.

44. On the politics of the INF deployment question in Germany, see Leon V. Sigal, *Nuclear Forces in Europe: Enduring Dilemmas, Present Prospects* (Washington, D.C.: Brookings, 1984), pp. 71–86.

45. Ernst Weisenfeld, "Die Aussenpolitik Frankreichs," in Karl Kaiser and Hans-Peter Schwarz, eds., *Weltpolitik: Strukturen—Akteure—Perspektiven* (Bonn: Bundeszentrale für Politische Bildung, 1985), p. 342.

46. The communiqué is reprinted in Hans-Peter Schwarz, *Eine Entente Elémentaire: Das deutsch-französische Verhältnis im 25. Jahr des Elysée-Vertrages* (Bonn: Forschungsinstitut der Deutschen Gesellschaft für Auswärtige Politik, 1988), pp. 46–47.

47. André Adrets (pseud.), "Franco-German Relations and the Nuclear Factor in a Divided Europe," in Robbin F. Laird, ed., *French Security Policy: From Independence to Interdependence* (Boulder, Colo.: Westview, 1986), p. 106.

48. See the *Frankfurter Allgemeine Zeitung*, October 23, 1982.

49. On the structure and activities of the commission, see especially Lothar Ruehl, "Der Aufschwung der sicherheitspolitischen Zusammenarbeit seit 1982," in Kaiser and Lellouche, *Deutsch-französische Sicherheitspolitik*, pp. 27–47, and Adrets, "Franco-German Relations," pp. 106–7.

50. Isabelle Renouard, "Die deutsch-französische Zusammenarbeit heute," in Kaiser and Lellouche, *Deutsch-französische Sicherheitspolitik*, p. 53. On the activities of the second working group, see also Ruehl, "Aufschwung," pp. 38–39.

51. Interviews with German and French defense ministry officials.

52. Yost, *France's Deterrent Posture*, Part I, p. 50.

53. *Le Matin*, October 16–17, 1982.

54. On the structure and equipment of the FAR, see especially *International Defense Review*, 8/1987, pp. 1023–26.

55. See Charles Hernu, "Equilibre, dissuasion, volonté: La voie étroite de la paix et de la liberté," *Défense nationale*, December 1983, p. 16; also the interview with Hernu in *Le Monde*, June 18, 1983, and the remarks by Armed Forces Chief of Staff Jeannou Lacaze quoted in *Le Monde*, May 9, 1984.

56. This point was heavily emphasized by French defense officials in interviews with the author.

57. Interviews with French defense officials.

58. On this point see the remarks by General Llamby, commander of the First Army, quoted in *Le Monde*, November 20–21, 1983; also General Lacaze, "The Future of French Defense," in Laird, ed., *French Security Policy*, p. 54. General Valentin, meanwhile, argued that the FAR would involve so much advance planning and dependence on allied support that it would amount to reintegration into the NATO command system. "L'arête étroite," p. 54.

59. *Le Matin*, March 8, 1984; *Washington Post*, April 20, 1984.

60. *International Defense Review*, 8/1987, p. 1025.

61. *Neue Zürcher Zeitung*, October 1, 1983.

62. This point was made explicitly by Dominique David, a proponent of the FAR, in *La Force d'action rapide en Europe: Le dire des armes* (Paris: Fondation pour les Etudes de Défense Nationale, 1984). General Valentin, an opponent of the project, contended that under existing financial constraints creating the FAR would reduce the First Army at best to a corps capable only of minor and localized actions; at worst, it would mean the First Army's demise. "L'arête étroite," p. 54.

63. According to *The Economist*, March 10, 1984, the German government would have preferred to see France strengthen its divisions in Germany rather than create the FAR.

64. See Yost, *France's Deterrent Posture*, Part I, p. 60.

65. *Le Monde*, June 1, 1983.

66. See Lucien Poirier, "La greffe," *Défense nationale*, April 1983, pp. 5–32. A similar view is presented in General Georges Fricaud-Chagnaud, "L'Armée de Terre face à ses missions en Europe," *Défense nationale*, May 1983, pp. 35–44.

67. See the discussion in David S. Yost, *France and Conventional Defense in Central Europe* (Marina del Rey, Calif.: European American Institute for Security Research, 1984), pp. 88–89.

68. Ingo Kolboom, "Im Westen nichts Neues? Frankreichs Sicherheitspolitik, das deutsch-französische Verhältnis und die deutsche Frage," in Kaiser and Lellouche, *Deutsch-französische Sicherheitspolitik*, p. 84.

69. *International Herald Tribune*, October 8, 1982.

70. See Robbin F. Laird, *France, the Soviet Union, and the Nuclear Weapons Issue* (Boulder, Colo.: Westview, 1985), pp. 45–65, and Patricia Chilton, "French Nuclear Weapons," in Jolyon Howorth and Patricia Chilton, eds., *Defence and Dissent in Contemporary France* (New York: Croom Helm/St. Martin's Press, 1984), pp. 135–69.

71. Total military expenditures in this period grew 7 percent in real terms, or 1.4 percent a year. François Heisbourg, "French Security Policy under Mitterrand," in Laird, ed., *French Security Policy*, p. 30.

72. Chilton, "French Nuclear Weapons," p. 143.

73. A useful discussion of these concepts and the weapon technologies associated with them is Yves Boyer, "Strategic Implications of the New Technologies for Conventional Weapons and the European Battlefield," in Catherine M. Kelleher and Gale A. Mattox, eds., *Evolving European Defense Policies* (Lexington, Mass.: D. C. Heath, 1987), pp. 99–121.

74. See Bernard W. Rogers, "Follow-on Forces Attack (FOFA): Myths and Realities," *NATO Review*, December 1984, pp. 1–9.

75. *Strengthening Conventional Defense in Europe: Proposals for the 1980s*, Report of the European Security Study (London: Macmillan, 1983).

76. Henry A. Kissinger, "The Future of NATO," in Douglas J. Murray and Paul R. Viotti, eds., *The Defense Policies of Nations* (Baltimore: Johns Hopkins University Press, 1982), p. 123.

77. Robert S. McNamara, "The Military Role of Nuclear Weapons: Perceptions and Misperceptions," *Foreign Affairs*, Fall 1983, p. 79.

78. McGeorge Bundy, George F. Kennan, Robert S. McNamara, and Gerard Smith, "Nuclear Weapons and the Atlantic Alliance," *Foreign Affairs*, Spring 1982, pp. 753–68.

79. For an overview of the alternative defense debate in Germany, see Günther Schmid, "Positionen in der Sicherheitspolitischen Diskussion und ihre Vertreter in der Bundesrepublik Deutschland," *Österreichische Militärische Zeitschrift*, 1983, no. 6, pp. 504–13.

80. See Gert Krell, Thomas Risse-Kappen, and Hans-Joachim Schmidt, "The No-First-Use Question in West Germany," in John D. Steinbruner and Leon V. Sigal, eds., *Alliance Security, NATO and the No-First-Use Question* (Washington, D.C.: Brookings, 1983), pp. 147–72.

81. See Alain Carton, "'Perceptions allemandes du plan Rogers': Les réactions officielles à la 'nouvelle doctrine' de l'OTAN en Europe," *Défense nationale*, July 1983, pp. 55–72.

82. The report is reprinted in Hans Günter Brauch, ed., *Sicherheitspolitik am Ende?* (Gerlingen: Bleicher, 1984), pp. 275–90.

83. *General-Anzeiger* (Bonn), April 23, 1983.

84. See Charles Hernu, "Face à la logique des blocs, une France indépendante et solidaire," speech of November 16, 1982, *Défense nationale*, December 1982, pp. 12–13. See also the remarks by Hernu quoted in *Le Monde*, December 2, 1982 and April 30, 1983, as well as similar criticisms of conventional deterrence by Foreign Minister Cheysson, quoted in *Le Monde*, July 9, 1983, and by Prime Minister Laurent Fabius, "La politique de défense: Rassembler et moderniser," *Défense nationale*, November 1984, p. 14.

CHAPTER 6

The Continuing Difficulty of Armaments Collaboration, 1975–1987

Between 1975 and 1987, the French and German governments continued to seek opportunities for collaboration in the development and production of major weapon systems. The incentives for cooperation were much the same as they had been in the 1950s and 1960s: for Germany, cooperation was a means of demonstrating solidarity with its key allies (including France), and of further developing the technological expertise of German industry in sectors such as aeronautics where Germany lagged behind. For France, cooperation was a means of obtaining indirect financial support for its policy of strategic independence vis-à-vis the United States.

The generally disappointing results of France's efforts at intra-European cooperation during the 1950s and 1960s led subsequent French governments to rely more heavily on the export of French arms outside Europe in order to maintain an independent arms industry. Whereas French arms exports had averaged $600 million per year in 1970–1972, by 1978 they rose to an average of $4.8 billion per year.[1] Exports accounted for about 20 percent of total output of the French armaments industry at the beginning of the 1970s, but about 40 percent at the end of the decade.[2] The 1970s also witnessed a highly significant shift in the destination of French arms exports. Whereas the majority of arms exported by France in the 1960s had gone to other Western industrial democracies, from 1970 onward the majority of orders for French arms came from less-developed states. The oil price increases of 1973 accelerated this trend. Between 1973 and 1982, only 11 percent of foreign orders for French weapons came from other European countries. The majority of orders in this period came from states in the Middle East and North Africa.[3]

Paradoxically, France's success in exporting arms outside Europe made Paris more anxious than ever to build a strong French position in the West European arms market. European arms sales were important to France for several reasons. Western Europe represented too large a proportion of the total world arms market for the French simply to concede it to the United States. Given the economic and political volatility of most developing countries, moreover, it was quite possible that the Third World arms market could rapidly become saturated.[4] There were also potential political risks involved in weapons exports to some Third World states. From the French government's perspective, therefore, a strong presence in the European arms market was the essential corrective to overreliance on sales of arms to the developing world. Besides, exports to other European countries were something of a precondition for continued strong sales of French arms to the Third World. If no West European states bought advanced arms from France, French arms would be in danger of losing credibility among Third World customers who wanted the best weapon systems available. Finally, the French considered sales of French arms within Europe vital in fore-stalling U.S. domination of Europe in military technology, a development that would, if it occurred, seriously undermine France's effort to maintain defense policy independence.

One event in particular mobilized French anxieties: the June 1975 decision by Belgium, the Netherlands, Denmark, and Norway to buy the General Dynamics F-16 fighter instead of Dassault's Mirage F1.[5] Until their debacle in what was widely referred to as the "deal of the century," the French had seemed to think they could sustain their arms industry through a combination of aggressive marketing and the cultivation of their previous export customers in Europe and elsewhere. The loss of the deal of the century—and above all the defection of the Belgians, whom Dassault had regarded as a sure buyer for the F1—thus came as a devastating setback. In the wake of the F-16 deal, the French government once again took the initiative in seeking intra-European cooperation in armaments develop-ment and production.

In contrast to their failed past initiatives in intra-European arms col-laboration, which had usually been too ambitious and too structured (the 1954 armaments pool, the 1957 armaments triangle, the 1963 Elysée Treaty), the French proceeded this time on a more pragmatic basis. On the one hand, France did seek to promote a long-term structural basis for European arms cooperation through the Independent European Program Group (IEPG). Created in 1976, the IEPG consisted of NATO's European members including France. The IEPG provided for regular meetings of the national armaments directors of its member states. These meetings were intended to promote the harmonization of arms procurement activities in Europe through exchanges of information on equipment replacement schedules and the identification of possible cooperative projects.[6]

In concrete terms, however, France sought to rebuild its position in the European arms market primarily through intensified bilateral and trilateral discussions of specific projects with Germany and Britain. The renewed French interest in joint weapons development was welcomed in Bonn and London, where officials were also eager to reduce the costs of developing advanced weapons while continuing to improve the technological capabilities of their arms industries.

From the perspective of Franco-German defense relations, several major arms production projects considered after 1975 are of interest. These include the proposals for a joint battle tank, a fighter aircraft (together with Britain, Italy, and Spain), an attack helicopter, a military observation satellite, and a variety of tactical missiles. Examination of the origin, evolution, and outcome of each of these projects provides important insights into the dynamics of arms procurement cooperation as well as the dynamics of the evolving Franco-German strategic relationship.

THE TANK

In 1977, after discovering that their schedules for replacing existing battle tanks were potentially compatible, the French and German governments began discussions on the possibility of jointly developing and producing a third-generation successor tank. About two-thirds of Germany's tank fleet consisted of Leopard 1s, which had been introduced into service from 1965 to the mid-1970s. The remainder were older American-made M-48s acquired in the 1950s, which were due to be replaced beginning in 1979 by the new German Leopard 2, of which Bonn had ordered 1,800 units. The French tank corps, meanwhile, consisted of about 1,200 AMX-30s. The Leopard 1 and the AMX-30 had both been developed in the early 1960s, and both would need to be replaced during the 1990s.

The French government and arms procurement bureaucracy strongly supported the idea of a joint Franco-German tank. France needed to develop a new tank in any case, and the French government saw collaboration with Germany as a way to save money while insuring that the new tank would be of the best possible quality. On the German side, the tank had two strong proponents in Chancellor Schmidt and Armaments Director Hans-Ludwig Eberhard, both of whom placed a high value on its symbolic significance.

Despite the high-level political support enjoyed by the tank, talks between the two defense ministries soon bogged down. The French and German army staffs, each wedded to its own ideas concerning tank design, were unable to reach agreement on the basic parameters of a common vehicle. Impatient with the lack of progress, Schmidt and French President Giscard d'Estaing ordered that the project move forward anyway.[7] A formal statement of intention to reach a common tank concept was signed by Eberhard and by his French counterpart, Henri Martre, on January 31, 1979.

In the months that followed, intensified talks between the two defense ministries came to grips with the concrete disagreements that still existed. Four problems stood out. First, there was disagreement over replacement schedules. The French wanted to begin deploying a new tank in 1991, whereas the Germans did not anticipate replacing the Leopard 1 before 1996. The German army staff was reluctant to begin designing the Leopard 1 successor in cooperation with France for fear that the resulting tank would be on the verge of obsolescence by the time of its introduction into the German army. Second, the two sides disagreed over the extent to which the new tank should draw on existing models. The Germans wanted the joint tank to be merely an improved version of the Leopard 2. The French government, on the other hand, favored developing an entirely new tank. A new tank would be a more expensive option than the German proposal, but would be better received by French arms manufacturers. It would also provoke less resistance from nationalist sentiment in France. Third, Paris wanted a relatively light tank (i.e., one under 50 tons) whereas the German side wanted a tank in the 50–60-ton range. The German preference was dictated by a desire for increased armor, especially on the turret. The lighter tank preferred by the French, on the other hand, would more easily find export customers, particularly outside Europe.

Finally, the question of exports was a major worry in itself. Because of the historical association between German tanks and German military aggression, successive governments in Bonn had refused to allow German arms makers to export tanks to countries other than Western industrial democracies. Bonn's de facto policy on weapons exports was, in fact, much more restrictive for armored vehicles than for other categories of weaponry manufactured in Germany.[8] The potential export of a Franco-German tank outside Europe thus touched an especially sensitive nerve in Germany. The French demanded a free hand in deciding whether and where to export the co-produced tank—an unhappy prospect for Bonn.

As the tank discussions continued, the French side gave in on many of the points at issue. It was agreed that the Franco-German project would not be an entirely new tank; instead, the Leopard 2 would be utilized as a test bed, and collaboration would focus on areas where improvement was possible. In effect, this meant adopting a large part of the Leopard 2 virtually without changes. The tank chassis, for example, was to remain unchanged, and only minor changes at most were foreseen for the Leopard 2's motor and 120–millimeter smooth-bore cannon. On the other hand, the two sides planned to develop an altogether new turret, with the German side having responsibility for developing an automatic cannon loading mechanism and the French side concentrating on the targeting and firing system. The possibility of extensive changes in the tank's armor and drive train was also to be investigated.[9] In addition, the French accepted that the joint tank would weigh more than 50 tons.

The one point of dispute that proved intractable was the export question. Paris was unwilling to accept any arrangement that would allow Bonn to veto French exports of the joint tank. High-level French and German foreign ministry officials undertook negotiations on the issue but were unable to resolve it.

The tank discussions took a surprising turn at the February 1980 Franco-German summit in Paris. Schmidt, acutely worried by the air of crisis in East-West relations following the Soviet invasion of Afghanistan, desperately sought a symbol of solidarity with France (see Chapter 5). Giscard sympathized with the chancellor's wishes. The symbol chosen by the two leaders to demonstrate their solidarity was the Franco-German tank. A variety of considerations prompted the choice. First, of the several major cooperative armaments projects under discussion between the two countries, the tank was the only one on which agreement seemed within reach. Second, co-production of a battle tank would be a high-profile symbol of cooperation, signaling a new level of trust and friendship between France and Germany at a time when Germany's leaders felt ever less able to trust their primary ally, the United States. Finally, the tank offered an opportunity for highly tangible cooperation with France despite the underlying incompatibility of French and German defense doctrines.

Thus Schmidt and Giscard decided to commit themselves to the tank project. The final details of the agreement were worked out only at the summit itself. The major obstacle was the export question; Schmidt finally resolved it by accepting the French position. Exports of the new tank were to be governed by guidelines like those agreed in 1972 for other Franco-German co-produced weapon systems. That is, neither side could veto an export desired by the other, but in exceptional cases the objecting side could raise the issue at the ministerial level. The export in question would then receive discussion in bilateral consultations before going forward.[10]

The tank agreement was received without enthusiasm in Germany. Indeed, it soon became evident that the project had few backers other than Schmidt and Eberhard. The two German tank producers, Krauss-Maffei and Krupp MaK, both opposed the accord. Regarding West German tank technology as the best in the world, they saw no advantage in a close association with the French. During the 1960s the Leopard 1 had been a resounding export success, with export sales of 4,500 units to Australia, Canada, and seven European NATO states. The German tank producers hoped many of these countries would buy the Leopard 2 as a successor tank when they began to replace their first-generation Leopards in the mid-1990s. They worried that the French would cooperate on a joint tank only until they had mastered Germany's technology, then produce a tank of their own which they would sell at state-subsidized prices to Leopard 1 users, thus depriving Germany of its tank export clientele among Western democracies. Because Bonn (unlike Paris) prohibited its tank producers from exporting to the Third World, the German tank firms guarded their limited export market all the more jealously.

Strong opposition to the tank project also came from the Bundestag, where the SPD, CDU, and FDP all took a stand against it. The Defense Committee and the Budget Committee were especially unfavorable. Members of the Defense Committee deeply resented not having been informed of the tank agreement before it was signed.[11] Even more importantly, the tank accord came at a time of deepening crisis in Germany's military equipment procurement budget. Planning miscalculations in the late 1970s had led, by 1980, to a spectacular shortfall in procurement funds.[12] Under the circumstances, the relevant Bundestag committees found it unthinkable that they should finance development of a new tank, especially at a time when the ultramodern Leopard 2 was just entering into production.

SPD and FDP deputies further objected to the joint tank because of the foreseeable political fallout from French export policy. It was clear that the French would attempt to sell the co-produced tank in the Middle East, and that West Germany would be powerless to stop them from doing so. This raised the extremely distasteful prospect that tanks containing 50 percent West German content might end up being employed in Middle Eastern wars.[13] The project also lacked allies within the West German military, who preferred to wait several more years before developing a Leopard 1 successor.

In contrast to the tide of criticism in Germany, the idea of a Franco-German tank collaboration was widely approved in France. Enthusiasm over the project was not, however, universal. Right-wing nationalists regarded the idea with some suspicion, and the Communist-controlled Confédération Générale de Travail (CGT) campaigned vigorously against the project under the slogan, "A French Tank for the French Army."[14]

Amid mounting opposition in West Germany, the tank agreement suffered a serious blow in March 1981 when Defense Minister Hans Apel announced sharp cuts in the government's planned arms purchases because of the budget crisis. In the revised procurement plan, Apel provided no funds for the Franco-German tank. If Schmidt wished the project to go forward, in other words, he would have to come up with the necessary funding for it from elsewhere in the government's budget.[15]

As the months dragged by without further West German action, the French side began to press Bonn for a decision on its participation in the venture. If Germany was not interested, France would need to begin developing a tank on its own. François Mitterrand, having succeeded Giscard as French president in 1981, wrote Schmidt in January 1982 to reiterate France's interest in the project.[16] Schmidt made a last-ditch effort to win the support of his own party members in the Bundestag. "We must fulfill this wish of France's," he pleaded. "We no longer have many friends in the world."[17] Schmidt's effort was unavailing, and with his departure from office in September 1982 the project was effectively finished off. Talks between the French and German defense ministries were renewed under Chancellor Kohl and his defense minister, Manfred Wörner, but they encountered the same problems as before and were soon allowed to lapse.

In the wake of the project's demise, the German defense ministry temporarily shelved plans for a Leopard 1 successor. In France, the state-owned tank producer GIAT went ahead with its own development program. In 1987 GIAT unveiled an experimental prototype of its new battle tank, named the Leclerc, which was to be ready for serial production beginning in 1991. French officials initiated talks with Spain, Belgium, and other countries to consider the possibilities for multilateral cooperation in the Leclerc production program.[18]

THE EUROPEAN FIGHTER AIRCRAFT

Beginning in 1976, French, German, and British armaments officials initiated discussions on the possibility of jointly developing a tactical fighter aircraft for the 1990s. The exploratory talks revealed rather consid-

erable divergences among the three states in their specific military requirements. Germany needed an aircraft early in the 1990s to replace its F-4F
and RF-4E Phantoms in a variety of air-to-air roles, particularly air-superiority missions. The German air force also wanted the aircraft to be able
to carry out ground-attack missions as a secondary role. France, meanwhile,
had decided in 1975 to acquire Dassault's Mirage 2000 as its major new
combat aircraft in the 1980s. Delivery of a preliminary batch of 130 aircraft
to the French air force was to begin in 1983, with a possible later order for
an additional 200 aircraft. The Mirage 2000s, together with the Mirage F1s
acquired during the latter 1970s, gave France an adequate air-to-air capability through the 1990s. On the other hand, France did have a requirement
for a new aircraft in the 1990s to serve in air-to-ground roles. Britain, for
its part, needed a multirole fighter—but with priority to ground-attack
missions—to replace its Harriers and Jaguars beginning as early as 1985.
Finally, Italy (another possible participant in the project) needed an
air-superiority fighter to replace its aged F-104 Starfighters no later than
the beginning of the 1990s.[19]

The European fighter aircraft discussions intensified in 1978, when the
French, German, and British defense ministers created a series of working
groups to study the possibility of reaching a common military requirement
for the fighter aircraft. Simultaneously, British Aerospace, Dassault, and
Messerschmidt-Bölkow-Blohm (MBB) were commissioned to examine the
possibilities for industrial collaboration on the aircraft.[20]

Over the subsequent several years, three major disputes emerged which
prevented the project from advancing to the development phase. The first
dispute concerned whether the aircraft should incorporate major components purchased from the United States, or if instead all contracts for
production work on the European Fighter Aircraft (EFA) should be reserved to manufacturers located in the participating countries. The German defense ministry favored allowing U.S.-made components to be
included on an equal basis with European components in the competition
for contracts. In fact, German defense officials explicitly favored equipping
the EFA with a number of major subassemblies purchased from American
producers, including the aircraft's engine and radar. The radar under
consideration, the APG-65 manufactured by Hughes, was regarded by
German officials as superior to anything that could be obtained in Europe
within the anticipated time frame. Similarly, General Electric's F-404
engine was considered by the Germans to be ideally suited for the planned
aircraft. Equipping the EFA with the APG-65 radar and the F-404 engine
would minimize the expense and risk involved in its development. If

suppliers for the EFA were limited to European firms, by contrast, it would be necessary to develop a new radar and a new engine specifically for the project, which would vastly increase development costs and probable delays.[21]

In line with its established policy on co-production of major weapon systems, the French government flatly rejected the idea of obtaining major components of the EFA from American suppliers. Predictably, the German defense ministry's preferences also encountered resistance from engine and electronics producers in France, Germany, and Britain, who wanted the EFA engine and avionics contracts for themselves.

The debate over the engine to be used in the EFA was further complicated by Anglo-French industrial rivalry. The French and British agreed that the joint aircraft should not be equipped with an American engine. But while the British wanted to use a more advanced version of the Rolls Royce RB-199 engine originally developed for the Tornado fighter aircraft, the French wanted to develop an entirely new engine, the M-88, based on a design by Snecma.[22] The disagreement was later to prove insurmountable, since neither the French nor the British government was willing to give way on the engine question under any circumstances.

The second major dispute dividing participants in the EFA project concerned the aircraft's operational specifications. France, Germany, and Britain each sought an aircraft with capabilities and equipment different from those desired by the other participants. In previous collaborative aircraft projects, divergences of this sort had been resolved in one of two ways: by building the aircraft in several vastly different versions (for example, the Franco-German Alpha-Jet) or by incorporating the demands of all sides into a single aircraft capable of performing diverse roles (as had occurred with the Tornado). Either solution would be extremely expensive. With France, Germany, and Britain all confronting tight procurement budgets, both these "traditional" options were largely foreclosed. The German side in particular was adamant that the new aircraft be designed-to-cost, that is, that its design specifications be determined by preset price limits rather than vice-versa.[23] Design-to-cost meant establishing priorities for the aircraft's performance characteristics and, if necessary, sacrificing secondary capabilities in order to stay within the established price constraints. The need to keep the project relatively inexpensive made definition of the aircraft much more difficult than if the participants had been able simply to add together the performance criteria sought by all sides. As the discussions dragged on, it became ever more doubtful whether any solution for a specialized fighter existed that would satisfy all the major participants.

The third major dispute concerned the questions of program organization and design leadership. France and Britain each claimed the overall leadership of the program. To buttress its position in the multilateral negotiations, each began developing a prototype aircraft that could be presented as an experimental basis for the EFA. The French prototype, developed by Dassault and later named the Rafale, was initiated early in 1983. British Aerospace began developing an analogous demonstrator aircraft, called EAP (Experimental Aircraft Program), in September 1982. The EAP was built in cooperation with West Germany and Italy; following France's withdrawal from the EFA program, the EAP was widely regarded as a pre-prototype for the EFA.

The West Germans, meanwhile, sought to establish the EFA program on a basis such that no one country could dominate it. In its previous experiences co-producing military aircraft—the Transall and Alpha-Jet with France, the Tornado with Britain—Germany had always found itself compelled to do most of the compromising on the definition of the aircraft. In the case of the EFA, the Germans hoped that the inclusion of both France and Britain in the program would prevent either from attaining a dominant position.

Closely related to the question of design leadership was that of the project's administrative organization. The Germans favored creating a multilateral organization to oversee the project, the so-called "integrated management" option. This would involve setting up an intergovernmental steering commission to supervise the program, as well as a multilateral industrial consortium to act as the primary contractor. All significant decisions, in this arrangement, would be subject to discussion and negotiation among the program participants, enabling each to defend its own military and industrial interests. Such an organizational structure had been created to oversee the development and production of the Tornado. Indeed, it was suggested that the existing Tornado management structures could be used as a basis for managing the EFA project.

The French side strongly opposed the integrated management approach, preferring instead an arrangement that would place most of the management responsibility in the hands of a single government and a single prime contractor. This type of arrangement, known as the "pilot" approach, would be far more efficient than the unwieldy and expensive integrated management approach. On the other hand, as the Alpha-Jet program had shown, the pilot management approach tended to result in the pilot country imposing its own preferences concerning system design and industrial work-sharing at the expense of its partners.[24]

These disagreements did not prevent the signature of an agreement by the air force chiefs of France, Britain, Germany, Italy, and Spain in December 1983, which established the main lines of an operational requirement for the European Fighter Aircraft. (Spain had joined the EFA negotiations soon after becoming a member of NATO in 1982.) Under the five-country agreement, the EFA was to be ready for introduction around 1995. Following further negotiations over the specific characteristics of the aircraft, the defense ministers of the five countries met in Madrid in July 1984 and signed an agreement in principle to proceed with joint development of the EFA. France, Germany, and Britain were each to have 24.5 percent of the development work, with Italy having a 16.5 percent share and Spain getting 10 percent. As subsequent events showed, the agreement was premature. None of the key disagreements had been resolved. France and Britain continued to struggle for overall control of the program, and the rivalry between Snecma and Rolls Royce over the EFA's engine went on unabated.[25]

Ultimately it was France that had to back down. The British, unlike the French, were willing to go along with the integrated management approach favored by Bonn and to settle for a 24.5 percent share in the project. The French government and Dassault, unable to accept cooperation on the given terms and seeing that they would not be able to win a dominant role in the project against the combined opposition of the other participants, withdrew from the consortium in August 1985. They chose instead to proceed with the development of their own fighter aircraft, based on the Rafale. Meanwhile, Germany, Britain, Italy, and Spain decided to move forward with the development phase of the EFA. Shares in the development work were revised so that Germany and Britain each had 33 percent, Italy 21 percent, and Spain 13 percent.[26]

Despite its decision not to participate in the EFA, the French government continued to seek other forms of intra-European cooperation for the Rafale. In one initiative, Paris proposed that French companies be given a 5–10 percent share in the development and production of the EFA in exchange for subcontracting an equivalent share of the Rafale program to firms in the EFA consortium countries.[27] The exchange would enable both sides to save money by permitting a limited amount of specialization by the EFA and Rafale consortia in the production of components for their respective aircraft.

The other French initiative took the form of discussions with Belgium, Norway, Denmark, and the Netherlands on possible participation in the Rafale project.[28] These countries were expected to need a replacement for their F-16 fighters early in the next century. By attempting to involve the European F-16 user states in the Rafale at an early stage, Paris evidently hoped to assure the Rafale an export market within Europe. The F-16 user states would presumably be given a significant share of the Rafale development and production work in exchange for a commitment to purchase the aircraft for their own armed forces.

THE ANTITANK HELICOPTER

During the 1970s, the military staffs of the French and West German armies each developed a military requirement for an antitank helicopter capable of operating during both day and night and in all weather conditions. Because no existing helicopter ideally suited French or German requirements, the French and German military staffs initiated talks on the possibility of developing the desired helicopter through a joint project. These talks (which took place from 1975 to 1977) led to the establishment of a common Franco-German requirement, but also uncovered deep differences between the two sides in their concepts for the proposed helicopter. The Germans wanted a helicopter in the 5-ton class, equipped with both antitank and self-protective (i.e., air-to-air) weaponry. The French, by contrast, preferred to develop two lighter, more specialized helicopters: one equipped solely for an antitank role and the other designed for protection and support of the antitank helicopters. Equipped with air-to-air missiles and a 30–millimeter cannon, the protection/support helicopter would be used to defend the antitank helicopters against fire from enemy helicopters.[29]

These divergent tactical concepts gave rise to a long series of disagreements over the helicopter's physical configuration. For example, the French military wanted the two-man crew to be seated side by side, while the Germans wanted to place one crewman behind the other. Although neither the German nor the French air force staff could provide any compelling military rationale for its own preferred seating arrangement, neither side was willing to give in to the other. The disagreement proved so intractable that at one point it nearly caused the entire joint project to be terminated. The dispute was only resolved, in fact, after French and German political leaders finally imposed the German-preferred configuration by fiat.[30]

An even more tenacious dispute concerned the targeting and night vision system to be employed in the helicopter. The French and German military requirements agreed that the helicopter must have a day/night and all-weather operational capability. The disagreement, as in so many other Franco-German co-production projects, concerned whether the necessary equipment should be purchased under license from an American company or should be developed by European industry. The German defense ministry strongly favored acquiring the Target Acquisition and Designation System/Pilot's Night Vision System (TADS/PNVS) developed by Martin Marietta. Using TADS/PNVS would help minimize the costs and development time of the overall project. No device comparable to TADS/PNVS was yet available from European sources, and waiting for one to be developed was likely to introduce additional costs and delays.

The French position, by contrast, was that night-vision and related optronic technologies would be such an important element of the conventional weaponry of the future that an American monopoly on such technologies could not be accepted under any circumstances. The French insisted that the helicopter be equipped with a European (i.e., French) targeting and night-vision system, even if some delays in development resulted. There were also the usual export considerations at work: the use of TADS/PNVS would enable the U.S. government to impose restrictions on exports of the Franco-German helicopter, an eventuality that the French regarded as intolerable.[31]

In the fall of 1979, France and Germany signed an intergovernmental agreement to begin an eighteen-month definition phase for the helicopter.[32] The ensuing studies uncovered a further incompatibility in the French and German positions concerning the helicopter's targeting and night-vision system. The German side wanted the targeting system to be installed in the nose of the helicopter, the nose section being the only place that TADS/PNVS would fit. The targeting system envisaged by the French, on the other hand, would be mounted on a mast above the main rotor.

With the two sides unable to resolve their differences, the definition phase ended in April 1981 without having reached a conclusion. Meanwhile, the main French and German contractors, Aérospatiale and MBB, continued to be interested in the possibility of a helicopter collaboration. At the suggestion of the French and German armaments directors, the two firms worked during the fall of 1981 to define a helicopter proposal that could then be offered to their respective governments. The resulting proposal, which conformed closely to French preferences, was rejected by the German government. The German government's counterproposal, offered in March 1982, met with a corresponding French rejection. For all practical purposes, the project was dead.

Only a few months later, however, the Franco-German helicopter was revived on political grounds. At their October 1982 summit meeting, Mitterrand and Kohl had announced their intention to revitalize Franco-German military cooperation (see Chapter 5). Both sides naturally sought a tangible demonstration of the new relationship. Because French and German strategic doctrines remained irreconcilable, the only possibility for immediate and visible progress in defense collaboration was in armaments production. But here, too, the situation was difficult. A joint battle tank was out of the question: neither side wanted to subject Franco-German relations to a repetition of Schmidt's debacle in the Bundestag. As for the European Fighter Aircraft, the discussions were still too far from resolution to offer any prospect of a quick success; also, the involvement of Britain, Italy, and Spain in the EFA meant that Paris and Bonn could not control progress on the project in the interest of their own political goals. Thus the two governments settled on the helicopter as the most promising available alternative.

From this point, the helicopter discussions followed a rather peculiar evolution. On the one hand, Kohl and Mitterrand were insistent in public on the need to reach an accord on the helicopter as a means of giving substance to their defense cooperation initiative. At the same time, however, neither government was willing to give way sufficiently on its own design preferences so that agreement would become possible.

On May 29, 1984, the French and German defense ministers signed with much fanfare an accord for the joint development and production of an attack helicopter in three versions.[33] The first version would be the support helicopter sought by the French army as a protective shield for its antitank helicopters. Denoted by the acronym HAP (*Hélicoptère d'appui et de protection*), this version was to be equipped with a 30–millimeter cannon and French-made antihelicopter missiles. Production of the French order for seventy-five units would begin in 1992. The second version would be an antitank helicopter equipped with HOT missiles and designed to meet the German army's military requirement. This version, designated PAH-2 (*Panzerabwehrhubschrauber*, second generation), was to go into production in 1993, with Germany scheduled to receive 212 units. Finally, a third version, the HAC-3G (*Hélicoptère anti-char*, third generation), would be an antitank helicopter equipped with the Trigat third-generation antitank missile being developed by France, Germany, and Britain (see below). France was due to accept delivery of 140 units of the HAC-3G beginning in 1996. In addition, Germany's PAH-2s were to be equipped retroactively with Trigat missiles once the Trigat became available.

The May 1984 agreement, dictated by political considerations, was on paper only. The key disputes were no nearer resolution than before. Chief among these was the ongoing disagreement over the helicopter's targeting and night-vision system. The accord signed by the defense ministers evaded this problem by providing that the two sides would collaborate in producing a "basis" helicopter not equipped with a targeting system or armaments. Each of the two governments would be free to equip its own helicopters with the targeting system and weaponry of its choice. France had already announced that it would employ a European-developed targeting system in its own helicopters in any event. West Germany expressed its preference in principle for a European targeting system, but with the proviso that an appropriate European system must be available early enough to prevent delays in the delivery of the PAH-2, and that the European system must be competitive with TADS/PNVS in cost and performance. If not, Germany would choose the American-made system.

As it turned out, even the decision to "solve" the targeting and night-vision dispute by letting each government install the system of its own choosing failed to provide a workable answer to the problem. Because TADS/PNVS would have to be installed in the helicopter's nose, and because the Germans gave priority to the helicopter's antitank mission, they insisted that the gunner be placed in the front seat and the pilot in the rear. The French, who began from the assumption of a mast-mounted targeting system and gave priority to the helicopter's support/protection role, demanded that the pilot be in front and the gunner behind.[34] The alternative seating arrangements created enough incompatibilities that the entire project appeared endangered.

A noteworthy feature of the May 1984 agreement was that it gave West Germany the primary responsibility for managing the helicopter project. The German government obtained the status of program leader despite the fact that MBB, the major German firm involved in the venture, did not want to be named prime contractor for the overall project. MBB worried that if Germany came to occupy a dominant position in the program, Aérospatiale might lose interest and instead construct a rival helicopter of its own.[35] After all, the helicopter division of Aérospatiale had a stronger technological base and a broader range of experience than MBB in helicopter construction, and might therefore grow dissatisfied with a subordinate role.

Despite MBB's qualms, the German government insisted throughout the negotiations with France that overall program leadership for the helicopter belong to the German side.[36] Bonn's claim to the managerial leadership of the project rested above all on the fact that the French had held the role of managerial "pilot" in the most recent major Franco-German co-production program, the Alpha-Jet. If France was serious about cooperating with West Germany on a basis of true partnership, argued Bonn, then it should be willing to allow the Germans their turn at managing a joint project.

The seemingly irresolvable argument over the Franco-German helicopter's optronic system delayed a production agreement until November 13, 1987.[37] In fact, the decision to go ahead with production was ultimately possible only because the German government finally gave in and agreed that all versions of the helicopter would employ a "European" targeting system (to be jointly developed by France and Germany) rather than TADS/PNVS. The gunner's sights would be mast-mounted, as preferred by the French.[38]

THE OBSERVATION SATELLITE

In the fall of 1983, the French government proposed to Bonn that the two countries join in constructing a military observation satellite. The German military, after reviewing the French suggestion, was favorable to the idea. West Germany had always depended on the United States for satellite-derived intelligence, which meant making do with whatever information Washington chose to share. The prospect of possessing their own independent source of satellite intelligence was thus highly attractive to the West Germans.

At their May 1984 summit meeting, Kohl and Mitterrand decided to establish a study group to examine the satellite idea in closer detail. In the discussions that followed, two major stumbling blocks became evident. First, there was disagreement over the allocation of development and production work on the satellite. The French proposal was based on an existing national program, SAMRO (*Satellite militaire de reconnaissance optique*). SAMRO had been initiated at the beginning of the 1980s, but the cost of carrying the program to completion forced the French government to suspend it in 1982. Under the French proposal, France and Germany were to contribute equally in funding the joint satellite, with each making a commitment of approximately one billion marks to the program.

The German government, if it was to provide half the project's funding, expected to obtain half of the development work and production contracts involved. But the development of SAMRO had already been largely completed by the French government in collaboration with French indus-try; German participation in the program was desired primarily as a means of putting the existing SAMRO design into production. If this were done, German industry would obtain only about 25 percent of the production work, with the remainder going to French firms. This was unsatisfactory to the German side, which insisted that any joint satellite be developed from scratch so that Germany could participate on an equal basis with France in terms of development and production.[39]

An even more serious dispute concerned the capabilities of the proposed satellite. As envisaged by the French, SAMRO would be a simple optical satellite able to gather intelligence only in clear weather. The Germans, however, were interested in an observation satellite for obtaining inde-pendent intelligence on the size and movements of Warsaw Pact forces, and potentially for verification of arms control agreements. Satisfactory performance of these functions would require a capability for virtually continuous observation. This would require not one but several low-orbit satellites, each equipped with heat sensors and radar equipment in addition to optic devices so as to provide intelligence in all weather conditions. Sophisticated satellites of this sort would take ten to fifteen years to develop, and the total cost of the project was likely to be closer to ten billion marks than to the estimated two billion marks needed to produce SAMRO. Given this situation, Bonn was decidedly unenthusiastic about pursuing the satellite proposal. Neither the military nor German industry was satisfied with France's SAMRO. Both would be much more interested in a joint project to develop an all-weather observation satellite. But the German defense ministry, already caught in a budget squeeze, had higher priorities than a multibillion-mark satellite program. The German space agency, meanwhile, was oriented entirely toward civilian space projects and strongly opposed the use of funds from its own budget to finance a military satellite.[40]

In September 1984, therefore, the German government decided not to participate in the project. The French government did not hide its disap-pointment with the German decision. At the Franco-German summit of November 1985, Mitterrand raised the satellite issue once again, in effect asking the West Germans to reconsider their position. A few days later, Kohl's government declined a second time to join the project.[41]

Subsequently the French government became even more firmly committed to the project. Eventually it persuaded Italy and Spain to join in financing a modified version of the program, which was renamed Hélios. Of the total projected program cost of 7.6 billion francs, Italy's share was to be 15 percent and Spain was to contribute 5 percent. The total program was expected to consist of three to four satellites, with the first satellite ready for launching in 1993.[42]

TACTICAL MISSILES

The final major area of Franco-German weapons cooperation was in tactical missiles. During the period covered in this chapter, two collaborative programs made substantial progress toward realization. One was the Trigat third-generation antitank missile program, which encompassed two distinct weapon systems. The Trigat-MR, successor to the Milan antitank missile, was to be a portable, medium-range weapon. The Trigat-LR, a successor to the HOT, was to be a long-range antitank missile designed for launching from helicopters and armored ground vehicles. The two missiles were to be developed by Euromissile Dynamics Group, a Paris-based industrial consortium formed in 1980 by Aérospatiale, MBB, and British Aerospace Dynamics Group (a division of British Aerospace). Under an October 1979 agreement, Britain was to participate equally with France and Germany in the development and production of the Trigat. Series production was to begin in 1991 for the Trigat-MR and in 1995 for the Trigat-LR.[43]

The other tactical missile program, a strictly Franco-German undertaking, was the ANS supersonic naval missile project. The missile, with a fire-and-forget guidance system and a range of up to 200 kilometers, was to be developed in several versions: ship-to-ship, land-to-ship, and air-to-ship. The development phase began in 1986, with Aérospatiale as the program leader and MBB as the main German contractor.[44]

The Trigat and ANS projects were noteworthy in that they were the only Franco-German armaments co-production projects described in this chapter that advanced without major public disputes and without visible resistance from at least some of the interested military and industrial participants. This unusual circumstance appeared to derive largely from historical factors. The major French and German industrial participants for both programs were Aérospatiale and MBB. As noted in Chapter 3, these two firms had a long history of continuous cooperation in the development of tactical missiles dating from the late 1950s. Because the tactical missile divisions of the two companies had literally grown up together, collaboration had become second nature to them by the 1980s. The Milan and HOT antitank missiles jointly developed earlier by Aérospatiale and MBB had proved exceptionally successful from a technical as well as a financial standpoint. When it came time to develop a new generation of antitank missiles, it was natural for the governments and firms involved in the Milan and HOT programs to want to continue such a profitable collaboration.

With regard to profitability, it is worth recalling that German firms received half of the production work as well as half of the profits generated by French exports of Milan, HOT, and Roland missiles to other countries. Many of France's missile customers were Middle Eastern states to which Germany would not itself sell arms; hence, collaboration with Aérospatiale opened export markets to MBB that would otherwise have remained off-limits to it. For Aérospatiale, meanwhile, cooperation with MBB insured that Germany would not develop its own family of advanced antitank missiles to compete with French products among Western industrial states.

Similar considerations help to explain the apparent ease of Franco-German agreement to cooperate in developing the ANS. Beginning in 1968, Aérospatiale and other French firms had been subcontractors in the development and production of MBB's Kormoran air-to-ship missile. Franco-German cooperation in the Kormoran development program had in turn contributed to the development of the French Exocet antiship missile family.[45] Thus Franco-German cooperation in the area of naval missiles was already well established when the notion of a supersonic naval missile came under discussion, and the same considerations and incentives that made Aérospatiale and MBB partners in the Trigat program also led them into partnership on the ANS.

THE GROWING DIFFICULTY OF COOPERATION

The history of attempts at armaments collaboration between France and West Germany from 1975 to 1987 demonstrated that the obstacles to successful weapons co-production were more formidable than ever. Five years of intensive discussions on a Franco-German battle tank yielded nothing despite the personal commitment of the German chancellor and the French president to the project. In the case of the antitank helicopter, a final production agreement required both an overt commitment by the French and German political leaderships as well as twelve years of difficult negotiations. The project for a European Fighter Aircraft, meanwhile, broke down into two separate programs after seven years of intensive talks.

From the mid-1970s onward, both French and German political leaders expressed a strong desire for cooperation in weapons production. Paris, for its part, showed time and again its willingness to compromise with Bonn in order to make Franco-German weapons collaboration succeed. In the case of the tank, for example, the French side accepted nearly all of the German government's demands concerning the basic parameters of the tank and the use of the Leopard 2 as the basis for the joint project. In the case of the helicopter, Paris accepted German leadership of the program despite the fact that French industry had much greater expertise than its German counterpart in the construction of military helicopters. It was Germany, not France, which rejected cooperation in two major instances: the tank and the military observation satellite. The one major project where France chose to go alone was the European Fighter Aircraft.

On the West German side, the political will to cooperate was also evident. It was perhaps strongest during the tenure of Helmut Schmidt, for whom the tie to France became pivotal as his confidence in American leadership plummeted. Under Helmut Kohl, Germany continued to favor armaments cooperation with France, although Kohl's government appeared somewhat less willing than Schmidt's to promote cooperation with France at the expense of other German political and industrial interests. Nevertheless, the Kohl government was quite anxious to have at least one major arms co-production project under way with France, as the saga of the attack helicopter demonstrated. Under Kohl as under previous chancellors, Bonn worried lest too little Franco-German armaments collaboration send the wrong signal to Paris, or to Moscow. As the most visible—and perhaps most substantive—facet of Franco-German defense cooperation, joint armaments projects with France were a favored political instrument of German leaders from the 1950s through the 1980s.

If both the French and German governments consistently favored arms procurement collaboration, however, then why did cooperation prove so difficult to carry out in practice? The blame could not be laid at the doorstep of any one actor or group in either country. Franco-German armaments cooperation had few consistent opponents. In fact, only the French Communist party and its allied trade union, the CGT, systematically opposed armaments cooperation between the two countries. The attitudes of industry, military planners, and budget authorities toward proposed co-production projects all tended to vary with the specific circumstances of each case.

Where the arms industry was concerned, for example, support or opposition for proposed projects depended on the technological capabilities of the industries involved, on the proposed work-sharing arrangements, and on the habits of individual companies. West Germany's tank manufacturers, Krauss-Maffei and Krupp MaK, were unenthusiastic about a Franco-German tank because they felt they had little to gain and much to lose in a joint project. Dassault, the French aircraft maker, supported or resisted cooperation depending on whether the cooperative arrangements would enable it to retain control over key design decisions. The German aeronauatics firm MBB, meanwhile, was a consistently strong supporter of cooperation. The long history of cooperation between MBB and Aérospatiale in the construction of aircraft and tactical missiles (including, among others, Transall, HOT, Milan, and Roland) made agreement between the two firms on new projects easier to achieve. In fact, MBB sometimes showed itself more willing than the German government to compromise in order to reach co-production agreements with Aérospatiale, as occurred during the industrial negotiations over the Franco-German attack helicopter.

The attitude of the military staffs toward cooperative projects also tended to be situation-dependent. Where battle tanks were concerned, the German military was decidedly nationalistic. In the case of helicopters and fighter aircraft, on the other hand, the German air force often displayed a marked preference for American-made equipment, and accepted the idea of a European substitute only with some reluctance. As to the attitude of France's military toward weapons collaboration, information is scarce because of the French officers' tradition of public silence. If one generalization held true in both the French and the German cases, however, it was that military staffs tended to prefer the best equipment available, and were sympathetic to whichever method—national production, collaborative procurement, or foreign purchase—would bring them state-of-the-art weapons within the desired time frame.

National budget authorities, for their part, tended to favor collaboration in cases where it was expected to produce savings and to oppose it where it would make procurement more expensive. The question of costs was far from simple. On the one hand, cooperative development of a complex weapon system was usually significantly cheaper for each participating country than developing the needed weapon entirely on its own. For example, the total cost of developing the EFA as a five-country project was estimated in 1985 at 7.5 to 12.4 billion German marks, of which Germany's share would have been around DM 3.6 billion. This was much less than the estimated DM 6.5 billion it would have cost Germany to develop an air-superiority fighter by itself.[46] On the other hand, a purely national project might well have been more *cost-effective* than co-production even if it was more expensive, because co-production projects involved higher administrative overhead and frequently yielded weapons that were both more complex than needed and less suited to the specific military requirements of each participant than the weapon system it might have produced by itself.[47] For this reason, no general assertion can be made about how decision makers judged the economic merits of proposed collaborative projects. The one generalization that can be made is that budget authorities usually opposed cooperative projects that appeared to derive solely from political considerations rather than from genuine military requirements. Certainly this was an important reason why the Bundestag's budget committee was so unfavorable in 1981 to the idea of a Franco-German tank.

Thus, trying to account for the difficulty of armaments cooperation in terms of individuals or interest groups opposed to it does not provide a great deal of insight into the nature of the problem. The difficulty was more general: any proposed major collaborative project brought into play a vast number of military and industrial actors and interests. For a complex weapon system like a fighter aircraft, a helicopter, or a main battle tank, hundreds or even thousands of firms would be involved in the design and production of components. Providing work to each of these companies, and helping each of them to enhance its technological capabilities, proved to be a major preoccupation of European governments in their arms procurement decisions.

The geometric growth in the cost of developing advanced weapon systems, and the extraordinarily high prices of certain weapon systems such as combat aircraft, meant that the economic and technological stakes of individual weapon projects often grew to life-or-death proportions for the firms involved. In the case of the European Fighter Aircraft, for example, European aircraft engine manufacturers believed that the firm that obtained the design leadership for the EFA's engine would gain a decisive competitive edge over all its rivals in Europe. It was for this reason that the two main candidates for the EFA engine design leadership, Rolls Royce and Snecma, treated the competition virtually as a fight to the death. The same could be said about Dassault's attitude toward design leadership of the EFA's airframe. Analogous rivalries existed between contractors for other high-technology components in the EFA and for other proposed collaborative projects. European governments proved extremely reluctant to divide up a given co-production program in ways that would come at the expense of any of the dozens of domestic firms with a major industrial or technological stake in the program. As a result, deciding how to parcel out the development and production work for large co-production projects such as the Franco-German tank, the attack helicopter, or the EFA became a nightmarish and often insurmountable problem.

The high economic and technological stakes involved in producing advanced conventional weapon systems exerted pressures which both promoted and limited cooperation. Before launching major weapon projects, European governments generally attempted to secure the collaboration of one other major European state. This effort had a triple goal: first, to save on development costs by sharing them with a partner; second, to insure that the weapon system would be sold to at least two governments, thereby reducing unit production costs; third, to co-opt a potential export competitor and thus improve the weapon's export prospects. At the same time, cooperation initiated with the goal of co-opting competitors tended to be self-limiting. Because each of the major states wanted to retain its existing capabilities in weapons design and technology, it was disinclined to include too many other major states in a key project: each additional state could in turn be expected to demand a substantial share of the design and development work, leaving less for the initial participants.

Part of the increasing difficulty of Franco-German armaments cooperation also appeared to stem from structural factors, especially the growth and increasing sophistication of the West German aeronautics sector. The West German aerospace industry, which employed fewer than 3,000 workers in 1957 (compared to 300,000 in Britain) had grown by 1985 to nearly 80,000 workers. Although Germany's aeronautics industry was still not equal to those of Britain or France in size or capability, the emergence of a substantial German aeronautics sector made Bonn more reluctant to take a back seat to Britain and France in joint aircraft projects. While France was the dominant partner in the Franco-German aircraft co-production projects of the 1960s and 1970s (Transall and Alpha-Jet), and Britain dominated Germany in the Tornado project, Germany's new attitude was visible in its insistence that it be given the management leadership in the Franco-German helicopter project.

Two factors came into play. First, Germany's aeronautics industry, as an economically significant and technologically progressive sector of the West German economy, was increasingly viewed by German leaders as an important national investment to be preserved and maintained. In other words, Germans began to look at their country's aerospace industry in much the same terms as the French and British viewed theirs. German leaders

were consequently less satisfied than before with co-production arrangements that allocated the most interesting research and development work
to French or British firms. Second, armaments collaboration confronted
German governments with difficult choices between the partly incompatible goals of intra-Alliance cooperation and intra-Alliance equality. In the
1960s and 1970s, the disparity in size and sophistication between Germany's aeronautics industry and its French and British counterparts had
made genuinely equal partnership unachievable. Bonn therefore focused
on the goal of cooperation, postponing its goal of equal industrial partnership to the day when the German aeronautics industry could hold its own
in joint projects with other European countries. By the late 1970s that day
had arrived, and since political equality within the Alliance remained an
important West German objective, Bonn became a more demanding
partner in joint aircraft projects.

As Germany became more insistent on equality of partnership in its arms
co-production agreements, finding contractual arrangements capable of
satisfying both Paris and Bonn became more difficult. The result was one
of the more ironic aspects of Franco-German armaments collaboration in
the 1980s: despite the trumpeted revitalization of Franco-German defense
cooperation beginning in 1982, the overall trend in armaments procurement was toward a lesser degree of Franco-German cooperation and toward
increased cooperation between France and the European states with
smaller armaments industries. After Germany declined to cooperate on the
battle tank, for example, Paris initiated talks with Spain and Belgium on
participation in its own Leclerc tank. Following its inability to agree with
Germany and Britain on the EFA, France began negotiations with the F-16
user states (Belgium, Norway, Denmark, and the Netherlands) on joining
its Rafale program. And after Bonn twice turned down the Hélios observation satellite proposal, the French government managed to persuade
Italy and Spain to help in financing it.

The trend toward weapons collaboration between France and the
smaller NATO allies appeared to reflect a deliberate decision by French
armaments authorities to develop alternatives to the traditional partnerships with Germany and Britain. Germany remained France's favored
partner for weapons co-production, but there were signs that France was
gradually giving up its long-standing effort to create a Franco-German
armaments axis. During the first half of the 1980s, for example, Paris signed
a series of bilateral "framework agreements" on defense equipment cooperation with other West European states.[48] The agreements were concerned more with the creation of new bilateral consultative procedures

than with specific arms projects.[49] The existence of the agreements suggested increased determination on France's part to look beyond Germany and Britain if necessary to find partners in conventional weapons production. The unpromising record of Franco-German efforts at armaments collaboration in the first half of the 1980s could only have reinforced this determination.

On the whole, France in the 1980s remained as devoted as ever to the Gaullist objective of national independence in all essential military technologies. There was, perhaps, a degree of narrowing in the French definition of what constituted an essential technology. Public statements by armaments officials during the Mitterrand years stressed France's eagerness to cooperate in conventional weapons production, and underlined French willingness to accept industrial and operational compromises in the development of conventional weapons in order to make cooperation possible.[50] French actions in its discussions with Germany on the tank, attack helicopter, and observation satellite programs lent credibility to such statements.

On the other hand, the key elements of Gaullist armaments policy remained in place. Even though the French seemed to be more intent than ever on intra-European cooperation, they continued to show a strong preference for asymmetrical partnerships that would allow France to remain in control—hence the visible drift away from joint projects with Germany and Britain toward co-production arrangements with countries like Belgium and Spain.

Second, French insistence on the freedom to export its arms remained absolute. In every instance, the French made clear that they would break off Franco-German arms collaboration rather than accept a German right to veto exports of co-produced weapon systems. Similarly, the French flatly rejected the inclusion of components in co-produced weapons that might be subject to U.S. export controls. More than ever, France remained entrenched in its self-reinforcing circle of producing armaments for export.

Above all, France continued to insist on maintaining an independent design and production capability for nuclear-related technologies, including all conventional weapon technologies essential for nuclear delivery systems. For example, although Paris might be willing to give up the design leadership on Franco-German projects such as the attack helicopter or the battle tank, it preferred to develop an advanced fighter aircraft by itself rather than accept a minority share of the EFA project. Paris also gave an increasingly high priority to the development of its own independent military satellite capability, regarding such a capability as a precondition for a credible independent nuclear deterrent in the twenty-first century.

Although the basic Gaullist premises of French policy on armaments cooperation remained intact, there were signs of a limited relaxation in the French attitude toward armaments collaboration with the United States. For example, France was a participant in the Multi-Launch Rocket System, a co-production project undertaken in collaboration with the United States, Germany, and Britain. France also joined the United States and several European countries in the (ultimately unsuccessful) NATO Frigate-90 project. And France participated in six of the seven projects approved in 1986 in the framework of the Nunn Initiative, under which the United States authorized expenditures of up to $2.9 billion by 1992 for joint U.S.-European military equipment projects.[51] Perhaps the most significant development was the December 1984 announcement that France would acquire the Boeing E-3A AWACS early-warning aircraft. In earlier years, French purchase of such a major system from the United States would have been difficult to imagine.

As for West Germany, its policy on weapons co-production continued to be buffeted by conflicting goals. The desire to use arms co-production as an instrument of European integration and Alliance unity, for example, made Bonn sympathetic in principle to the demands of smaller allies to be included in projects at the development stage. The search for cost-effective procurement choices, however, generated contrary pressures to develop weapons on a bilateral or even purely national basis.[52] An even more basic contradiction concerned Bonn's simultaneous desire for intra-Alliance cooperation and intra-Alliance equality in arms co-production, even though the two did not always go together.

Finally, unlike the situation in the United States, France, or Britain, substantial segments of the West German public and political elite regarded the industrial and technological successes of Germany's arms manufacturers with misgivings. Conscious that sustaining a world-class armaments industry would require aggressive pursuit of Third World sales, many Germans were deeply ambivalent about having a large national economic stake in arms production. That the West German public was far from comfortable with Germany's role as an arms supplier was demonstrated by the acrimonious public debate which broke out in 1980 following reports that Bonn had approved the export of submarines to Pinochet's Chile and was considering the sale of Leopard 2 tanks to Saudi Arabia.[53] The debate subsided only after the Schmidt government published new guidelines for weapons exports showing that no major liberalization of the existing policy was envisaged.[54] The new guidelines did, notably, clarify Bonn's policy on armaments co-production. They stated that the German government would attempt to adhere to its export restrictions as far as possible where co-produced weapons were concerned, but that Germany's interest in cooperation would be given a fundamentally higher priority. Thus the 1982 guidelines made official the de facto policy followed by Bonn since 1971.

The net result of the conflicting pressures on German arms co-production policy was a decided lack of coherence. Armaments cooperation, German officials frequently declared, was a means rather than an end in itself. But an instrument in service of several contradictory objectives would not easily accomplish any of them.

NOTES

1. Kolodziej, *Making and Marketing Arms*, p. 174.

2. Pierre Dussauge, *L'Industrie française de l'armement* (Paris: Economica, 1985), p. 14.

3. Kolodziej, *Making and Marketing Arms*, pp. 176–78.

4. Cf. the remarks by French armaments director Jean-Laurent Delpech in *Le Monde*, December 12, 1975.

5. For the history of this decision, see Ingemar Dörfer, *Arms Deal: The Selling of the F-16* (New York: Praeger, 1983).

6. See D. C. R. Heyhoe, *The Alliance and Europe: Part VI—The European Programme Group*, Adelphi Paper no. 129 (London: IISS, Winter 1976/77).

7. Interviews with French and German officials.

8. Eckehart Ehrenberg, *Der deutsche Rüstungsexport: Beurteilungen und Perspektiven* (Munich: Bernard & Graefe, 1981), pp. 100–101. In the 1970s, for example, German shipyards exported torpedo-equipped submarines to such countries as Indonesia, Colombia, and Venezuela. Minesweepers were exported to Brazil, and customers for German-built patrol boats included Argentina, Ecuador, Ghana, and Nigeria. See Ulrich Albrecht, Peter Lock, and Herbert Wulf, *Arbeitsplätze durch Rüstung?* (Reinbek bei Hamburg: Rowohlt, 1978), pp. 159–64.

9. Interview with former German armaments official. See also *Wehrtechnik*, September 1980, p. 60, and *Die Welt*, March 8, 1982.

10. Interviews with French and German officials.

11. Interview with Bundestag deputy.

12. For details, see *Aviation Week and Space Technology*, August 18, 1980, pp. 18–19.

13. *Frankfurter Allgemeine Zeitung*, January 26, 1982.

14. *Wehrtechnik*, May 1981, p. 18; *Le Monde*, August 28, 1980 and January 23, 1981.

15. *Le Monde*, March 10, 1981.

16. *Le Monde*, March 5, 1982.

17. *Der Spiegel*, 1982 no. 10, p. 26.

18. *International Defense Review*, 6/1987, pp. 755–60.

19. *Wehrtechnik*, June 1977, pp. 26–43 and 68–70; and *International Defense Review*, 3/1978, pp. 335–46.

20. Assembly of Western European Union, Committee on Scientific, Technological and Aerospace Questions, *The European Combat Aircraft and Other Aeronautical Developments*, Document 874, April 1981, p. 5.

21. *Wehrtechnik*, May 1980, p. 46.

22. *Wehrtechnik*, May 1980, p. 43.

23. *Wehrtechnik*, May 1980, p. 46.

24. For a general comparison of the integrated management and pilot approaches, as well as French and German views on them, see *Wehrtechnik*, February 1984, pp. 29–30.

25. See the *Frankfurter Allgemeine Zeitung*, June 15, 1985; and *Le Monde*, April 3, April 6, and September 10, 1985.

26. *Wehrtechnik*, October 1985, p. 20.

27. *Le Monde*, November 10–11, 1985.

28. *Le Monde*, March 12, 1986.

29. See Henri Louet, *Rapport d'information par la Commission de la défense nationale et des forces armées sur la coopération industrielle franco-allemande en matière d'hélicoptères de combat* (Paris: Assemblée Nationale, Troisième session extraordinaire de 1985–86, no. 249), pp. 7–15.

30. François Heisbourg, "Für einen neuen Anfang," in Kaiser and Lellouche, *Deutsch-französische Sicherheitspolitik*, p. 131.

31. Interviews with German armaments officials.

32. For chronologies of the Franco-German helicopter negotiations, see Louet, *Rapport*, pp. 20–23, and *L'Armement*, December 1984, pp. 8–11.

33. The agreement is reprinted in Louet, *Rapport*, pp. 43–64.

34. See *Interavia*, March 1984, pp. 258–61.

35. Interview with MBB official.

36. See the interview with Joachim Heyden, a German armaments official, in *Wehrtechnik*, June 1986, especially p. 33.

37. See *Le Monde*, November 14, 1987.

38. *Wehrtechnik*, June 1986, p. 33, and *International Defense Review*, 5/1987, pp. 610–13. Because of the delay in reaching a production accord, planned delivery of the first HAPs and PAH-2s was postponed to 1998, and that of the first HAC-3Gs to the year 2000.

39. Interviews with German defense ministry officials. See also the *Süddeutsche Zeitung*, October 12, 1984, and *Der Spiegel*, October 15, 1984, pp. 23–24.

40. *Quotidien de Paris*, October 30, 1984.

41. *Le Monde*, November 16, 1985.

42. *Le Monde*, April 10, 1987.

43. *International Defense Review*, 9/1984, pp. 1379–81, and *Wehrtechnik*, January 1985, pp. 28–32.

44. *Wehrtechnik*, January 1985, pp. 44–46.

45. Bittner, "Eine positive Bilanz," p. 124.

46. *Frankfurter Allgemeine Zeitung*, June 15, 1985.

47. For a discussion of the price variables involved in national vs. multilateral procurement projects, see Keith Hartley, *NATO Arms Cooperation: A Study in Economics and Politics* (London: Allen and Unwin, 1983).

48. Accords were signed with Norway, Britain, Denmark, Belgium, Italy, the Netherlands, Spain, Greece, Switzerland, and Sweden. See *Armées d'aujourd'hui*, November 1984, p. 32, and Kolodziej, *Making and Marketing Arms*, p. 166.

49. Interview with French defense ministry official.

50. See, for example, the remarks by Georges Lemoine, a high defense ministry official, in *Le Monde*, February 21, 1982.

51. These included projects in the areas of command and control, precision-guided munitions, and stand-off weapons. See Timm R. Meyer, "Die Rüstungs-zusammenarbeit zwischen Grossbritannien und der Bundesrepublik Deutschland," in Karl Kaiser and John Roper, eds., *Die Stille Allianz: Deu'tsch-britische Sicherheitskooperation* (Bonn: Europa Union Verlag, 1987), pp. 278–79.

52. Interview with Joachim Heyden, *Wehrtechnik*, June 1986, p. 40.

53. See Cowen, *Defense Procurement*, pp. 269–71.

54. The 1982 guidelines are reprinted in the Bulletin of the German Press and Information Office, May 5, 1982, pp. 309–11. On the evolution of German arms export policy in the 1980s, see Frederic S. Pearson, "Of Leopards and Cheetahs: West Germany's Role as a Mid-Sized Arms Supplier," *Orbis*, Spring 1985, pp. 165–81.

————————————————————

CHAPTER 7

The Long Road to Genuine Dialogue, 1983–1988

The peace movement that had emerged in West Germany during the early 1980s, and the accompanying erosion of German confidence in nuclear deterrence, were sources of profound worry in Paris. The rise of the peace movement made French leaders conscious once again that France's strategic position depended on Germany remaining a solid and loyal member of NATO. And, as during the Pompidou years, the mere suggestion that Germany might set out on a course of its own led to exaggerated fears and an acute sensation of vulnerability on the part of the French political elite.

The French saw themselves as having an enormous stake in the INF deployment question, which they viewed as the litmus test of Germany's reliability. For Germany not to carry out the Pershing II and cruise missile deployments, they felt, would be tantamount to capitulation before Soviet intimidation, and this in turn would have potentially disastrous psychological consequences for the West.[1] Panicking in the realization of their limited leverage over Germany, French commentators conjured up the ghost of Rapallo and constructed fearful scenarios of German neutralization, unilateral disarmament, or of a separate Bonn-Moscow deal that would harshly compromise France's security.[2] Speaking for the French government, Defense Minister Hernu warned that "the energies rising in the young people of our neighbors are now expressed through the distorting prism of pacifism; they are likely to give in to the temptations of a disastrous neutralism which would create a void."[3]

French anxiety peaked in the months before the March 1983 German parliamentary elections. It appeared more and more likely that the Social Democrats, if they regained power, would refuse to carry out the scheduled

INF deployments. Viewed from Paris, the March elections thus loomed as a watershed for the Atlantic Alliance. This was the background of Mitterrand's famous speech to the German Bundestag on January 20, 1983. Mitterrand used the occasion, which commemorated the Elysée Treaty's twentieth anniversary, to insist on the absolute necessity of carrying out the 1979 two-track decision. What this meant, of course, even though the French president did not express himself in such bald terms, was that Germany should go forward with the scheduled Pershing II and cruise missile deployments.

The French leader's remarks drew a predictably mixed reception. On the one hand, Kohl and his government were delighted to have such a high-profile French endorsement for the unpopular deployment decision, and appreciated Mitterrand's courage in taking a stance that would expose him to criticism from domestic opponents and from Moscow. The opposition Social Democrats, by contrast, were enraged that Mitterrand had so emphatically cast his support behind Kohl only six weeks before the general election. As it turned out, the Social Democrats were soundly defeated in the election and the CDU-CSU-FDP coalition remained in place. The French government breathed a great sigh of relief. Somewhat anticlimactically, the Bundestag decided on November 22 by a vote of 286 to 226 to proceed on schedule with the INF deployments, finally laying to rest the most contentious defense issue in Germany since the 1950s.

THE CONTINUING ABSENCE OF COMMON GROUND

With the beginning of the INF deployments, French motivation for closer defense and security ties to Bonn started to ebb. As the earlier panic faded, in fact, it became increasingly obvious to Paris that the obstacles to closer Franco-German defense cooperation were as large as ever. Indeed, whereas Schmidt had sought to use the Franco-German partnership as a basis for greater European self-assertion vis-à-vis the United States, Kohl's team pursued the more traditional German strategy of using its special ties to Paris to try to pull France into closer strategic alignment with NATO.[4] Also, as noted in Chapter 5, Bonn's willingness to accept a greater role for conventional deterrence conjugated poorly with the Mitterrand government's reaffirmed commitment to strategic nuclear deterrence.

In 1982, when the expanded Franco-German discussions on defense and security issues began, observers in Germany had believed that the initiative signaled a new willingness on France's part to allow Bonn a consultative role in French tactical nuclear planning.[5] The German government soon began to probe along these lines, proposing that the Franco-German Commission discuss the targeting and employment concepts for French tactical nuclear weapons. Paris immediately quashed such suggestions by reiterating its view that questions touching on the use of French nuclear forces were for France to decide alone. As Prime Minister Pierre Mauroy underlined in a September 1983 speech: "Our nuclear systems constitute a totally independent strategic force, in the service of a doctrine which is our own. It is a question of arms of last resort for assuring the survival of our country. Our solidarity with our allies may not in any case infringe on this autonomy of decision."[6]

Once the initial novelty of the high-level defense consultations wore off, therefore, mutual disillusionment started to set in. By 1984 the bilateral talks had begun to stagnate, as each of the working groups rediscovered the barriers to cooperation that had plagued previous French and German governments. In the working groups on military cooperation and politico-strategic affairs, progress was blocked by the absolute French refusal to accommodate Germany on the question of tactical nuclear consultation. It was clear that the French plan to replace Pluton with Hadès did not resolve the problem as far as Bonn was concerned. Meanwhile, France's continued priority to nuclear modernization made it likely that its conventional forces would undergo further decline, a consideration that dampened initial German enthusiasm over the possibilities created by the *Force d'action rapide*. Finally, the talks on armaments co-production had yielded no notable breakthroughs. Tight procurement budgets, as well as the complications imposed on both sides by military and industrial interests, had defeated all attempts to reach agreement on joint production of a major weapon system.

German disappointment with the results of the talks took on an increasingly hard edge in the spring of 1984. Not surprisingly, much of the German criticism of Paris came from the SPD. Relations between the French and German Socialist parties had been strained from the beginning of Mitterrand's presidency. The SPD was annoyed that Mitterrand's government got along so well with the Kohl team (especially after its rather chilly treatment of Schmidt's government) and was alienated by Mitterrand's close alignment with Ronald Reagan and Margaret Thatcher on East-West issues. The memory of Mitterrand's 1983 Bundestag speech and the role it played in the SPD's subsequent electoral defeat was also a source of continuing resentment. SPD officials showed their discontent by stepping up their public criticism of France's policy of defense independence.[7] Much to the

French government's irritation, the SPD also began calling for the inclusion of French and British nuclear forces at the U.S.-Soviet INF negotiations under way in Geneva.[8]

The first half of 1984 also witnessed strong criticism of French defense policy by German conservatives. Alfred Dregger, chairman of the CDU/CSU Bundestag delegation, wrote an article for *Die Zeit* denouncing France's unwillingness to participate in the forward defense of Germany or to consult with Germany on the targeting and employment doctrine of its nuclear weapons.[9] CDU defense spokesman Jürgen Todenhöfer also joined the debate, remarking bitterly that Germany enjoyed only a "third-class security." "A Europe," he wrote, "in which the Federal Republic of Germany always stands at the head of the line when it is a question of financial sacrifices, [but] at the back of the line when it is a question of its security, is not an acceptable prospect for us."[10] A February 1984 meeting in Bonn between members of the French and German parliamentary defense committees revealed similar sentiments. The CDU, CSU, and SPD representatives all joined in calling on France to consult with Germany over the conditions of employment of its tactical nuclear forces.[11]

The situation that had emerged was highly uncomfortable for the French government. Across the German political spectrum, attitudes of impatience and disappointment toward France were evident. Although Kohl's government refrained from public criticism of French defense policy, and indeed tried to emphasize the positive in its statements about Franco-German security cooperation, it was clear that Dregger's article reflected the views of much of the CDU leadership.[12]

The possibility that a new defense policy consensus might form in Germany on the basis of despair at French nuclear nationalism was a chilling prospect for Paris. In 1984 the potential implications of German disillusion with France were perceived to be much greater than they had been for de Gaulle in the mid-1960s. Not only was the Germany of the 1980s far more self-confident and assertive than the Germany of the 1960s, but the INF debate had shattered Germany's former consensus over NATO nuclear strategy. In the Germany of the 1980s, a growing political movement—the Greens—called for withdrawal from the Atlantic Alliance. In the German public at large, varying degrees of unilateral disarmament were seriously debated as alternatives to existing Alliance defense arrangements. Perhaps worst from the French perspective was that mainstream political figures like Egon Bahr, the architect of *Ostpolitik*, were advocating the removal of all allied nuclear weapons from German soil, a policy that would undermine France's existing nuclear strategy as much as it would NATO's.[13]

Again, Antitank Helicopters

The French government therefore found itself anxiously searching for some impressive, tangible demonstration of progress in Franco-German defense relations to quell the tide of criticism pouring from Bonn. However, Paris remained unwilling to reverse the long-established French position on nuclear consultations, which had been solemnly incorporated into the Gaullist catechism during the Pluton stationing controversies of the 1970s. Instead, Mitterrand's government reached for the predictable solution: co-production with the Germans of a major weapon system. Thus it was that at the conclusion of the Franco-German summit of May 28–29, 1984, the two sides announced the joint development and production of an antitank helicopter.

The helicopter project, under intermittent discussion between the two governments since 1975, had already been rescued from the grave by Kohl and Mitterrand once before in the context of getting the new Franco-German security consultations off on a good footing (see Chapter 6). Since that point, however, disagreement on major aspects of the helicopter program had persisted. The memorandum of understanding signed at the May 1984 summit failed to resolve the disputes that had previously combined to block an accord. Significantly, however, the French did concede the overall program leadership to Germany and had made a major concession regarding the aircraft's targeting and night vision systems. The highly premature co-production announcement reflected above all the French government's urgent desire to demonstrate that the bilateral security talks could yield mutually advantageous results.

The Schmidt Proposal

Despite the nominal helicopter accord, Paris and Bonn remained far from achieving any fundamental breakthrough in their defense relationship. This underlying reality was perhaps best illustrated by reactions to an important speech delivered by former Chancellor Helmut Schmidt to the Bundestag on June 28, 1984.[14] In the speech, Schmidt proposed that France and Germany join in creating the basis for an autonomous West European defense system. Germany would contribute an army of eighteen divisions to the enterprise, while France would provide twelve divisions. Together, argued Schmidt, these thirty divisions would suffice to defend Central Europe and to deter a Soviet attack. The German forces would be entirely conventional, while France would make clear that its national nuclear force would be used to defend Germany as well as itself. In recognition of France's status as a permanent member of the United Nations Security Council, a guarantor of Berlin, and an independent nuclear power, the Franco-German defense arrangements would be under French leadership and command.

Carrying out the proposal, Schmidt noted, would require substantially increased defense expenditures by both sides. Germany would have to underwrite a large part of the development and production costs for shared conventional arms. France would probably need to spend more on conventional forces and less on nuclear forces. Finally, although the proposed arrangement would make France and Germany more self-reliant in defense questions, both countries would remain members of the Atlantic Alliance.

Schmidt's far-reaching proposal was especially interesting because it came very close to the type of arrangement that de Gaulle had apparently envisaged with the Fouchet Plan and the Elysée Treaty, namely, an autonomous European defense system led by a nuclear-armed France, but in which a non-nuclear Germany would provide a large part of the requisite manpower and funding. That Schmidt should make such a proposal indicated how little faith he continued to have in the existing Alliance system, which left Germany highly dependent on an unpredictable United States, and in which deterrence rested on nuclear scenarios that seemed less credible with each passing day.

Schmidt's speech met with complete silence on the part of the French and German governments. That Kohl's conservative government did not rush to embrace the ideas of a former Social Democratic chancellor was, to be sure, not very surprising. Not only would Schmidt's plan be costly, but its notion of a German defense under French command was contrary to the nationalist and Atlanticist orientation of Kohl's foreign policy team. More surprising was the utter lack of a French response to the speech, especially since Schmidt's proposals so closely resembled de Gaulle's own European design. By its silence Paris revealed how unwilling it was to move away from its established military doctrine, even if doing so could elevate France to the leadership of an autonomous and powerful Europe.

Mutual disillusionment with the Franco-German defense talks grew through the remainder of 1984 and into 1985. If the German side was dissatisfied with French inflexibility on the questions of nuclear consultations or an automatic commitment to Germany's defense, Paris for its part was increasingly disgruntled over the Kohl government's failure to treat France as a preferred partner in cooperative weapons projects. Indeed, despite the intensity of Franco-German discussions on weapons co-production from 1982 onward, Bonn still appeared to give as high a priority to armaments cooperation with the United States, Britain, and other European allies as with France. The Franco-German working group on armaments cooperation registered a daunting series of failures. In the autumn of 1984, Bonn declined to participate in two projects very important to the French: the SAMRO military observation satellite (see Chapter 6) and an advanced air defense system to succeed the aging Hawk missile system. The Germans also hesitated to join the French project for a European space shuttle (Hermès). In August 1985, plans for a European fighter aircraft broke down into two separate projects, one by the French and one by a British-German-Italian-Spanish consortium. As for the helicopter project, renewed disputes over the program's basic characteristics soon called the May 1984 agreement into question.[15]

Discord over Strategic Defense

The period 1984-1985 was also marked by tensions over the question of how to respond to the Strategic Defense Initiative (SDI) announced by President Reagan in March 1983.[16] As the project gradually took shape, the French government's attitude toward it grew increasingly hostile.[17] After all, an independent nuclear force was the cornerstone of France's security strategy, as well as the basis of its political weight in European and world affairs and the heart of its foreign policy consensus. To the extent that SDI called into question the long-term viability of strategic nuclear deterrence, all major parties in France regarded the program as utterly inimical to France's national interest.

In Germany, official skepticism toward SDI was more muted.[18] Although dubious of SDI's technical merits and deeply apprehensive about its implications for Alliance strategy, the Kohl government was unwilling to declare outright opposition to a project that was clearly a top priority for the Reagan administration. Instead, Bonn adopted a position, announced by the chancellor in February 1985, of highly conditional support for SDI.

Bonn's acquiescence in SDI, no matter how unenthusiastic, was resented in Paris as evidence of an underlying German willingness to see key French security interests betrayed. That Bonn's stance did not lead to a major breach in Franco-German relations, in fact, was due largely to the fact that by 1985 the French had concluded that neither superpower would be able to master the technical requirements of ballistic missile defense for many years to come.[19] Meanwhile, Washington's March 1985 invitation to the Europeans to participate in the SDI research program furnished Paris and Bonn with an additional apple of discord. Bonn's halfhearted acceptance of the idea of a European Research Coordinating Agency (Eureka), launched by Paris in response to the implications of SDI for Europe's industrial competitiveness, provided the French with still another grievance to add to their already long list of disappointments in the areas of armaments and technological cooperation.[20]

THE CONGEALED STATUS QUO

A quite striking feature of Franco-German defense relations in the first half of the 1980s was the way in which both France and Germany had become wedded to the European status quo, to the point that the strategic policies of both countries revolved essentially around efforts to preserve the existing situation from disruption. The late 1970s and early 1980s were not good years for the Western Alliance. Challenges to French and German foreign policy seemed to come from several directions at once. These included the gradual weakening of the U.S. security guarantee to Europe, the confidence-eroding leadership of the Alliance under Carter and Reagan, an apparently endless military buildup by the Soviet Union, and the breakdown of domestic consensus on defense policy in West Germany.

For Helmut Schmidt, these developments were worrisome enough to make him contemplate reviving de Gaulle's blueprint for a self-reliant Europe led by France. Schmidt gradually came to conclude that Bonn could carry out a foreign policy corresponding to German interests only if it succeeded in reducing its military dependence on Washington while at the same time retaining sufficient military capabilities to deflect Soviet political pressures. Accomplishing this feat would require a closer relationship with France—a relationship, in short, that would extend French nuclear deterrence to include West Germany, and that would present a unified Franco-German front to Washington as well as to Moscow. In effect Schmidt's proposal, as it had evolved by mid-1984, was a program for Western Europe—built around a Franco-German core—to begin striving again toward the essentials of great-power status.

Yet Schmidt's 1984 proposal found no resonance at all in Mitterrand's France or Kohl's Germany. Why not? The answer, fundamentally, is that both France and Germany had lost interest in recovering true great-power capabilities. During the first three decades after World War II, France and West Germany had both gradually ceased to strive for the military capabilities essential to a genuine great-power role. In the French case, this process had begun during the 1960s with the development of France's nuclear forces and the corresponding evolution of French strategic policy. In concentrating its limited resources on nuclear weapons, the French state consciously opted for a strategy of deterrence at the expense of its ability to defend itself (whether alone or in tandem with its NATO allies) against a full-scale conventional offensive by the Warsaw Pact. Of course, France continued to be protected indirectly by the NATO forces arrayed along the inter-German border, supplemented by U.S. extended nuclear deterrence; indeed, indirect protection by NATO was France's foremost strategic asset throughout the Cold War era. Secondarily, France was protected by its own national nuclear deterrent. France's strategic situation thus granted it a broad margin of maneuver at the rhetorical level, but meant that the French state lacked the conventional military capabilities to control its own immediate external environment, much less intervene effectively against the activities of either superpower elsewhere in the world. The evolution of French strategic doctrine in the 1960s and early 1970s contributed to this limitation: by subordinating France's conventional forces to strategic deterrence and explicitly forswearing a conventional defense of French territory, the French state effectively abjured great-power status.

This being the case, it was in no way apparent to French leaders in 1984 what they stood to gain by returning to de Gaulle's plan for a Franco-German military axis. To do so would require substantially increased expenditures on conventional forces as well as much closer coordination of French foreign policy with that of West Germany, two measures sure to encounter strong domestic political opposition. Schmidt's proposals, because they would be politically costly for any French government to pursue, and because they aimed to recover a military option that France had already given up and did not really believe in anyway, held little attraction for French leaders. What Paris wanted from the strategic dialogue renewed with Bonn in 1982 was not to lay the basis for an autonomous West European defense, but rather to encourage Germany to maintain its commitment to NATO so that France's existing strategic position would not be jeopardized.

The Germans, meanwhile, had given up great-power aspirations even more decisively than had the French. The tacit U.S. acceptance of Soviet domination in Eastern Europe (as demonstrated by the lack of an American military response to the Berlin Wall or to the Soviet interventions in

Hungary and Czechoslovakia), as well as the Western powers' denial of full political *Gleichberechtigung* to West Germany (as demonstrated by the nuclear control-sharing debate) had brought home to Bonn the strategic limitations of a policy of military strength. Under Brandt, the Social Democrats and the Free Democrats had increasingly viewed peaceful dialogue and détente rather than military capability as the means to reshape West Germany's relations with its eastern neighbors.

During the 1970s and 1980s, as the implications of flexible response gradually sank in and the credibility of U.S. nuclear guarantees continued to erode, German leaders came increasingly to believe that any extended conventional or tactical nuclear defense of Germany against a Warsaw Pact onslaught would be intolerably destructive of German lives and property. The nuclear modernization debates which began in the late 1970s did much to reinforce such views. By the mid-1980s, leaders in all of Germany's major political parties had begun to view the Bundeswehr more as a symbol of German solidarity with the Western Alliance than as an effective instrument for defending West German territory against the Soviet army. The Bundeswehr remained important as a necessary condition for American, French, and British alliance commitments to Germany, but as German leaders began to move away from a military conception of national security, the Bundeswehr's actual war-fighting capability became secondary to its symbolic functions. Like the French, the Germans were beginning to give up on the idea of conventional defense and therefore to attribute less importance to upgrading conventional capabilities. But whereas French strategic doctrine emphasized national nuclear capabilities as the key to effective deterrence, German doctrine increasingly emphasized the prevention of war through détente and arms control. Although Manfred Wörner, Kohl's first defense minister, strongly supported conventional defense and sought to enhance the Bundeswehr's war-fighting capabilities through systematic procurement of advanced conventional weapons, his approach failed to gain a solid constituency even in the CDU. Instead, Kohl's government, like those of Brandt and Schmidt, embraced détente wholeheartedly.

In this context, Kohl and his advisers were interested in closer defense cooperation with France for two main reasons: first, as a way to gain influence over French tactical nuclear doctrine; second, as a way to make France's strategic commitment to Germany more tangible, thereby increasing its value for deterrence. Kohl's government showed no desire to use defense cooperation with Paris as a basis for West European military self-reliance. To do so would be completely at odds with the underlying evolution of West German policy. It would require large and politically unpopular increases in Germany's conventional military effort. It would create a potential pretext for Washington to withdraw additional forces from Europe. It would accentuate Bonn's political deference toward Paris, which could hardly be appealing to the German public. And it would involve a military buildup that might endanger Germany's hard-won relations with the Soviet Union and the states of Eastern Europe.

These were the considerations that caused the governments in both Paris and Bonn to ignore Schmidt's far-reaching proposal of June 1984. Even had Schmidt still been chancellor at the time, it is difficult to imagine that he would have gotten far with such a proposal had he made it officially. There appeared to be little constituency for it on either side of the Rhine.

THE BREAKTHROUGH

By the summer of 1985, Franco-German defense relations had reached a virtual deadlock. The intensified discussions since 1982 had highlighted for both Paris and Bonn the divergences of their national interests and the incompatibility of their strategic doctrines, without yielding any compensating breakthroughs. Disillusion was mutual. It had become increasingly apparent, moreover, that the deadlock would be broken only if Paris went partway in meeting German demands for tactical nuclear consultations and for closer coordination of French and allied operational plans concerning the defense of German territory. The basic fact was that Kohl, with his Atlanticist orientation and cordial personal relations with Ronald Reagan, felt much less need for French support than Schmidt had felt in 1981 when he proposed a stronger Franco-German link. Once the INF deployment crisis had passed, the German government settled comfortably back into its traditional approach of putting ties to Washington ahead of ties to Paris. Developments in the Soviet Union had further reduced any pressure on Bonn to make innovations in its security policy. With Gorbachev's ascendance to the Soviet leadership in March 1985, U.S.-Soviet relations had finally begun improving from their five-year nadir.

Thus as long as the French remained unwilling to go beyond existing commitments regarding the use of their conventional or nuclear forces to defend Germany, the high-level bilateral meetings were of limited value to Bonn. It appeared likely that a continued French refusal to compromise might eventually cause the collapse of the entire consultative structure established in 1982. Given the enormous fanfare surrounding the establishment of the talks and the commitment of many high-level officials to the project, such a collapse would be a major foreign policy debacle for the Mitterrand government. It would likely also be a fatal setback to armaments co-production with Germany, already difficult enough in the best of times. Worst of all, feared the French, overt failure of the talks might cause a backlash that would push Germany toward precisely the nationalist-neutralist posture France wanted to prevent.

French fears about a potential "neutralist drift" in Germany had temporarily eased after Kohl's 1983 election victory, but began to revive as the direction of Kohl's evolving foreign policy became clearer. One source of French anxiety was the Kohl government's *Deutschlandpolitik*. Traditionally the CDU/CSU had taken a hard line toward the Soviet-backed regime in East Germany. On returning to power under Kohl, however, the CDU/CSU made no attempt to reverse the policy of inter-German détente set in place by the SPD governments of the 1970s. Instead, it became evident that Kohl's government would go to great lengths to promote rapprochement with East Germany despite the poor overall climate of East-West relations.[21] Under Kohl, official and unofficial links between the two Germanys multiplied. Even the harshest onetime critics of ties to East Germany, including Franz Josef Strauss, appeared by the mid-1980s to have accepted the idea of sheltering inter-German relations from the fallout of other East-West tensions.

Second, the French began to worry about Gorbachev's public relations offensive and its potential effects on Bonn. In his first months in office Gorbachev had announced a moratorium on Soviet nuclear weapons tests, proposed a chemical weapons-free zone in Central Europe, and in general conveyed an image of much greater flexibility on arms control issues than his predecessors. Gorbachev's dynamism and apparent readiness to strike deals held appeal for broad segments of the German political elite. Once again the French confronted their recurring nightmare of a separate German-Soviet deal at their expense. If they were unwilling to offer Germany anything of value, the French were in danger of becoming expendable.

As France's alternatives came into focus, therefore, the pressure to make a significant gesture toward Germany's basic demands increased. Ultimately the Mitterrand government decided it had too much at stake in the bilateral security talks to accept the idea of their complete breakdown. The first substantive French step toward meeting German concerns came in the joint declaration on military and strategic questions issued at the February 1986 Franco-German summit meeting in Paris.[22] In the statement, the two sides announced an agreement to expand the operational military cooperation between their armed forces. Joint studies were to be conducted on how best to employ French forces, especially the FAR, if they should be used in a military action on German soil. Appropriate joint maneuvers by French and German forces were to be arranged later. Also announced was a project for joint training of military officers. Finally, the statement declared that the French president would, "within the limits imposed by the extreme speed of such decisions," try to consult with the German chancellor before using French prestrategic nuclear arms on German territory. The two sides acknowledged, however, that "decisions in this matter cannot be divided."

At a minimum, the February announcement represented a new French willingness to move beyond long-established taboos in declaratory policy. Just how much significance should be attached to the announcement regarding nuclear consultations was open to some doubt. The French pledge did not amount to allowing Germany a veto over France's resort to nuclear arms, and in any case was conditional on having sufficient time for meaningful consultations to take place—something that might well not be the case if a situation calling for resort to tactical nuclear weapons in the Central European theater were to arise. Nevertheless, the announcement did mark an important departure from France's previous statements regarding consultations on its use of tactical nuclear weapons. As such, it was a first step toward meaningful reconciliation of French and German defense strategies.

Meanwhile, the idea of troop maneuvers based on joint Franco-German studies was an important practical breakthrough. Given France's continued absence from the integrated NATO command, joint maneuvers were an especially useful means of developing effective procedures for the employment of French forces in an allied defense of West Germany. The first major exercise carried out under the new agreement took place near Würzburg in September 1986. Entitled "Franconian Shield," the maneuvers involved some 50,000 German, American, and French troops based in southern Germany, and included substantial components of the 1st French tank division.[23] The 3,500 French troops that took part represented the largest French participation in a military exercise on German territory since 1966.

Even more significant were the widely noted "Bold Sparrow" maneuvers of September 1987, in which components of the FAR came from their bases inside France to support German forces in central Bavaria.[24] The exercise involved 20,000 French troops, about half the FAR's total strength, together with 50,000 German troops. Intended to demonstrate France's willingness to help repulse an invasion of West Germany, the Bold Sparrow maneuvers provided an important symbol of Franco-German solidarity.

However, the positive significance of the exercise was overshadowed in part by the political flap that occurred when the French side refused to allow NATO officers to attend the maneuvers as observers. France's insistence on the strictly bilateral basis of the exercise, which also meant refusing to allow military units from other NATO countries to take part, contradicted Germany's desire to share the insights gained from the maneuvers with its other allies. The exercise also revealed serious problems in coordinating the battle actions of French and German units, raising once again old questions about France's ability to contribute effectively to European defense as long as its forces remained outside NATO's integrated command structure.[25]

GERMANY TURNS TOWARD FRANCE

Beginning in the autumn of 1986, Franco-German relations underwent a sharp turn toward closer strategic coordination. The fundamental reason for this shift was German dismay over the course of U.S. foreign policy. Whereas Kohl's government had earlier been impatient with French intransigence and had appeared to regard its ties with Paris as a matter of secondary importance, new developments began pushing the German government to reconsider its priorities.

One development was cumulative West German concern over the condition of the American economy. Under Reagan, U.S. government spending had swung sharply into deficit. Beginning in 1983, deficits in the federal budget averaged more than $200 billion per year. Contrary to the Reagan administration's assertions, moreover, it had become clear that the deficits were structural rather than cyclical in nature.[26] Given the apparent lack of political will in both the administration and Congress to undertake serious deficit reduction, many West Europeans feared a drastic erosion in America's international capabilities. Whatever Reagan's rhetoric about renewed American strength, a pattern of massive annual budget deficits must inevitably lead to cutbacks and underfunding for U.S. strategic commitments abroad.[27] For Germany, the prospect of an economically weakened United States made France appear more valuable as a strategic partner.

A second and even more urgent source of German anxiety was the Reagan-Gorbachev summit meeting in Reykjavik in October 1986. Reykjavik deeply undermined European confidence in the United States. Events at the summit seemed to demonstrate, in spectacular fashion, the amateurism and unreliability of American foreign policy. Leaders throughout Western Europe were appalled to realize that Reagan had very nearly accepted a deal to eliminate all ballistic missiles within ten years, a step that would have abandoned the whole foundation of deterrence on which NATO strategy had rested for decades. Even worse, press reports soon made it evident that Reagan and his team had undertaken discussions on this and other far-reaching proposals with almost no advance preparation. It was stupefying to European leaders that Reagan had contemplated such a radical alteration of U.S. and Alliance strategy without thorough study and without prior consultations of any sort with allied governments.[28]

German leaders were also concerned by developments in the U.S.-Soviet negotiations on intermediate nuclear forces (INF) in Europe. At Reykjavik, Reagan and Gorbachev had reached the basic outlines of an agreement to eliminate from Europe all U.S. and Soviet nuclear weapon systems with a range of 1,000 to 5,000 kilometers, a plan known as the "zero option." In April 1987, Gorbachev proposed a "second zero": the elimination from Europe of all U.S. and Soviet short-range intermediate forces with ranges of 500 to 1,000 kilometers. Kohl opposed the second zero, fearing it might lead to the strategic decoupling of West Germany from the rest of NATO. He preferred instead a U.S.-Soviet agreement that would set low equal ceilings for all short-range nuclear systems, thereby limiting the buildup of Soviet short-range missiles in Eastern Europe but retaining Germany's nuclear coupling to its allies. Meanwhile, U.S. leaders including Reagan, Secretary of State George Schultz, and Defense Secretary Casper Weinberger strongly favored the second zero and placed heavy pressure on Bonn to give its assent. Kohl's government, isolated on the issue both domestically and internationally, had little choice but to give in.[29] In the aftermath of the affair, Kohl and other CDU leaders began to reconsider the importance of developing a more assertive West European posture on key security issues. Given that Washington seemed inclined to negotiate arms control accords that met its own needs but ignored important West German interests, Kohl began searching for ways to build the Franco-German link into a stronger counterbalance to U.S. positions.[30]

In the end, Reagan's actions had affected Kohl in much the same way Carter's had affected Schmidt: they created distrust toward Washington and a corresponding incentive to buttress reliance on NATO with a strengthened Franco-German partnership. In 1987, for the first time since joining the Atlantic Alliance, the West German government began to show an interest in developing Franco-German defense ties as a possible long-term alternative to NATO. The traditional West German view, which had regarded Franco-German defense ties as useful only insofar as they could pull the French back into NATO's orbit, began giving way to a new premise that intra-European defense relationships were valuable in themselves given American unreliability.

The French government, it should be noted, was also worried by the developments of 1986–1987. The French worried that the successful conclusion of an INF treaty might generate new pressures for the inclusion of French and British nuclear forces in arms control agreements.[31] Like the Germans, they were disturbed by the proceedings at Reykjavik, and they feared that both Reykjavik and the INF treaty signified the beginning of an American disengagement from Europe.[32] They worried that the implications of Reykjavik and the INF treaty might erode German faith in the U.S. nuclear guarantee and thereby reinforce tendencies toward neutralism.[33] They worried that the German government was being seduced by Gorbachev's disarmament proposals, and were dismayed when German leaders, including Foreign Minister Hans-Dietrich Genscher, stated that Gorbachev should be taken at his word.[34] Finally, the French were concerned over German reactions to the Chernobyl nuclear disaster. Although the Chernobyl accident had no logical connection to the issue of nuclear armament, it nonetheless exacerbated the popular anxieties about nuclear war that had appeared in Germany during the INF modernization debate.[35] For all these reasons, French leaders perceived the need to show solidarity with West Germany in a way that would counteract sentiment for denuclearization.[36]

Still the practical question remained: what could be done to strengthen the Franco-German defense partnership while remaining faithful to the policy of independence on which France's defense consensus still rested? Neither President Mitterrand, a Socialist, nor Jacques Chirac, a leader of the French Right and prime minister since March 1986, had any intention of abandoning the Gaullist framework of French defense policy. Both leaders, however, were willing to engage in incremental steps to deepen Franco-German defense cooperation and to build up Western Europe's assertion of its defense interests vis-à-vis the United States.

Beginning in the fall of 1987, it was possible to detect some slight modifications in French declaratory doctrine which seemed intended to reassure Germany about French intentions. In a speech on December 12, for example, Chirac went beyond the statements of previous French governments in declaring that if Germany were attacked, France's military response would be "immediate and without reservation."[37] Mitterrand, on a visit to West Germany in October 1987, also sought to reassure the Germans about French nuclear doctrine. He made a point of implying that even if French tactical nuclear weapons were employed in battle against an aggressor, such weapons would not necessarily land on German territory.[38] The French government showed that these were not just empty words by its subsequent announcement that the range of the Hadès missile, intended for deployment in the early 1990s, would be increased yet again, from 350 kilometers to 500.[39] The longer range would create more possibilities for the missile to overshoot Germany if it were ever actually used in battle.

A second new development in 1987 was the announcement that France and Germany would create an army brigade consisting of troops from both countries.[40] It was Kohl who, in June, initially suggested the formation of a joint Franco-German military unit. Such a unit would have great significance as a symbol of deepened bilateral cooperation. It would give a concrete existence to Franco-German ties which summit meetings and formal declarations alone could not provide. The idea of a joint brigade had a certain practical logic in that a brigade-sized unit would be large enough to convey seriousness of intent, yet small enough not to cause a major controversy in the Alliance or in French domestic politics. Both Paris and Bonn agreed that the brigade should be militarily functional, not just a showpiece for parades. It was decided that the brigade would consist of 4,200 troops and would be assembled from existing French and German forces. The unit would not be part of NATO's integrated command structure, but could be placed under operational NATO control if circumstances warranted. The unit would serve as a laboratory for the development of multinational military units, and for improving the interoperability of French and German forces as a whole.[41]

The French and German governments also agreed in 1987 on a further initiative, the creation of a bilateral Defense and Security Council. Like the joint brigade, the joint defense council began as a German idea but quickly gained French support.[42] On paper, the council was a far-reaching and ambitious project. Given its membership, which was to consist of the French and German heads of government, foreign ministers, defense ministers, and armed forces chiefs of staff, the council would possess the political authority for genuine coordination of French and German strategic policies. The council was to meet at least twice per year, alternately in France and Germany, and to oversee the work of the Franco-German Defense and Security Commission established in 1982. To give it institutional structure, the council would also have a secretariat based in Paris.

The council's main purposes were to be (1) the development of common concepts in the area of defense and security; (2) the progressive harmonization of French and German positions on all questions having to do with

European defense and security, including the areas of arms control and disarmament; (3) responsibility for decisions in regard to joint military units such as the Franco-German brigade; (4) responsibility for decisions in regard to bilateral military maneuvers, joint officer training, and other mutual support arrangements; and (5) upgrading of the equipment and interoperability of the French and German armed forces and improvement of cooperation in armaments production. Because of the importance of the initiative, the two governments decided to put it into the form of an official protocol to the 1963 Elysée Treaty. Mitterrand and Kohl signed the protocol in January 1988 (on the treaty's twenty-fifth anniversary), and the French and German parliaments ratified it in December.[43]

In 1987 Paris and Bonn also finally overcame the obstacles holding up progress on their only major ongoing joint weapons project, the antitank helicopter. Since the initial development and production agreement of May 1984, the project had experienced repeated setbacks. The 1984 accord had itself been signed for political reasons before several of the key issues regarding the helicopter's development were settled (see Chapter 6). As those issues remained unresolved, the projected costs of the program rapidly increased, leading both the French defense ministry and the Bundestag's defense committee to have second thoughts about the program. But Mitterrand and Kohl, each of whom had a large political investment in the project, adamantly insisted that it move forward. For Kohl in particular, the collapse of the helicopter project was unacceptable given his determination to deepen Germany's defense relationship with France. The German side therefore finally gave in on the issue of greatest concern to Paris, namely, the helicopter's targeting and night-vision system. Instead of equipping its own helicopters with the U.S.-made TADS/PNVS system, Bonn agreed that all versions of the helicopter would employ a European-developed targeting system. This concession paved the way for a new framework agreement signed in July 1987 by the French and German defense ministers.[44] Under the revised agreement, Germany also gave up its role as program leader. Aérospatiale and MBB instead established a joint subsidiary company, Eurocopter, to oversee the project. Following the signing of a formal Memorandum of Understanding in November 1987, the development of the helicopter at last got under way.

The European Dimension

At the same time that Paris and Bonn were taking steps to expand and intensify their bilateral defense cooperation, they were also taking steps to intensify defense cooperation among West European states as a group. But in contrast to the bilateral measures, where the German government had tended to take the initiative, leadership for innovations at the European level came principally from the French.

One important development was the successful negotiation of the Single European Act, which renewed a process of economic integration in the European Community that had languished since the Luxembourg Compromise of 1966. Although proposals to reform the EC had been gestating for years, real progress toward reform occurred only in 1984, when Mitterrand's government indicated its willingness to move beyond the constraints which the 1966 compromise had imposed.[45] During 1984–1985, even as Franco-German defense cooperation appeared to have reached its limits, Mitterrand and Kohl together launched an initiative aimed at deepening the Community's economic and political integration. Support for the initiative among other EC member states led to a conference of the EC governments, which in turn led to agreement on the Single European Act. The act, which was signed in February 1986 and went into force in July 1987, reintroduced elements of majority voting into EC decision making, broadened the EC framework, and provided for the establishment of a single market among the EC states by 1992. Importantly from the perspective of European defense cooperation, the act also expanded EC competence in the area of foreign policy. Article 30.1 of the act called on EC members to "endeavor jointly to formulate and implement a common foreign policy"; Article 30.6 affirmed the readiness of the members to "coordinate their positions more closely on the political and economic aspects of security."[46] While defense policy per se remained outside the Community's responsibilities, the Single European Act represented a significant step toward incorporating defense and security issues into the process of European integration.

A second French initiative on European defense concerned the Western European Union (WEU), the organization established by the modified Brussels Treaty of 1954. WEU was the only European body with formal responsibilities for military defense. Under Article V of the modified Brussels Treaty, member states pledged themselves to provide "all the military and other aid and assistance in their power" to any other member subjected to armed attack in Europe.[47] Since France, Germany, Britain, and Italy were all members of WEU, it was possible, at least in theory, for the organization to provide the basis of an autonomous West European defense system. From the outset, however, WEU had in effect handed over its defense responsibilities to NATO. WEU appeared redundant, and although it continued to exist, its periodic meetings had little real significance and were widely ignored.

But in late 1981, Mitterrand's government began to show interest in reactivating the WEU.[48] This interest had its sources chiefly in French anxiety over the growing German peace movement. French proposals to revive the WEU began shortly after the first large peace demonstrations in West Germany opposing the decision on INF modernization. In the French view, the German peace movement demonstrated the need for an organization that could discuss the political aspects of defense and security questions from a purely European perspective.[49] The French believed, for example, that if the two-track decision on INF modernization had been discussed and approved by a purely European defense body, it would have commanded much greater support among the German public. As it was, many Germans felt (even if inaccurately) that the decision had been imposed on them by the United States and that they had no control over their own fate. The INF decision thus produced neutralist sentiments which made it difficult for the German government to maintain public support for a strong defense.

Kohl's government agreed with the rationale behind the French proposal and quickly became a strong supporter of reactivating WEU.[50] The British and Dutch governments took somewhat longer to persuade, but finally it was agreed that the foreign and defense ministers of the seven WEU states would meet in a special session of the WEU to mark the thirtieth anniversary of the modified Brussels Treaty. At the meeting, which took place in Rome in October 1984, it was decided to reactivate the organization through twice-yearly meetings of the WEU foreign and defense ministers and the establishment of working groups to follow up on their decisions. The ministers agreed that they would "seek to harmonize their views on the specific conditions of security in Europe." Particular areas of focus were to include arms control and disarmament, East-West relations, burden-sharing in the Alliance, the political aspects of European armaments cooperation, and defense questions in general.[51]

The first substantive topic to come before the revived WEU, as it turned out, was the difficult question of a common European position on the American SDI program.[52] Although misgivings about SDI were widely shared among WEU member states, U.S. pressure on the Europeans to support SDI made both the British and the Germans unwilling to adopt an openly critical stance. As a result, it proved impossible to develop a common position. After this discouraging start, the WEU again faded from view for a time.

In the wake of Reykjavik, however, the French and German governments agreed once again on the need to develop common European positions on key security issues such as arms control.[53] Prodded by both Paris and Bonn, the WEU drafted a Platform on European Security Interests, approved on October 27, 1987.[54] The platform declared the WEU states' intention to develop "a more cohesive European defense identity" consistent with their commitment to the Atlantic Alliance. Although the platform was only a statement of intent that did not in itself alter the U.S.-European relationship, the second awakening of WEU in 1987 did signal a new determination among European governments to develop a more unified voice on security issues as a counterbalance to American unilateralism. The concept of European defense identity would acquire increasing significance in the years to follow.

Again, Limits to Cooperation

The developments of 1987 marked a genuine turning point in the history of the Atlantic Alliance. Paris and Bonn had initiated a broad spectrum of measures intended to give their defense relationship more substance and to lay the basis for greater defense coordination in the future. For the first time in its history, the Bonn government appeared ready to move toward the type of Franco-German political union which de Gaulle had proposed to Adenauer in 1962 but which few German leaders other than Adenauer had been willing to consider in earnest.

As it turned out, however, world events overtook the evolving Franco-German partnership before the new initiatives of 1987 had time to bear fruit. In particular, the accelerating renovation of Soviet domestic and foreign policies under Gorbachev transformed Bonn's own strategic calculus. Traditional Soviet foreign policy, whose main instrument in Europe had been the steady buildup of military forces, never really allowed Bonn any option other than constantly attempting to reinforce its alliance partnerships with the United States, France, and Britain. But under Gorbachev, the cooperative side of Soviet-German relations rapidly expanded.[55] In 1987–1988, the Soviet Union greatly increased the number of ethnic Germans it permitted to emigrate to West Germany. Moscow and Bonn signed new bilateral agreements in several areas including cultural exchanges, environmental protection, and maritime safety. The Soviet government invited a variety of leading German politicians to Moscow for official visits, culminating in Kohl's trip to Moscow in October 1988. Gorbachev himself visited Bonn in June 1989.

The growing cordiality of Soviet-West German relations took place in the context of Moscow's apparent readiness for serious disarmament measures. In a December 1988 speech at the United Nations, for example, Gorbachev announced substantial unilateral reductions of Soviet forces in Eastern Europe and the European Soviet Union, and stated that Soviet military doctrine would shift to a strictly defensive posture. In effect, Gorbachev's initiatives overshadowed the accomplishments of closer Franco-German military cooperation. If Gorbachev could in fact be taken at his word, West Germany stood to gain much more by negotiating a reduced threat from Moscow than by obtaining firmer assurances of solidarity from Paris. In the late 1980s as in the early 1970s, French leaders found themselves increasingly on the sidelines as West Germany and the Soviet Union joined to reshape the European order.

NOTES

1. See, for example, Dominique Moïsi, "La France et la crise des euromissiles," *Défense nationale*, August–September 1983, pp. 39–40.

2. Examples include André Glucksmann, *La force du vertige* (Paris: Grasset, 1983); Joseph Rovan, "Réflexions sur la crise allemande," *Politique étrangère*, 1983, no. 1, pp. 39–46, and "Le problème allemand," *Défense nationale*, December 1982, pp. 27–35; and Gabriel Robin, "The German Problem Revisited," *Atlantic Quarterly*, Autumn 1983, pp. 191–200. For a comprehensive and pointedly ironic overview of foreign anxieties regarding Germany, see Eberhard Schulz and Peter Danylow, *Bewegung in der deutschen Frage? Die ausländischen Besorgnisse über die Entwicklung in den beiden deutschen Staaten* (Bonn: Europa Union Verlag, 1984).

3. Hernu, "Equilibre, dissuasion, volonté," p. 19, quoted in Joffe, *The Limited Partnership*, p. 36.

4. Kolboom, "Im Westen nichts Neues," p. 87.

5. See, for example, Ernst Weisenfeld, "Flankenschutz aus Paris," *Die Zeit*, October 29, 1982, p. 11.

6. Mauroy, "La stratégie de la France," speech of September 20, 1983, *Défense nationale*, November 1983, p. 11.

7. See, for example, the remarks by SPD foreign policy spokesman Karsten Voigt reported in *Die Welt*, March 1, 1984.

8. See, for example, the remarks of Hans-Jochen Vogel, the SPD's 1983 candidate for chancellor, cited in *Le Monde*, September 25–26, 1983.

9. Alfred Dregger, "Paris muss Farbe bekennen," *Die Zeit*, March 23, 1984, p. 4.

10. Jürgen Todenhöfer, "Eine europäische Atomstreitmacht als zweite Säule," *Die Welt*, April 17, 1984.

11. *Die Welt*, February 23, 1984.

12. *Washington Post*, April 20, 1984.

13. See Egon Bahr, "Atomare Klassenunterschiede," *Der Spiegel*, February 13, 1984, pp. 36–37.

14. The text of the speech is reprinted in Deutscher Bundestag, Stenographische Berichte, 10. Wahlperiode, 77. Sitzung, June 28, 1984, pp. 5596–5603.

15. See Heisbourg, "Für einen neuen Anfang," pp. 132–36.

16. On the implications of SDI for Europe, and European reactions to the U.S. initiative, see Ivo H. Daalder, *The SDI Challenge to Europe* (Cambridge, Mass.: Ballinger, 1987); Hans Günter Brauch, ed., *Star Wars and European Defense* (New York: St. Martin's Press, 1987); Sanford Lakoff and Randy Willoughby, eds., *Strategic Defense and the Western Alliance* (Lexington, Mass.: D. C. Heath, 1987); and Pierre Lellouche, ed., *L'Initiative de défense stratégique et la sécurité de l'Europe* (Paris: IFRI, 1986).

17. Pierre Lellouche, "Frankreich, SDI und die Sicherheit Europas," in Kaiser and Lellouche, *Deutsch-französische Sicherheitspolitik*, p. 243.

18. See Karl Kaiser, "SDI und deutsche Politik," in Kaiser and Lellouche, *Deutsch-französische Sicherheitspolitik*, pp. 266–68, and Wolfram Hanrieder, *Germany, America, Europe* (New Haven: Yale University Press, 1989), pp. 122–30.

19. Article by Bernard Brigouleix in *Le Monde*, March 2, 1985.

20. For details on Eureka see Jean-Baptiste Main de Boissière, "Le programme Eurêka," *Défense nationale*, December 1986, and Wayne Sandholtz, *High-Tech Europe* (Berkeley: University of California Press, 1992), pp 257–97.

21. See Richard Löwenthal, "The German Question Transformed," *Foreign Affairs*, Winter 1984/85, pp. 303–15; Walther Leisler Kiep, "The New Deutschlandpolitik," *Foreign Affairs*, Winter 1984/85, pp. 316–29; and Hanrieder, *Germany, America, Europe*, pp. 214–17.

22. The text appears in *Europa-Archiv*, 1986, no. 9, pp. D235–37.

23. See Rolf Födisch, "'Fränkischer Schild'—Manöver des III. Korps der Bundeswehr," *Österreichische Militärische Zeitschrift*, 1986, no. 6, pp. 529–40.

24. See Horst Pleiner, "'Kecker Spatz—Moineau hardi'—Deutsch-französische Heeresübung 1987," *Österreichische Militärische Zeitschrift*, 1987, no. 6, pp. 512–27; also the reports in *Défense nationale*, December 1987, pp. 176–79, and *International Defense Review*, 11/1987, p. 1458.

25. See Jörg Baldauf, "The Accomplishments of Bilateral Security Cooperation—A West German View," in Laird, *Strangers and Friends*, pp. 120–22, and Leimbacher, *Die unverzichtbare Allianz*, pp. 167–71.

26. Michael Kreile, "Aufschwung und Risiko: Die Wirtschafts- und Haushaltspolitik der Reagan-Administration," in Hartmut Wasser, ed., *Die Ära Reagan: Eine erste Bilanz* (Stuttgart: Klett, 1988), pp. 162–84.

27. See, for example, Michael Howard, "A European Perspective on the Reagan Years," *Foreign Affairs*, America and the World 1987/88, pp. 478–93.

28. See James Schlesinger, "Reykjavik and Revelations: A Turn of the Tide?" *Foreign Affairs*, America and the World 1986, pp. 426–46, and Howard, "A European Perspective."

29. See Thomas Risse-Kappen, *The Zero Option: INF, West Germany, and Arms Control* (Boulder, Colo.: Westview, 1988), pp. 114–42, and Leimbacher, *Die unverzichtbare Allianz*, pp. 136–47.

30. Leimbacher, *Die unverzichtbare Allianz*, pp. 145–53.

31. Dominique Moïsi, "French Foreign Policy: The Challenge of Adaptation," *Foreign Affairs*, Fall 1988, p. 155.

32. Philip H. Gordon, *A Certain Idea of France* (Princeton: Princeton University Press, 1993), p. 149.

33. For example, François-Georges Dreyfus, "RFA: Le péril national-neutraliste," *Politique internationale*, Autumn 1987, pp. 185–200.

34. Ingo Kolboom, "Der Blick nach Osten—Von der französischen 'Détente' und der deutschen 'Ostpolitik' zu einer gemeinsamen Öffnung nach Osten?" in André Brigot, Peter Schmidt, and Walter Schütze, eds., *Sicherheits- und Ostpolitik: Deutsch-französische Perspektiven* (Baden-Baden: Nomos, 1989), pp. 130–31.

35. See Dieter Mayer-Simeth, "La peur de l'atome: Une nouvelle composante de l'âme allemande?" in Bernard Brigouleix and Joseph Rovan, eds., *Que devient l'Allemagne?* (Paris: Editions Anthropos, 1986), pp. 147–54.

36. See, for example, the essay by Jean-Pierre Chevènement in *Le Monde*, June 18, 1987.

37. Jacques Chirac, "La France et les enjeux de la sécurité européenne" (speech of December 12, 1987), *Défense nationale*, February 1988, p. 16.

38. Gordon, *A Certain Idea*, p. 154. See also the interview with Mitterrand published in *Le Nouvel Observateur*, December 18, 1987, p. 25.

39. Peter Schmidt, "The Franco-German Defence and Security Council," *Aussenpolitik*, 1989, no. 4, p. 366.

40. See *Le Monde*, June 21–22 and July 19–20, 1987.

41. Leimbacher, *Die unverzichtbare Allianz*, pp. 155–58.

42. For details on the origins of the council and its activities in 1989–1990 see Leimbacher, *Die unverzichtbare Allianz*, pp. 174–80.

43. The protocol is reprinted in Reinhardt Rummel, ed., *The Evolution of an International Actor: Western Europe's New Assertiveness* (Boulder, Colo.: Westview, 1990), pp. 307–9.

44. *Frankfurter Allgemeine Zeitung*, July 17, 1987, and *Le Monde*, July 18, 1987.

45. See Andrew Moravcsik, "Negotiating the Single European Act: National Interests and Conventional Statecraft in the European Community," *International Organization*, Winter 1991, pp. 19–56.

46. See Rummel, *Evolution of an International Actor*, pp. 325–27.

47. Text in Radoux, *France and NATO*, p. 21.

48. See, for example, *Le Monde*, December 3, 1981, February 12, 1982, and December 2, 1982; and *Le Figaro*, June 16, 1982.

49. Interviews with French foreign ministry officials.

50. *Le Monde*, February 25, 1984.

51. See Western European Union, Document 989, *The Rome Declaration*, October 27, 1984.

52. See *Le Monde*, April 3, 1985, and the *Frankfurter Allgemeine Zeitung*, November 14, 1985.

53. For a statement of official French views in this regard, see the remarks by Prime Minister Jacques Chirac reprinted in *Le Monde*, December 4, 1986.

54. The platform is reprinted in Rummel, *Evolution of an International Actor*, pp. 310–15.

55. See F. Stephen Larrabee, "The View from Moscow," in Larrabee, ed., *The Two German States and European Security* (New York: St. Martin's, 1989), pp. 182–205.

——————————————————————

CHAPTER 8

Strategic Adaptation in a Post–Cold War World, 1989–1995

The political transformation of Eastern Europe during the second half of 1989 had enormous implications for Western foreign policies. With the astonishing collapse of Communist regimes throughout Eastern Europe and the wholly unexpected opening of the Berlin Wall on November 9, Western leaders suddenly found that key assumptions of the Cold War era no longer held true. The post-1945 order seemed to have disappeared for good, and old bearings seemed meaningless in the unknown waters of the new era. One of the principal implications of the wall's demise was that German reunification, which had long seemed an impossibly remote prospect, abruptly emerged as a concrete possibility. Chancellor Kohl, ordinarily hesitant in articulating a clear position on controversial issues, reacted in this case decisively to the new opportunity. On November 28, less than three weeks after the wall was down, Kohl delivered a speech to the German Bundestag in which he outlined a ten-point program for the eventual confederation of the two German states.[1] With the nearly total disintegration of Communist party authority in East Germany during the first week of December, almost anything seemed possible.

Predictably, the French government reacted with anxiety. Throughout the Cold War era, anything that seemed to lead to a major change in Germany's status had revived old fears that Germany might become "unstuck" from the West and begin pursuing policies antithetical to French interests.[2] As in 1970, Paris became uneasy because of its obviously limited influence over the pace and scope of developments in the German question. Officially the French government was in favor of eventual German reunification, a position stated by de Gaulle in 1959 and reiterated by subsequent French governments. Mitterrand had himself publicly endorsed reunification as a long-run goal on several occasions. But French leaders (like everyone else) had never anticipated that the barriers between the two Germanys might fall so quickly.

If it took place, German reunification would have significant implications for France's international status. Not only would it make Germany bigger and more powerful (and France smaller by comparison), but it would deprive France of one of its principal sources of leverage over Germany and one of its major claims to great-power rank, namely, its status as one of the Four Powers legally responsible for Berlin and for Germany as a whole. With German unification would come a final end to the restrictions on German sovereignty that France, together with Britain, the United States, and the Soviet Union, had exercised since 1945. In the French view, any development so momentous must occur in a framework that took account of the interests of other European states and with appropriate safeguards to protect existing boundaries and European stability.[3] If reunification were going to occur, the French wanted to exercise fully their formal legal rights to manage the process. The French government was profoundly irritated that Kohl seemed to be taking the question of reunification into his own hands. In addition, Mitterrand took it as a personal affront that Kohl had said nothing to him about the ten–point plan even though the two leaders had dined together on the Saturday preceding Kohl's speech.[4]

The French also felt placed on the defensive by U.S. policy. President Bush seemed to encourage the German government in the very self-assertiveness that the French found so unsettling. Visiting West Germany at the end of May 1989, Bush had described the Germans as America's "partners in leadership."[5] He also specifically and publicly supported the idea of German unification on several occasions between April and December 1989.[6] After the Berlin Wall came down, Washington adopted a policy of full support for Kohl's efforts at unification, but with an active U.S. engagement aimed at preventing destabilizing developments during the transition to a unified German state. This approach was sharply at odds with the French (and British) view that unification should proceed slowly and that the Four Powers should have primary responsibility for overseeing the process.[7]

On December 12, U.S. Secretary of State James Baker delivered a major speech in West Berlin on the future role of the Atlantic Alliance, calling for expanded NATO involvement in arms control and the settlement of regional disputes. The French government began to see itself as the victim of an implicit Washington-Bonn axis, in which Washington allowed Bonn a free hand in dealing with the Soviets for unification in exchange for Germany's support of U.S. attempts to dominate post–Cold War Europe through the expansion of NATO's political dimension.[8] And in fact, Bush and Kohl did make a crucial bilateral deal at Camp David on the weekend of February 25, 1990, when Bush agreed to the idea of reunifying Germany as quickly as possible in exchange for the chancellor's promise that a reunified Germany would remain fully integrated in NATO.[9]

Mitterrand's actions in late 1989 and early 1990 can be understood as an attempt to reassert French interests in the rapidly evolving situation. The French president traveled to meet with Soviet and East German leaders in December, and on both occasions called for caution in proceeding toward German unification. These maneuvers, which of course greatly annoyed Kohl and his advisers, were aimed not so much at preventing unification as at reminding the Germans that Paris could make life unpleasant for them if they did not take care to respect French interests and rights.[10] Mitterrand's March 1990 meeting with Polish leaders, at which he sympathized publicly with Polish concerns about a unified Germany's commitment to the Oder-Neisse boundary, was in the same vein. To a certain extent the French president's actions also seemed motivated by personal vindictiveness toward Kohl for having omitted to consult with him before setting his unification policy in motion. Certainly Mitterrand's failure to notify Kohl before announcing his December trip to East Germany, and his snub of Kohl's invitation to attend the official opening of the Brandenburg Gate, seemed to serve no purpose beyond a private settling of scores.[11]

But by the early months of 1990, the need for a more constructive French policy was manifest. The pace of events was accelerating, and France ran the risk of being left behind with nothing to show for its stubbornness. Meeting with Kohl and Genscher at the Kremlin in February, Gorbachev conceded that "the Germans themselves should decide on the course, the forms and time-frame of their unification."[12] From this point on, it was less a question of whether unification would occur than of how quickly and under what terms it would take place. On March 18, free elections were held in East Germany for the first time, and pro-unification parties won a decisive victory. With East Germany seemingly moving toward spontaneous unification with the Federal Republic, Four-Power leverage over the process of unification dwindled.

Even if the internal aspects of unification were to be left to the Germans alone, it remained to work out the key "external" aspects: the formal termination of Four-Power rights in Germany, the question of a unified

Germany's membership in NATO, and the withdrawal of Soviet troops from East Germany. These issues were addressed at a series of negotiations, which took place from March to September 1990, involving the two German states and the Four Powers.[13] The most difficult problem confronting these "Two-plus-Four" talks proved to be the issue of NATO membership for unified Germany. Some elements of the Soviet leadership adamantly opposed the idea of a unified Germany in NATO, and Gorbachev himself evidently had misgivings. Gradually, however, the Soviet side gave up its attempt to obtain German neutrality in exchange for unification. Having consistently ruled out the use of force to secure its interests in Germany, Gorbachev's government proved to have little leverage in the negotiations despite the presence of 380,000 Soviet troops on East German soil. Moreover, the Soviet regime was preoccupied with an economic crisis and the rapid erosion of its own political authority at home. In the end Gorbachev appeared to decide that a unified Germany anchored to the United States through NATO membership was probably preferable anyway to a neutralized and insecure Germany flailing about at the center of Europe.

All the same, winning final Soviet acceptance for the idea of a unified Germany in NATO required a variety of incentives and assurances. The main elements of the bargain that took shape in July 1990 were as follows: Germany agreed to limit its armed forces after unification to a combined total of 370,000 troops; in addition, Germany promised to remain a non-nuclear state, to renounce all claims to Polish or Soviet territory, to negotiate a treaty of friendship and cooperation with the Soviet Union, and to provide the Soviets with extensive financial assistance. Germany further promised not to deploy NATO troops on former East German territory until all Soviet units had been withdrawn. There was also agreement to modify NATO to make the alliance appear less threatening to the Soviets. The key changes to NATO doctrine were announced by Alliance leaders in the July 1990 London Declaration. These included statements of intent to transform NATO's relationship with Eastern Europe from an adversarial to a cooperative one, to limit the offensive capabilities of NATO forces in Europe, to reduce the reliance on nuclear weapons in NATO strategy, to move away from "forward defense" to a reduced forward presence, and to support an upgraded role for CSCE in managing European security. The Soviet government, for its part, accepted Germany's right to remain in NATO after unification and pledged to withdraw all its troops from German territory within three to four years.[14]

With this deal in place, German unification followed rapidly. A Treaty of Final Settlement on Germany was signed by the two German states and the Four Powers in Moscow on September 12. The next day, Genscher and Soviet Foreign Minister Shevardnadze signed a Soviet-German treaty of friendship and cooperation. The Four Powers terminated their remaining occupation rights on October 1, and on October 3 Germany officially became a single state.

Amid this dizzying rush of events, French discontent was evident. Most of the key elements of the July package had emerged in bilateral meetings among the Soviets, Americans, and West Germans. At times the Two-plus-Four format seemed to exist merely to give an imprimatur to agreements that France had had little voice in constructing. The French were uneasy that so much of the final deal seemed to emerge from bilateral Soviet-German understandings. The upper limit of 370,000 on the future size of the Bundeswehr, for example, had been agreed between Kohl and Gorbachev at their mid-July meeting in the Caucasus, as had the arrangement on the transitional status of East Germany and the withdrawal of Soviet troops. These were issues with potential to affect French security. The French could also not help but have misgivings over the negotiation of a Soviet-German friendship treaty. The treaty signed by the German and Soviet governments in September included a mutual non-aggression pledge as well as agreement that the two sides would immediately contact each other in times of crisis "with a view to coordinating their positions."[15] These were terms that brought unwelcome recollections of past Soviet-German pacts.

The French were also displeased at the proposed changes to NATO strategy that emerged in July 1990. Among the changes announced in the London Declaration were the intention of reducing reliance on tactical nuclear weapons, cutting back the number of short-range nuclear systems deployed in Europe, and making nuclear arms into "weapons of last resort." From the French perspective, these changes further undermined the credibility of U.S. nuclear strategy in Europe.[16] The French also disagreed with allied plans, announced in London, to begin restructuring NATO forces around "multinational corps." Since France participated neither in the integrated command structure nor the Nuclear Planning Group, its official position on both the nuclear strategy changes and the move toward multinational corps was that the proposed changes did not involve France and were therefore not of concern to it. In reality, however, the French government viewed the proposed changes as reorganizing NATO to correspond to German wishes.[17] As German reunification approached, in other words, Germany was not moving toward a more "European" conception of its defense identity. Instead, the United States and Germany were trying to adapt NATO for a post–Cold War world in which NATO would continue to enjoy priority over European defense institutions. French leaders foresaw that before long they might come under pressure from Germany to include their own troops based in Germany in one of the NATO multilateral corps.

At the conclusion of the London NATO conference, Mitterrand abruptly announced that all French forces stationed in Germany would be withdrawn to French territory.[18] It may be, as Mitterrand hinted in various statements on the subject, that he assumed a unified Germany would no longer want French troops on its soil. This explanation seems improbable, however, since Mitterrand announced the move without first consulting the Germans to ascertain their views. More likely is that Mitterrand wanted to preempt any German proposal that the French forces in Germany be integrated into a NATO multilateral corps. It may also be that, once again, Mitterrand had simply decided to make the Germans pay a price for having failed to coordinate changes in their security policy ahead of time with France.

The sourness in Franco-German relations lasted through the September 1990 Franco-German summit in Munich.[19] There was a good deal of rancor on both sides from accumulated grievances since the Berlin Wall's demise. At the summit Kohl appealed personally to Mitterrand to reconsider his decision on withdrawing French troops, but the French president refused to budge.

THE PUSH FOR EUROPEAN UNION

Despite the mutual disillusionment in Franco-German relations during 1990, the fact was that both Paris and Bonn had strong reasons to look beyond their existing disappointments with each other and begin laying the bases of a strengthened bilateral relationship. The Germans, for their part, were acutely conscious of the suspicions and uneasiness that a reunited Germany might arouse on the part of its West European partners. To allay such fears, German leaders believed, Germany must reaffirm and deepen its commitment to European integration at the same time that it carried out reunification.[20] Such a policy would be to Germany's own benefit, by ruling out any return to the destructive rivalries of Europe's past. Indeed, Kohl often described German unification and European unification as "two sides of the same coin."[21] And successful European integration depended, first and foremost, on the Franco-German tandem. Meanwhile the French, for their part, also viewed German unification as necessitating a deepening of European integration. Having regained unity, Germany had much less need of France's support than before. The new Germany enjoyed new strategic options. For France to protect itself against the possible exercise of those options, it needed to draw Germany into a tighter embrace than ever.

There was thus full agreement between Paris and Bonn on the need to deepen European integration in parallel with German unification. Kohl and Mitterrand had taken an initial step in this direction in April 1990, when they addressed a joint letter to the president of the European Council proposing to accelerate the political construction of the European Community. At the time, plans were already in place for the EC states to begin negotiating the terms of economic and monetary union.[22] The Kohl-Mitterrand letter proposed that negotiations on *political* union be initiated alongside the talks on economic and monetary union. The other EC governments agreed, and parallel EC conferences on political union and economic/monetary union opened in Rome in December 1990.

REVISING THE EUROPEAN SECURITY ARCHITECTURE

France and Germany also shared the initiative in seeking to give the European Community a strategic and military dimension, something it had never possessed in the past. In a proposal dated February 4, 1991, the French and German foreign ministers called for the creation of an "organic relationship" between the EC and the Western European Union. Historically, there had been no formal link between EC and WEU. Under the Franco-German proposal, the WEU would become an integral part of the EC, in effect, the EC body responsible for European defense and security policy. The French and German governments followed up their initial proposal with a joint letter to other EC governments dated October 14, 1991.[23] In the October letter, France and Germany proposed that the European political union under negotiation should commit member states to the eventual establishment of a common defense.

Both Franco-German proposals encountered resistance from some other EC states, who were anxious that steps toward the creation of a European defense identity not have the effect of undermining NATO.[24] Even so, the compromise that emerged went well beyond previous efforts at incorporating defense policy into European institutions.

Final agreement on the terms of European union took place at a meeting of the EC heads of government at Maastricht on December 10, 1991. The Treaty on European Union (also known as the Maastricht Treaty) spelled out ambitious objectives toward endowing the European Community with a military and defense dimension.[25] The treaty instructed member states to define and implement a common position in "all areas of foreign and security policy" (Article J.1). The treaty went on to say that this common policy should "include all questions related to the security of the Union, including the eventual framing of a common defense policy, which might in time lead to a common defense" (Article J.4). In line with the Franco-German initiatives mentioned above, the treaty also formally recognized WEU as "an integral part of the development" of the European Community. The Community itself was renamed the "European Union" (EU). A declaration attached to the treaty invited all European Union member states to become members of WEU, and announced the creation of a WEU military planning body.[26] The inclusion of defense policy in the European Union framework was a key step toward creating the possibility for Western Europe to emerge as a unitary strategic actor in world politics.

In addition to its provisions on a common foreign and security policy, the Maastricht agreement was important because it laid the basis for substantial further pooling of sovereignty among its member states. For example, the treaty established a timetable for the creation of a European central bank and a single European currency. Carrying out the Maastricht provisions would significantly advance the overall process of European integration, presumably creating a stronger foundation for the emergence of a common European defense.

The Eurocorps

In their October 1991 proposal on a common European security policy, the French and German governments had included a statement of their intent to create further joint military units in addition to the existing Franco-German brigade. They suggested that such units could eventually form the basis for a European army incorporating forces from other WEU states as well. In May 1992, Kohl and Mitterrand officially decided to establish such a force. Widely referred to as the "Eurocorps," the force was to be headquartered at Strasbourg and to become fully operational in the autumn of 1995. Initially, Germany and France would each contribute one armored division to the corps, together with related logistical and support units. The armored division contributed by the French would be comprised of forces already deployed on German territory, which would remain at their existing garrisons. However, the majority of French forces in Germany would continue withdrawing to France as announced in 1990.[27]

At a meeting in Bonn in June 1992, Mitterrand and Kohl together with other WEU leaders issued an important statement, known as the Petersberg Declaration, on the future development of the WEU's operational military role. In addition to its traditional mission of helping defend Europe from attack, the WEU announced its willingness in principle to make forces available for missions under U.N. or CSCE mandates. These could include humanitarian, rescue, and peacekeeping missions, as well as combat operations intended to restore peace.[28]

While the establishment of the Eurocorps had considerable symbolic importance, it did not signal a German intent to abandon NATO in favor of a united and militarily powerful Europe. Indeed, far from trying to get rid of NATO and its integrated command structure as an intrusion on the ambitions of a united Germany, Kohl's government actively sought to revitalize NATO and adapt it to a post–Cold War environment. Germany took a leading role, for example, in prodding NATO to create a framework for strategic dialogue and military contacts with the states of the former Warsaw Pact. Such a dialogue came into existence when NATO established the North Atlantic Cooperation Council (NACC) in November 1991.[29] Germany also played a key part in shaping the new NATO strategic concept announced in November 1991, which had grown out of the reevaluation of Alliance strategy announced in July 1990 in London. The new concept placed greater emphasis on dialogue and cooperation with non-NATO states and downplayed the Western Alliance's military aspects. Under the new concept, NATO stated its intention to reduce its forces in Europe, to limit its forces' offensive capabilities, and to reduce its reliance on nuclear weapons.[30]

The German government's efforts in 1991–1992 to reinforce NATO while also promoting greater European defense integration caused a certain amount of uneasiness in both Washington and Paris.[31] Washington was suspicious that a European military force under WEU control might eventually emerge as a competitor to NATO despite Bonn's avowed commitment to the Atlantic Alliance. Paris was concerned that attempts to adapt NATO for the post–Cold War environment might perpetuate American political domination of Europe into the indefinite future, regardless of Germany's evident commitment to the process of European integration.[32] The controversy finally eased at the beginning of 1993 with an agreement that clarified command relationships between NATO and the

Eurocorps.[33] Under the agreement, the Eurocorps would be able to under-take military actions under WEU command if NATO were not involved, but would be placed under NATO command for military operations involv-ing the Atlantic Alliance as a whole. This solution eased most of Wash-ington's anxiety about possible conflicts of interest between NATO and WEU military operations.

Despite Germany's leading role in promoting both the renovation of NATO strategy and the deepening of European defense cooperation, German security policy in 1991–1992 demonstrated strong continuity with Bonn's pre-unification policy. Germany's strategy at both the European and Atlantic levels seemed aimed above all at preserving alliance ties forged during the Cold War. Bonn's foremost strategic priority, throughout the Cold War, had been to prevent Germany from becoming isolated diplo-matically. This objective seemed unchanged even after unification was accomplished. The announcement of the Eurocorps, for example, seemed motivated in part by Germany's desire to forestall a complete pullout of French troops from German territory. As such, the Eurocorps arrangement bore an interesting resemblance to the Franco-German troop stationing agreement of 1966. In both cases, France had announced its intention to withdraw all troops from German territory, and Germany responded by proposing a new arrangement that would keep French troops in Germany and thus preserve a material symbol of French commitment to Germany's defense. Germany's initiatives in the Atlantic Alliance appeared to reflect an analogous effort to define a post–Cold War role for NATO and thus forestall American or British decisions to terminate their military presence in Germany.

TOWARD A COMMON EUROPEAN DEFENSE?

From late 1993 to mid-1994, a series of developments seemed on the surface to indicate movement toward the strengthening of a genuine European defense identity built around a Franco-German core. There also seemed to be indications of a degree of convergence between France and Germany's overall strategic concepts. For one thing, the Maastricht Treaty entered into force in November 1993, officially opening the way to creation of a common European foreign and security policy. In early 1994 it also appeared that the United States and France had definitively resolved their earlier divergences over whether a European defense identity might under-mine NATO. The Brussels Declaration of January 1994, approved by the heads of state and government of the Atlantic Alliance, affirmed the

Alliance's "full support" for a common European security and defense identity, and also for the eventual emergence of a common European defense "compatible with that of the Atlantic Alliance."[34] The declaration also affirmed support for continued strengthening of WEU as the defense component of the European Union. Under President Clinton, the U.S. government seemed more relaxed about the idea of a European defense identity than the Bush administration had been.[35] With American support, the idea was likely to fare better than if faced by Washington's opposition.

It also appeared that overall French and German strategic concepts were moving closer together. In some ways, in fact, official French and German strategic concepts were more compatible in 1994 than at any time since the creation of the Fifth Republic in 1958. The French and German governments had both begun restructuring their armed forces to place greater emphasis on rapid reaction forces equipped for actions outside the Central European theater. This was a noticeable difference from previous years, when France had focused largely on its nuclear forces and Germany on its heavy armored divisions and fighter aircraft.

Evolution in French strategic concepts had been visible beginning in 1991, when the French government sharply cut spending on nuclear forces and increased spending on conventional forces proportionately.[36] The French government halted further development of the S-45 mobile missile, stretched out the procurement schedule for future nuclear missile submarines, and cancelled the Hadès tactical nuclear missile program.[37] The 1992–1994 military program law reduced spending on nuclear programs from 30 percent to about 20 percent of the defense budget. This spending allocation continued in the military equipment budget announced for the years 1995–2000, in which nuclear forces were to receive 21 percent of total equipment funds.[38] There were two principal reasons for the decreased emphasis on nuclear forces. The first was the end of the Cold War and the disintegration of the Soviet Union. In the absence of a powerful Soviet nuclear and conventional threat directed against Western Europe, the upgrading of French deterrent capabilities lost much of its urgency. The other reason was the amplification of threats to French security likely to require a response with conventional arms.

French analysts had begun to note with great concern the rise (or in some instances the intensification) of political turbulence in the regions along Western Europe's eastern and southern margins. In some places, such as Yugoslavia, the reemergence of ethnic-based conflicts followed as a direct consequence of Communism's collapse. Elsewhere, as in the Islamic states of the southern Mediterranean littoral, civil unrest was more the product of long-simmering discontent with the corruption and repressive tactics of entrenched political elites. The French were especially worried by the rise of militant fundamentalist movements in North Africa and the Middle East.[39] Because of France's large population of immigrant Arabs, and its close ties with some of North Africa's unstable regimes (especially that of Algeria), political upheaval in North Africa created the possibility of increased terrorist activity in France, a deluge of new refugees, and a loss of regional influence. While economic and political measures were likely to be more important in restoring stability to North Africa than military actions, the Gulf conflict of 1990–1991 had shown the need for adequate military means to be held in readiness.

In fact, the Gulf conflict exerted a profound effect on French strategic thinking about the relative importance of conventional versus nuclear forces. Mitterrand and other French leaders viewed the Gulf crisis as a case in which France must assume a position of international leadership.[40] In a region where fundamental French interests were involved, they believed, France could not allow itself to be marginalized politically. As the U.S.-Iraqi confrontation moved toward war, however, the French discovered that their autonomy in the crisis was tightly circumscribed. To exert influence in a military conflict requires a military presence, and the French had difficulty assembling even the 14,000 troops they eventually sent to the Gulf. By contrast, the United States had more than half a million troops in the Gulf in January 1991, and the British had 43,000. The limited French military presence in the Gulf translated into limited diplomatic leverage. French forces were placed under tactical U.S. control during the war, and overall allied military strategy was directed almost entirely from Washington. After the war was over, the Bush administration launched a major initiative aimed at resolving the Arab-Israeli dispute. Much to their frustration, the French found their own peace proposals ignored while the United States established near-monopoly control over the peace process.

In the aftermath of the Gulf experience, the French government began taking a variety of steps to upgrade its power projection capabilities. One special source of frustration during the conflict had been France's lack of independent satellite intelligence as events unfolded and its resulting dependence on the United States for satellite data. Acquiring independent satellite observation and communications capabilities emerged after the war as one of France's foremost strategic priorities.[41] The French government increased its spending on military space programs, and also stepped up its efforts to engage other West European countries in the development of a European military satellite capability independent of the United

States. One measure along these lines was a June 1991 agreement to establish a multilateral satellite data processing center under WEU auspices. Located in Torrejon, Spain, the center was expected to analyze photos taken by the French-Spanish-Italian Hélios satellites, the first of which was due for launch in 1995.[42]

In other steps to upgrade its power projection capabilities, the French government budgeted funds to buy five additional KC-135 tanker aircraft from the United States, and initiated a multilateral European program to develop a new military transport aircraft.[43] The French also began promoting plans to create a French-Spanish-Italian rapid reaction force capable of taking military action in the Mediterranean region.[44] The rapid reaction force would draw on existing air-naval capabilities in the armed forces of the participating states. A small, permanent military staff was to be established for planning purposes, so that any joint action could be coordinated effectively.

The new French White Book on Defense, published in February 1994, confirmed the alteration of French strategic priorities. Under the official strategic doctrine of the 1970s, France's conventional forces had existed primarily as an extension of strategic nuclear deterrence. The ability to carry out conventional military engagements at a distance from France had been only a secondary mission. The 1994 White Book reversed these priorities.[45] The revised doctrine recognized that the ability to carry out missions of conflict prevention and crisis management, where involvement would be limited and nuclear escalation would not be in question, had gained in strategic importance.

Meanwhile, a superficially similar evolution was under way in Germany's view of its conventional forces. During the Cold War, the Federal Republic had shied away from any use of its armed forces outside Germany. Awareness of Germany's political vulnerability created a consensus among leaders of all the major parties that Germany should not use its forces except within the NATO command structure and geographic area. This view caused Germany to encounter growing criticism from U.S. leaders, who regarded force contributions as an appropriate part of burden-sharing when Western interests were at stake outside the NATO area.

Soon after unification, the Kohl government began moving incrementally toward a policy of using the German armed forces to participate, at least in a symbolic capacity, in U.N. peacekeeping missions and multilateral humanitarian actions. Between 1991 and 1994 such missions included participation in relief supply airlifts in Bosnia, naval support for the NATO embargo of Yugoslavia's coastline, participation in Arabian Gulf mine-clearing operations after Operation Desert Storm, and participation in the distribution of relief supplies to Kurdish and Somali refugees.[46] These actions proved to be intensely controversial in Germany and stimulated a passionate domestic debate regarding the acceptability and even the constitutionality of deploying German forces in out-of-area contingencies.[47] The parties of the governing coalition, though initially divided on the issue, gradually reached a consensus that German troops should be able to take part in out-of-area peacekeeping and humanitarian missions, as well as in peace enforcement (i.e., combat) missions, as long as all such missions took place in a multilateral framework and with U.N. approval. The opposition Social Democrats, on the other hand, remained strongly opposed to any combat operations except those conducted for immediate self-defense within the NATO area. The German public's views on military action evolved significantly during the early 1990s, and by 1994 a majority of public opinion favored in principle the idea of German participation in U.N. peacekeeping missions as well as in NATO out-of-area operations.[48] However, the German public continued to tend to oppose a German military role when actual situations requiring such a role were in question.

The debate over the constitutionality of out-of-area uses of the Bundeswehr was also resolved in 1994. In an important decision, the German Constitutional Court ruled in July 1994 that out-of-area uses of the Bundeswehr, pursued within the framework of collective security institutions, were in fact constitutional and did not (as some had argued) contradict Articles 24 and 87 of the German Basic Law as long as prior authorization was obtained from Parliament.[49]

It was clear that Kohl's government had begun moving toward a greater role for German troops in out-of-area contingencies in large part because of American pressure and criticism. Germany's new policy was politically astute: contributing forces to allied out-of-area missions would help prevent isolationists in the United States from using the burden-sharing issue as an excuse to dissolve NATO. However, there were other reasons as well for the adaptation of the Bundeswehr to new missions. One was the need to provide the Bundeswehr with a meaningful role. If the Bundeswehr's only purpose was to defend against a nonexistent Soviet threat, then public support for it was bound to wane and morale within the armed forces was sure to suffer. The governing coalition also seemed to be trying to move German public opinion toward the idea that Germany had a positive obligation to make forces available for international peacekeeping and humanitarian missions, and that participation in such missions was an inescapable responsibility for Germany as a major state in the international system.[50] To uphold a peaceful world order required that each contribute to the maintenance of peace and the rule of law according to its abilities.

In addition, the Germans (like the French) had come to understand that as long as Russia continued to behave as a partner rather than an opponent of the West, the military tasks of defending European interests and promoting an international order based on the rule of law would take place outside rather than inside Western Europe. If Germany did not take part in these military tasks, it would have less influence than it wanted over the world's political evolution. Beginning in 1992, Germany began to publicize its desire for a permanent seat on the U.N. Security Council; the German government realized it had little chance of achieving this objective unless it were willing and able to carry out the responsibilities, including those of a military nature, which a Council seat would entail.[51]

Thus Germany, like France, announced the restructuring of its armed forces to adapt them for out-of-area rather than Central European situations, and for tasks involving peacekeeping and humanitarian objectives rather than all-out warfare with a heavily armed opponent.[52] German government statements indicated that virtually all spending on new equipment would henceforth go to crisis-reaction forces. Such forces would comprise about one-quarter of the army, a third of the air force, and 40 percent of the navy. The Bundeswehr's territorial defense units, by contrast, were expected to receive little or no new equipment before the turn of the century.

Developments in Armaments Collaboration

French and German efforts to cooperate in developing and procuring armaments continued in the 1990s. Indeed, such efforts appeared to intensify at both the bilateral and the West European level. Two developments made European cooperation in arms procurement more imperative than ever. First, declining weapons acquisition budgets in all the major West European states meant that European arms producers faced dwindling orders from their own governments. Second, Europe's arms export markets shrank in the 1990s, the result of weakened demand for arms among developing states and increasing U.S. success in capturing sales of weapons to the developing world for itself.[53]

As a consequence of these developments, the French, German, and British arms industries all experienced sharp declines in employment beginning in the second half of the 1980s, declines that were expected to continue well into the 1990s.[54] For example, a French parliamentary report released in October 1993 predicted a further loss of 40,000 jobs in the French armaments industry by 1995.[55] European leaders, who continued to view their national armaments industries as important political and technological assets, regarded these trends with consternation. If European states were to preserve viable arms production capabilities, they no longer had the option of developing advanced weapon systems on their own. Multilateral collaboration would henceforth be a necessity.

The ongoing talks between France and Germany on weapons co-production had yielded a variety of prospective projects by the early 1990s.[56] In addition to the antitank helicopter discussed in Chapters 6 and 7, major Franco-German projects under consideration included a jointly developed armored personnel carrier, a transport aircraft (intended as a successor to the Transall), and a tactical transport helicopter, the NH-90, to be developed in collaboration with Italy and the Netherlands.[57]

The long-term effectiveness of multilateral collaboration in helping West European arms producers remain internationally viable depended in large part on making cooperation more systematic. French and German leaders promoted a variety of steps in the 1990s intended to lay the basis for more regularized collaboration. Increasingly they came to believe that achieving systematic cooperation in arms production would depend on incorporating weapons procurement into the overall process of European union. One important step in this direction came in 1993, when the IEPG became absorbed into the Western European Union and IEPG activities were transferred from Lisbon to Brussels.[58]

However, it remained as difficult as ever to find satisfactory ways of allocating development and production contracts for high-technology subsystems among competing firms. In the end it appeared that the problem could be solved effectively only if European arms manufacturers ceased to compete with one another and instead joined forces with their foreign competitors through the creation of transnational consortia or even outright mergers. There were in fact some indications in the late 1980s and early 1990s that such a process had begun.[59] Without the industrial consolidation of arms producers at a European level, the political obstacles that had plagued earlier Franco-German efforts at weapons co-production seemed likely to remain formidable.

CONTINUING LIMITS ON EUROPE AS A POWER

It seemed clear that the revisions to French and German defense policy in the early 1990s created new possibilities for at least a partial harmonization of French and German strategic concepts. Both countries had begun restructuring their forces to increase crisis-reaction and force projection capabilities. France's decision to denuclearize its ground forces also made it easier for the two countries to engage in joint operational planning. France's Pluton tactical nuclear missile, the object of so much Franco-German discord in the 1970s, was retired from service, and the Hadès missile designed to replace it was cancelled.

On the political plane, the ratification of the Maastricht Treaty and the creation of an organic link between WEU and the European Union laid the political groundwork for a common European defense. WEU member states began taking practical steps toward the concrete realization of a common defense: these included the establishment of the Eurocorps, the creation of the WEU satellite intelligence center in Spain, and attempts to coordinate West European arms procurement decisions more systematically.

Although these developments were important steps in the continuing process of European integration, Western Europe in the first half of the 1990s did not appear to be evolving in a direction that would eventually make it into a strategic superpower. Indeed, the emergence of a true West European superpower, possessing a superpower's strategic capabilities, remained a highly unlikely outcome.

First, there was no real reason to think that the Maastricht provisions on foreign and security policy would make joint European diplomatic or military action more strategically effective in the future than it had been in the past.[60] The Maastricht provisions sought to discourage member states from taking unilateral action on foreign or security problems; instead, members were supposed to strive for a unified position and to promote their interests through collective action. The basic problem, however, was that decisions to use force under EU auspices required unanimous agreement among member states. While it might be reasonably easy to reach agreement in a case where the territorial defense of Western Europe itself was in question, an external invasion of Western Europe was highly improbable. Far more likely were out-of-area contingencies like the Persian Gulf crisis or the Bosnian civil war. If European states actually adhered to the Maastricht guidelines and pursued military options only after obtaining a consensus decision from the EU Council of Ministers, the result was more likely to be a paralyzed Europe than a decisive and strategically effective Europe. (Of course, states like Britain and France appeared likely in any event to ignore European institutions and take action on their own when they had important interests at stake.) Thus, at least in the short run, it was difficult to see how the Maastricht accords would serve to enhance Europe's strategic importance in world politics.

Second, there was little reason to think that West European states were combining their military capabilities in a way that would create a greater whole. It would be more accurate instead to say that European states were trying to use increased cooperation to *replace* the military capabilities they were losing through downsizing and reductions in defense spending. During the period from 1990 to 1996, defense spending in real terms was projected to decrease by 26 percent for Germany and 19 percent for Britain. Only France, among Western Europe's major states, planned to keep real defense spending roughly constant. The armed forces of Britain, France, and Germany were all shrinking in manpower and equipment levels.[61] Whereas West Germany alone maintained nearly 500,000 active troops in the mid-1980s, the total troop strength of united Germany was expected to drop by the mid-1990s to 300,000 or even fewer. In France, the number of main battle tanks was scheduled to decrease from 1,000 to 650 as the new Leclerc tank was introduced, and combat aircraft were to decrease from 450 to 380. The French navy, which counted 150 ships in 1985, was expected to decrease to about 103 by the year 2004. In Britain, planned cuts to the armed forces were expected to eliminate more than a quarter of existing infantry battalions and two-fifths of armored regiments, and to reduce the number of aircraft by about one-quarter.

The preconditions for an effective national combat capability in today's world include high levels of personnel training, a broad base of advanced conventional weapon systems, and a high level of logistical capability to support such systems. European states, because of cutbacks in training and readiness levels, growing reliance on reserve troops, and gradually narrowing technological bases, began in the early 1990s to approach what Philip Zelikow called "the threshold of conventional debilitation." "In the not-too-distant future," wrote Zelikow, "no European country will be able to mount a unilateral conventional military campaign that can defeat any adversary able to conduct modern military operations."[62] Writing in 1993, Timothy Birch and John Crotts asserted that "European navies have deteriorated to the point that they require alliance with the U.S. Navy to undertake operations."[63] European armed forces remained especially deficient in force projection assets such as sealift, heavy airlift, and satellite reconnaissance and communications. These were precisely the capabilities, however, that Western Europe would most need if it sought to act as a strategic power independently of the United States.

Finally, for all its symbolic importance, it remained far from clear that the Eurocorps could actually function effectively as a fighting unit. On becoming operational in the fall of 1995, the Eurocorps was expected to comprise about 50,000 troops including the German 10th tank division, the French 1st armored division, the Belgian 1st mechanized division, and the Spanish 21st mechanized infantry brigade.[64] Two important practical problems were evident.[65] First, the national units designated for inclusion in the corps were based at widely dispersed locations. The Spanish brigade assigned to the Eurocorps, for example, was permanently located at Cordoba, which would seem to make any coordinated action with the German division at Sigmaringen difficult to execute. Second, there was little interoperability in the equipment of the various Eurocorps units. Even if the participating states closely coordinated their future equipment acquisitions to eliminate this problem, under normal equipment replacement schedules it would be a matter of decades before standardization was accomplished.

Of course, with adequate political will and financial investment, the WEU states certainly had the capability to remedy these deficiencies over time. If they were willing to invest the necessary resources, European countries could also provide themselves with an effective force projection capability not dependent on American operational assistance. But it remained unclear whether European states were willing to make such an investment, which would require tens of billions of dollars in new equipment spending.[66] As noted above, the French and German governments both assigned a high priority in the 1990s to improving their force projection capabilities. Nevertheless, given defense budgets that were either not growing (France) or rapidly shrinking (Germany and most other WEU states), improvements in such capabilities seem destined to develop in small increments rather than massive strides.

These mechanical and logistical obstacles to an effective European force projection capability were, however, only a part of the story. The most fundamental barrier to Western Europe's emergence as a true superpower was *political*: specifically, Germany's nearly total lack of interest in becoming a major strategic power.

GERMANY'S LACK OF GREAT-POWER AMBITIONS

Although Germany became more assertive in its foreign policy after unification, and even began to push for a permanent seat on the U.N. Security Council, this did not mean Germany was evolving toward the behavior pattern of a traditional great power. Germany's foreign policy remained distinctive among the major European states and reflected the singular nature of German history in the twentieth century.

One distinctive aspect of Germany's history was its defeat and occupation in two world wars. As a consequence of those wars, both leaders and the general public in Germany developed a sense of special responsibility in world affairs which combined a desire for atonement with a determination not to repeat the self-destructive policies of the past. Germany was also distinctive in having lost, under the constraints of the Cold War system, the habit of using armed force to protect its interests abroad. "Because Germany's security interests were limited to self-defence within NATO," Wolfgang Schlör has written, "the German public does not have a global view of security policy and does not readily accept the importance of security issues beyond the defence of its homeland."[67]

Germany's security concepts were strongly shaped by the nature of its post-1945 foreign policy experience. Military and economic integration with its Western partners was a cornerstone of German foreign policy in the Cold War era. The Federal Republic pursued its national strategic interests within the framework of multilateral organizations, above all NATO and the European Community. Integration was an enormous success for Germany, enabling it to obtain stable military security and international diplomatic acceptance. The acceptance of multilateral integration also allowed Germany to build vast export markets within Western Europe, helping propel it to a position as the world's third largest economy.

However, West Germany's strategic concepts were shaped not only by its successful experiences in integrated institutions, but also by its many foreign policy failures. Despite continuous attempts throughout the history of the Cold War, for example, Germany repeatedly failed to obtain the same level of security for German territory as other Alliance members obtained for their own. To a large extent (as the French often pointed out) this was simply a consequence of geography: West Germany was located on the front line of the Western Alliance, whereas France, or Britain, or the United States were not. Nevertheless, Bonn sought repeatedly to shape NATO policies in ways that would at least nominally give Germany the same degree of protection as its allies enjoyed. This was a battle Germany fought on many occasions, and repeatedly lost. Instances of such failures included NATO's long adherence in the 1950s to a fallback strategy that called for abandoning most of West Germany to Soviet troops in the event of a war; the U.S. adoption of flexible response, which made it more likely that a U.S.-Soviet nuclear war would be confined to German territory; the abandonment of plans (such as the Multilateral Force) which would allow Germany to have codetermination over the use of allied nuclear weapons in Central Europe; France's withdrawal from the NATO integrated command structure, which allowed it to develop military strategies that privileged its own national territory at Germany's expense; and the Reagan administration's SDI program, which (conceptually at least) implied an effort to sanctuarize U.S. territory while allowing Germany to remain a potential superpower battleground. The cumulative impact of these lost battles was to convince both German leaders and the German public that in any future great-power war in Europe, Germany would be the principal battlefield and thus the principal victim of the war's destructive impact.

The other cornerstone of Germany's early Cold War foreign policy which failed decisively was the "policy of strength," which sought to pave the way for eventual reunification by isolating the East German regime internationally and intimidating both the East German regime and the Soviet Union through NATO's military power and unity of purpose. This policy, which merely caused the Soviets to tighten their already rigid grip on East Germany, had led by the mid-1960s to a complete dead end. The policy of détente, inaugurated under Brandt, worked well by comparison, enabling the restoration of economic ties between the two Germanys and contacts between private individuals. By steadily multiplying these ties, and constantly seeking to reassure the East German regime that its intentions were not aggressive, Bonn succeeded in building a rapprochement that had proved unattainable under the policy of strength.

Even after unification, Germany's fundamental strategic concepts continued to reflect the lessons learned from its earlier foreign policy failures. The single most important consequence of Germany's Cold War experience was to move it sharply *away* from a military and nuclear conception of national security.[68] Each time in the Cold War era that Germany's allies or adversaries placed greater emphasis on military or nuclear assets as the basis of security, Germany found its strategic influence diminished and its vulnerability increased. By contrast, Germany's power was greatest at times of least tension in East-West relations, when the possibility of resort to military force was lowest and economic sources of power mattered more.

Around 1987, in the aftermath of Reykjavik, a consensus began to emerge among Germany's major parties that the only effective route to national security was to create a condition in which war at the center of Europe was simply *not an option* for the states of the Atlantic Alliance or the Warsaw Pact. In the wake of unification, this consensus solidified. The

1994 defense White Paper, for example, formulated Germany's fundamental security concept in the following terms: "German policy is committed to peace. Its foremost task is to safeguard, promote and shape peace, both within Germany and in the international community."[69] The German government appeared to recognize, however, that a stable and durable peace could not be achieved by primary reliance on conventional or nuclear deterrence. To emphasize retaliatory capabilities as the source of one's security would mean conceding that war remained a possibility. Rather, to transcend war completely among a given group of states required that those states redefine their national interests in such a way that a war in their midst could not serve the interests of any of them under any circumstances. To promote such a redefinition of national interests, Germany moved increasingly toward a three-pronged strategy that viewed economic integration, inclusive security partnerships, and disarmament as the cornerstones of the future European international order.[70]

The first element of Germany's post–Cold War security strategy was to maintain and further develop the successful multilateral institutions on which it had come to rely in preceding decades, the Atlantic Alliance and the European Community. Unification and the end of the Cold War, far from making Germany eager to dispense with NATO, instead caused it to become an even stronger supporter of the Western Alliance than before.[71] Given a reduced threat from the East, the military risks attached to NATO membership decreased, while the political benefits of American engagement in Europe persisted. As for the European Community, Germany after unification strongly and consistently supported deeper integration of the kind represented by Maastricht. Kohl and his government seemed determined to make the process of European integration irrevocable.

A second major element in Germany's security strategy was to extend and intensify the successful policies of *Ostpolitik*. Germany's fundamental idea in this regard was to enmesh Eastern Europe and Russia in a multilayered security partnership with the West that would reshape those countries' concepts of national interest. As the 1994 White Paper stated: "The objective is to tie the states of Eastern Europe as closely as possible to Western structures by pursuing a policy marked by cooperation and integration, thereby preventing a development that could result in a relapse into confrontational patterns of behaviour."[72] If Eastern Europe and Russia perceived no threat from the West, they would also perceive no possible national interest in war with the West. Constructing the desired East-West security partnership required that membership in NATO and the EU eventually be extended to East European states who shared those institutions' objectives.[73] For a stable peace to exist, all European states must enjoy an equal level of security, which in Germany's view was incompatible with policies of exclusion. Recognizing that it might be some time before NATO and the EU were ready to welcome East European states as full members, Germany also strongly supported transitional arrangements (such as "associate status" for potential future EU members and membership for non-NATO states in the North Atlantic Cooperation Council) as a sign to East European states of the West's commitment to treat them as partners.

Building a stable security partnership with Eastern Europe and Russia would also require expanding German investment and trade ties with those countries, as well as providing financial assistance for the transition to democracy. Germany viewed the consolidation of democratic institutions in East European states as crucially important: respect for the rule of law, which lay at the heart of liberal democracy, was also the foundation for durably peaceful relations between states. Democratic institutions were also a precondition for successful inclusion of East European states in NATO and the EU, since those organizations were based in part on a community of values among members.

The third principal element of Germany's post–Cold War strategy was disarmament. During the Cold War, conditions made it impossible for West Germany to go very far down the path of disarmament even after it had abandoned the "policy of strength" in favor of détente. East-West armaments rivalry was one of the principal methods by which the Cold War was waged, and Germany could not diverge much from an Alliance strategy that demanded the continuous upgrading of military capabilities. Germany's post–Cold War strategy, however, viewed arms reductions as a crucial aspect of the process of transcending war at Europe's center. For partner states to eliminate war as a possibility, they must set aside the option of offensive military action against one another. This meant, in the view of German leaders, reducing the military capabilities that made offensive military action conceivable. In the early 1990s, policy statements by Social Democratic leaders strongly emphasized the need for disarmament and denuclearization.[74] While not as explicit, a similar orientation was visible in the major policy statements—for example, the 1994 Defense White Paper—of the governing Christian Democrats and Free Democrats.

The Kohl government's efforts to widen Germany's military role in out-of-area situations thus took place in the context of a powerful underlying commitment to multilateralism and to peace within Europe. Germany's major parties all remained strongly averse to the idea of unilateral military action, and agreed that uses of German troops in out-of-area missions would occur only within multilateral settings. Germany's major parties also agreed that any use of Bundeswehr troops must be consistent with Germany's Western Alliance commitments, conform to the United Nations charter, and serve the objectives of peace and the rule of law in the international community.

EUROPEAN INTEGRATION AND NATIONAL IDENTITY

German strategic policy in the late 1980s and the first half of the 1990s thus evolved in a direction closely resembling the "civilian power" model described by Hanns Maull (see Introduction). In the negotiations surrounding unification, Germany categorically renounced nuclear arms and territorial ambitions. Following unification, Germany drastically reduced both its defense budget and the size of its armed forces, and oriented its long-range defense planning around the assumption of continued low military spending. Rather than detach itself from its Atlantic and European allies, as some had expected, Germany instead took a leading role in promoting deeper European integration and in seeking to adapt NATO for the challenges of future years. German policymakers moved systematically to construct a European security order based on the principles of integration, inclusion, disarmament, transparency, and support for democratic institutions and free markets.

Germany's growing commitment to a civilian strategic policy threatened to create a new point of discord between itself and France. Over time, German leaders of all major political parties had come to see international politics as a potentially positive-sum game in which Germany, its Western allies, and its former Warsaw Pact adversaries could all come out ahead. Given shared agreement on the principles of democracy and the rule of law, a definitive consolidation of peace in Central and Western Europe seemed not only possible but beneficial to both sides in the former East-West rivalry.

But French policymakers, in contrast to their German counterparts, remained oriented to a far more traditional strategic concept, one informed by the classical precepts of Realpolitik. In the 1990s, as in earlier decades, French leaders and political analysts continued to view the world as a fundamentally competitive realm in which states sought to assert their interests and expand their influence at the expense of other states. As became increasingly apparent, French and German leaders had very different views regarding the strategic implications of inclusion and exclusion. From a French viewpoint, Germany's efforts to construct an inclusive European security order stretching "from Vancouver to Vladivostok" smacked of strategic incoherence. To the French, who continued to define security in balance-of-power terms, a strategy of inclusion could make sense only in conjunction with a larger strategy of exclusion.[75] Thus, states might construct a commonality of interests among themselves, but only for the purpose of creating a joint front against a larger rival. Integration and inclusion were not ends in themselves, in the French view; they were instruments of the balance of power. Because Russia and the United States were inherently larger and more strategically potent than France by itself, France needed to find European partners in constructing a European strategic identity. Divided among themselves, individual European states could not hope to assert themselves effectively against the American and Russian behemoths.

To the French, in other words, asserting European interests vis-à-vis the United States and Russia remained central to the purposes of European integration. France's willingness to accept the higher degree of integration embodied in the Maastricht Treaty signified not the abandonment of national self-assertion but the progressive transference of French strategic ambitions from the national to the West European level.[76] The French view was not easily reconciled with a German approach that sought to bring as many states as possible into partnership with one another and that aimed, ultimately, to leave no one on the other side. The French continued to think in terms of security institutions with clear memberships and boundaries. They felt ill at ease with Germany's ongoing attempts to employ overlapping institutions (NATO, EU, CSCE) as well as transitional and intermediate membership arrangements (NACC, EU associate status) as a means of trying to bring the states of Western and Eastern Europe, plus the United States and Russia, into a quasi-universal security partnership.

As the Maastricht agreements began entering into effect, both France and Germany seemed to view the accelerating pace of European integration with anxiety more than anticipation. One problem was the visible lack of enthusiasm for the agreements among European publics. The contentious ratification debates in several European states, including France and Germany, suggested that as integration deepened, it might encounter growing resistance from electorates for whom European Union decision making continued to seem remote and technocratic.[77] Achieving

the political and monetary union foreseen by the Maastricht Treaty promised to be a difficult and domestically divisive undertaking.

There was also increased concern over the unresolved contradiction
between attempting to expand the European Union's membership while
also deepening integration among the Union's existing members. The end
of the Cold War made this contradiction more acute. East European
states—especially Poland, the Czech Republic, and Slovakia—began seeking admission to the European Union. The German government, with its
vision of an inclusive European economic and security system, favored
incorporating them into the process of European integration at the earliest
possible juncture.[78] Given the economic and cultural disparities between
Eastern and Western Europe, however, it seemed unlikely that such an
expansion could take place without sacrificing progress toward genuine
political union. One conceivable solution to the contradiction might be
to initiate a "multiple track" Europe in which some states (for example,
France, Germany, and the Benelux countries) would move quickly toward
full economic and political union, while other states would proceed more
slowly. Such an approach would allow the admission of East European states
into the EU without forcing a halt to the process of deepened integration.[79]

The French, however, seemed unwilling to contemplate any major new
steps toward integration. Indeed, Prime Minister Edouard Balladur's conservative government, which took power in March 1993, seemed increasingly to have second thoughts even about its commitments under the
Maastricht Treaty.[80] In effect, the French were having an identity crisis.
Each step toward greater integration brought them closer to the point
where fundamental aspects of national sovereignty would shift from the
national to the European level. This was a more daunting prospect for the
French than for the Germans, who were far more accustomed to constraints
on their national independence. Maastricht posed a challenge to many of
the basic myths and symbols of French national identity.[81] As such, it had
the potential to reignite explosive internal debates from the French past.
The French were also gnawed by fears that deeper integration might
ultimately mean the subordination of French sovereignty to a dominant
Germany.[82] Unification had increased the Federal Republic's size and
population while removing the practical and legal constraints that had
limited German strategic autonomy prior to 1990.

In addition to these concerns, the very disparity in their larger visions
of Europe's strategic destiny caused French and German leaders unease.
There was, as Dana Allin wrote, "an anxiety that the rush to European
unity was taking place without any clear agreement on the meaning of the

final goal."[83] The Germans, for their part, worried that political union might mean acquiescing in a French strategic concept that defined West European identity in balance-of-power terms, that is, as a counterweight to the United States and Russia. Such an outcome would contradict German hopes for a security partnership encompassing all the countries of the Atlantic Alliance and the former Warsaw Pact. The French, meanwhile, feared that political union might mean giving in to a German strategic perspective that downgraded European security independence and failed to distinguish Europe's strategic interests adequately from those of the United States or Russia. As long as the question of united Europe's fundamental strategic identity remained unresolved, misgivings about the prospect of political union seemed certain to persist on both sides.

NOTES

1. The speech is excerpted in Adam Daniel Rotfeld and Walther Stützle, eds., *Germany and Europe in Transition* (Oxford: Oxford University Press, 1991), pp. 120–23.

2. For a survey of panicky French reactions in late 1989 to the possibility of reunification, see Wolfgang Geiger, "'Wenn Deutschland erwacht . . . ': Die 'deutsche Frage' aus Französischer Sicht," *Die Neue Gesellschaft/Frankfurter Hefte*, January 1990, pp. 63–68; also Henri Ménudier, "Die deutsche Frage aus der heutigen Sicht Frankreichs," in Hannelore Horn and Siegfried Mampel, eds., *Die deutsche Frage aus der heutigen Sicht des Auslandes* (Berlin: Duncker & Humblot, 1987), pp. 25–50.

3. David S. Yost, "France in the New Europe," *Foreign Affairs*, Winter 1990/91, p. 112.

4. Stephen F. Szabo, *The Diplomacy of German Unification* (New York: St. Martin's Press, 1992), p. 50.

5. See the text of Bush's speech in the *Frankfurter Allgemeine Zeitung*, June 1, 1989.

6. Elizabeth Pond, *Beyond the Wall* (Washington, D.C.: Brookings, 1993), p. 55.

7. Pond, *Beyond the Wall*, pp. 163–64; Alexander Moens, "American Diplomacy and German Unification," *Survival*, November/December 1991, p. 533.

8. See François Armand (pseud.), "La relation avec l'Allemagne en matière de politique étrangère et de sécurité 1988–1992," *Relations internationales et stratégiques*, Spring 1993, pp. 151–52.

9. Moens, "American Diplomacy," p. 537.

10. Jérôme Paolini, "Les deux politiques européennes de François Mitterrand," *Relations internationales et stratégiques*, Spring 1993, p. 129; Szabo, *Diplomacy of German Unification*, pp. 50–51.

11. Pond, *Beyond the Wall*, pp. 159, 196.

12. Statement reprinted in Rotfeld and Stützle, *Germany and Europe in Transition*, p. 101. See also the account by Horst Teltschik, *329 Tage* (Berlin: Siedler, 1991), pp. 140–41.

13. For detailed histories of these negotiations, see Pond, *Beyond the Wall*; Szabo, *Diplomacy of German Unification*; and Teltschik, *329 Tage*. Many of the key documents on unification are reprinted in Rotfeld and Stützle, *Germany and Europe in Transition*.

14. As it happened, the last remaining Russian troops departed German territory at the end of August 1994.

15. For the text of the treaty, see Rotfeld and Stützle, *Germany and Europe in Transition*, pp. 190–94.

16. Szabo, *Diplomacy of German Unification*, p. 91.

17. Armand, "La relation avec l'Allemagne," p. 152.

18. See the excerpts from Mitterrand's July 6 press conference reprinted in *Le Monde*, July 8–9, 1990.

19. See Philip Gordon, "The Franco-German Security Partnership," in McCarthy, *France-Germany*, p. 151.

20. Wayne Sandholtz, "Monetary Bargains: The Treaty on EMU," in Alan W. Cafruny and Glenda G. Rosenthal, eds., *The State of the European Community*, vol. 2: *The Maastricht Debates and Beyond* (Boulder, Colo.: Lynne Rienner, 1993), pp. 130–31; Jeffrey J. Anderson and John B. Goodman, "Mars or Minerva? A United Germany in a Post–Cold War Europe," in Robert O. Keohane, Joseph S. Nye, and Stanley Hoffmann, eds., *After the Cold War* (Cambridge, Mass.: Harvard University Press, 1993), p. 56.

21. Roger Morgan, "France and Germany as Partners in the European Community," in McCarthy, *France-Germany*, p. 102.

22. See Niels Thygesen, "The Delors Report and European Economic and Monetary Union," *International Affairs*, Autumn 1989, pp. 637–52.

23. The February and October 1991 proposals are both reprinted in Peter Schmidt, *The Special Franco-German Security Relationship in the 1990s*, Chaillot Paper 8 (Paris: Institute for Security Studies, 1993), pp. 59–64.

24. See Anand Menon, Anthony Forster, and William Wallace, "A Common European Defence?" *Survival*, Autumn 1992, pp. 98–118.

25. The provisions of the treaty dealing with the Common Foreign and Security Policy are reprinted in Herbert Wulf, ed., *Arms Industry Limited* (Oxford: Oxford University Press, 1993), pp. 217–21.

26. See Scott A. Harris and James B. Steinberg, *European Defense and the Future of Transatlantic Cooperation* (Santa Monica, Calif.: Rand Corp., 1993), pp. 11–12.

27. During the 1980s France had maintained three armored divisions (totaling some 49,000 troops) in southwestern Germany. Between 1991 and 1993 these forces were reduced by two-thirds, to one division of 16,000 troops. See

Karl-Heinz Bender, "Les Forces Françaises en Allemagne: Ein Rückblick," *Dokumente*, 1993, no. 5, pp. 398–99.

28. Harris and Steinberg, *European Defense*, pp. 34–35.

29. For details see Guido Gerosa, "The North Atlantic Cooperation Council," *European Security*, Autumn 1992, pp. 273–89.

30. The new concept is reprinted in *NATO Review*, December 1991, pp. 25–32.

31. See Menon, Forster and Wallace, "A Common European Defence?" and Gordon, *A Certain Idea*, pp. 172–78.

32. See Bozo, *La France et l'OTAN*, pp. 181–94.

33. See Harris and Steinberg, *European Defense*, pp. 28–29.

34. The declaration is reprinted in *NATO Review*, February 1994, pp. 30–33.

35. On this point see *Le Monde*, June 9, 1994.

36. See Gordon, *A Certain Idea*, p. 181.

37. Fifteen Hadès missile launchers, which had already been produced, were placed in storage.

38. *Le Monde*, April 22, 1994.

39. On this point see Yves Boyer, "Europe's Future Strategic Orientation," *Washington Quarterly*, Autumn 1993, pp. 141–53, and Pierre Lellouche, "France in Search of Security," *Foreign Affairs*, Spring 1993, pp. 122–31.

40. See Pia Christina Wood, "François Mitterrand and the Persian Gulf War: The Search for Influence," *French Politics and Society*, Summer 1992, pp. 44–62.

41. See Gordon, *A Certain Idea*, pp. 181–82.

42. See *International Defense Review*, 1/1992, p. 11 and 1/1993, p. 12; also *Le Monde*, April 30, 1994.

43. See *Le Monde*, November 5, 1993, April 15, 1994, and April 22, 1994.

44. See *Le Monde*, October 30, 1993 and July 14, 1994.

45. France, Ministry of Defense, *Livre blanc sur la défense* (1994), pp. 93–95.

46. Germany, Federal Ministry of Defense, *White Paper on the Security of the Federal Republic of Germany and the Situation and Future of the Bundeswehr* (1994), pp. 66–69.

47. See Anderson and Goodman, "Mars or Minerva?" pp. 47–49, K.-Peter Stratmann, "The Future of West European Security and Defence Cooperation— German Perspectives," in Peter Schmidt, ed., *In the Midst of Change: On the Development of West European Security and Defence Cooperation* (Baden-Baden: Nomos, 1992) pp. 55–59, and Françoise Nicolas and Hans Stark, *L'Allemagne: Une nouvelle hégémonie?* (Paris: IFRI, 1992), pp. 48–52.

48. See Wolfgang F. Schlör, *German Security Policy*, Adelphi Paper 277 (London: IISS, 1993), and Philip H. Gordon, "The Normalization of German Foreign Policy," *Orbis*, Spring 1994, pp. 225–43.

49. See *The New York Times*, July 13, 1994.

50. Anderson and Goodman, "Mars or Minerva?" p. 48.

51. Schlör, *German Security Policy*, p. 83; *Le Monde*, October 2, 1993.

52. For details see Schlör, *German Security Policy*, pp. 41–43, and Germany, Federal Ministry of Defense, *White Paper 1994*, p. 99.

53. International trade in armaments, which reached $64 billion in 1984, had fallen by 1989 to $45 billion and was expected to remain at or below $40 billion per year through the end of the 1990s. See Ethan B. Kapstein, "America's Arms-Trade Monopoly," *Foreign Affairs*, May/June 1994, p. 15. On the reasons for declining Third World arms purchases, see Frederic S. Pearson, "Political Change and World Arms Export Markets: Impact on the Structure of West European Arms Industries," in Michael Brzoska and Peter Lock, eds., *Restructuring of Arms Production in Western Europe* (Oxford: Oxford University Press, 1992), pp. 44–58. Meanwhile, American exporters succeeded in establishing a quasi-monopoly on weapon sales to developing states, with the U.S. share of the Third World arms market growing to 73 percent in 1993. See *The New York Times*, August 2, 1994.

54. See Herbert Wulf, "Western Europe: Facing Over-capacities," in Wulf, *Arms Industry Limited*, pp. 144–46.

55. *Le Monde*, October 10–11, 1993.

56. See Alain Carton, "Coopération en matière d'armements entre la France et l'Allemagne," *Documents*, 1991, no. 4, pp. 28–29.

57. For details of the announcement on future development of a Franco-German armored personnel carrier, see *Le Monde*, June 21, 1994. On plans for the Transall successor, a project likely to involve Italy, Spain, Turkey, and Portugal in addition to France and Germany, see *Le Monde*, April 15, 1994. The development phase for the NH-90 tactical transport helicopter began in September 1992, with delivery of the first helicopter scheduled for 1999. See *Wehrtechnik*, February 1994, pp. 50–51, and September 1992, pp. 5–8.

58. See *Le Monde*, October 15, 1993.

59. See James B. Steinberg, *The Transformation of the European Defense Industry* (Santa Monica, Calif.: Rand Corp., 1992), pp. 65–93, and Elisabeth Sköns, "Western Europe: Internationalization of the Arms Industry," in Wulf, *Arms Industry Limited*, pp. 160–90.

60. See Philip Zelikow, "The New Concert of Europe," *Survival*, Summer 1992, pp. 20–22.

61. See Schlör, *German Security Policy*, p. 43; *Le Monde*, June 15, 1994; Sherard Cowper-Coles, "From Defence to Security: British Policy in Transition," *Survival*, Spring 1994, p. 151.

62. Zelikow, "The New Concert of Europe," p. 25.

63. Timothy J. Birch and John H. Crotts, "European Defense Integration: National Interests, National Sensitivities," in Cafruny and Rosenthal, *The Maastricht Debates and Beyond*, pp. 273–76.

64. *Le Monde*, July 14, 1994.

65. See *Le Monde*, July 12, 1994.

66. For estimates of the cost of achieving various levels of force projection capability, see M. B. Berman and G. M. Carter, *The Independent European Force: Costs of Independence* (Santa Monica, Calif.: Rand Corp., 1993).

67. Schlör, "German Security Policy," p. 5.

68. See Hans-Peter Schwarz, *Die gezähmten Deutschen: Von der Machtbesessenheit zur Machtvergessenheit* (Stuttgart: Deutsche Verlags-Anstalt, 1985).

69. Germany, Federal Ministry of Defense, *White Paper 1994*, p. 39.

70. For a detailed elaboration of this point, see James Sperling, "German Security Policy and the Future European Security Order," in Michael G. Huelshoff, Andrei S. Markovits, and Simon Reich, eds., *From Bundesrepublik to Deutschland: German Politics after Unification* (Ann Arbor: University of Michigan Press, 1993), pp. 321–46.

71. Elizabeth Pond, "Germany in the New Europe," *Foreign Affairs*, Spring 1992, pp. 114–30; Anderson and Goodman, "Mars or Minerva?" pp. 29–30.

72. Germany, Federal Ministry of Defense, *White Paper 1994*, p. 31.

73. Germany, Federal Ministry of Defense, *White Paper 1994*, pp. 51–52.

74. See Hans-Georg Ehrhart, "La sécurité européenne vue par le PS et le SPD," *Documents*, 1991, no. 5, pp. 25–31.

75. See Ole Waever, "Three Competing Europes: German, French, Russian," *International Affairs*, July 1990, pp. 477–93.

76. Daniel Vernet, "France in a New Europe," *The National Interest*, Fall 1992, pp. 30–38; Peter Schmidt, "French Security Policy Ambitions," *Aussenpolitik*, 1993, no. 4, pp. 335–43.

77. See Brigid Laffan, "The Treaty of Maastricht: Political Authority and Legitimacy," in Cafruny and Rosenthal, *The Maastricht Debates and Beyond*, pp. 35–51.

78. See Nina Grunenberg, "Was Wollen die Deutschen mit Europa?" *Die Zeit*, July 8, 1994, p. 3; also the interview with Helmut Kohl in *Le Monde*, October 1, 1994.

79. A proposal along these lines in September 1994 by a group of leading CDU and CSU Bundestag members ignited an extremely lively debate in France. See *Le Monde*, September 24, September 29, October 12, November 3, November 18, November 23, and November 30, 1994; and *The Economist*, November 26, 1994, pp. 55–56 and December 3, 1994, pp. 62–66.

80. See *Le Monde*, November 8, 1994.

81. See Stanley Hoffmann, "Thoughts on the French Nation Today," *Daedalus*, Summer 1993, pp. 63–79, and Gregory Flynn, "The New France and Post–Cold War Europe: Paradigm Lost . . . ?" Paper delivered at the Annual Meeting of the American Political Science Association, September 1–4, 1994.

82. Hoffmann, "Thoughts on the French Nation," p. 75; Hans Stark, "France-Allemagne: Entente et mésententes," *Politique étrangère*, Winter 1993/94, pp. 989–99; "La peur du colosse," unsigned article, *Documents*, 1993, no. 3, pp. 34–37.

83. Dana H. Allin, "Germany Looks at France," in McCarthy, *France-Germany*, p. 28.

Conclusion

From the mid-1950s to the mid-1990s, the strategic policies of both France and Germany evolved substantially. The purpose of this chapter is to summarize that evolution and to describe its underlying dynamics. As medium-sized states in a world dominated by two military superpowers, France and Germany found themselves forced repeatedly during the Cold War to sacrifice some of their objectives to achieve others. Strategic decisions made at key junctures during the Cold War altered the essential framework of the security debate in both countries, and those alterations in turn affected both countries' subsequent strategic choices. Inasmuch as their key strategic decisions both shaped and reflected fundamental national interests, French and German strategic choices during the Cold War revealed much about the likely future strategic orientations of both states.

FRENCH AND GERMAN STRATEGIC PERSPECTIVES DURING THE COLD WAR

The foreign policies of both France and Germany in the latter 1950s reflected ambitions to recover great-power status. In the final years of the Fourth Republic, French governments moved tentatively toward the creation of a continental bloc, based on a Franco-German tandem, that would provide France with the resources to resist American economic and cultural domination and to carry out its military-strategic objectives independently of Washington. Under the Fifth Republic this policy came even more clearly into focus. De Gaulle's design for a self-reliant, French-led Europe incorporated several elements: the establishment of a détente with the Soviet Union that would loosen Europe's rigid division into blocs; the forging of a European entity that would define its interests free from American tutelage; and the creation of a French national nuclear arsenal that would secure for France the leadership of Europe and justify its claims to an equal voice in the councils of the mighty. Like his predecessors in the late Fourth Republic, de Gaulle recognized that partnership with West Germany was the key to increased power and status for France.

Under Adenauer, West Germany like France had a program for improving its international position. Unlike France, however, West Germany could not mount a direct bid for great-power status. First it was necessary to overcome the constraints on German freedom of action imposed by the legacy of two world wars and by the Soviet military occupation of East Germany. To be genuinely autonomous, Germany needed to attain reunification by means that would not permanently restrict the options and instruments of its foreign policy. Adenauer hoped to achieve this objective through Western unity and strength, which would eventually prompt Moscow to accept German reunification on Bonn's terms. Because its foreign policy strategy depended on support from the major Western powers, Adenauer's Germany did all it could to promote allied and European unity. The German chancellor devoted particularly great effort to cultivating close defense relations with France, which was in many ways the key to European integration and Alliance solidarity.

Unfortunately for de Gaulle and Adenauer, their foreign policy strategies directly contradicted each other. The success of de Gaulle's strategy required that Bonn be weaned from its submission to Washington, while Adenauer's plan depended on cementing France ever more solidly to the Western bloc. The opposition of French and German goals could not be resolved. Finally, a frustrated de Gaulle gave up his attempt to bring Germany into France's orbit. Soon afterward, he announced his country's withdrawal from Alliance military integration. At the time, France's allies regarded the general's actions as proof of exaggerated national ambitions. By withdrawing from NATO integration, however, de Gaulle guaranteed France's political isolation in the Alliance and thereby implicitly ended France's attempt to develop a self-reliant European alternative to NATO. In retrospect it is clear that the French actions of 1966 marked the beginning of the French state's accommodation to the Cold War order. In effect de Gaulle had given up on the ambitious program underlying the Fouchet Plan and the Elysée Treaty. Having fallen short in his grand project to restore France to true great-power status, the general had decided to settle for the immediate political and psychological advantages of a largely symbolic independence.

Meanwhile, West Germany also found itself compelled to scale back its foreign policy objectives. The solidification of a two-class system of nuclear and non-nuclear countries, together with the slowing of supranational integration in Europe, put Germany's goal of equality of rights within the Alliance indefinitely out of reach. At the same time, it became increasingly apparent that Bonn's hard line toward the Soviet Union was a dead end, and that adhering to it would only assure Moscow's continued hostility while doing nothing to bring about reunification or a final European peace settlement. Bonn therefore decided on a deal with Moscow which, even though it was not a final settlement, at least provided a basis for the pragmatic development of political and economic relations between West Germany and the countries of Eastern Europe including East Germany.

Ostpolitik thus marked a fundamental shift away from Germany's initial strategy of attempting to unmake the results of World War II, to a policy of trying to live as comfortably as possible within the confines of a divided Europe and a divided Germany. Like France's withdrawal from NATO integration, *Ostpolitik* amounted in practice to the abandonment of great-power aspirations and essential acceptance of the existing structure of world power relations. In adopting a policy of détente, West Germany broadened the base of its own security. *Ostpolitik* recognized the limits of the American security guarantee and attempted to supplement it through a partial accommodation with Moscow. Although *Ostpolitik* did not end Germany's dependence on the United States, it did give Bonn greater room for maneuver between the superpowers. By enabling Bonn to establish its own independent dialogue with Moscow, *Ostpolitik* established an upper limit to Bonn's strategic vulnerability vis-à-vis its allies. Specifically, it curtailed American and French ability to manipulate Germany's vulnerabilities for their own ends.

German *Ostpolitik* thus had important implications for French foreign policy. France had been able to quit the NATO command structure precisely because its security was indirectly assured by the American defense commitment to Europe and by Germany's integration in NATO. Because it created at least the theoretical possibility of an eventual Soviet-German security agreement outside the NATO framework, *Ostpolitik* represented a latent threat to France's foreign policy autonomy.

Despite its new vulnerability to potential German strategic choices, Paris responded to *Ostpolitik* with dogmatism rather than adaptation. During the Pompidou years, French foreign policy lost the tactical agility that had been among its most pronounced features under de Gaulle. The increasing rigidity of France's strategic policy was due above all to the country's huge investment (financial, political, and psychological) in its national nuclear force. De Gaulle had wanted France to have its own nuclear deterrent both for the political gains an independent nuclear force would bring and as a step toward eventual military self-reliance. By the early 1970s, however, it was becoming evident that France by itself, with its finite resources, must choose one or the other: an independent nuclear force or an effective defense capability, the latter requiring greatly increased expenditures on conventional forces and much closer coordination of French military planning with that of other NATO states.

Given this choice, there was no chance whatever that the French government would opt for a policy based on military effectiveness. Choosing such a policy would have involved severe political drawbacks. For one thing, to choose the path of military effectiveness would mean sacrificing all the psychological advantages provided by the rhetoric of national independence. It would mean admitting that creating a national nuclear force had not liberated France from strategic dependence on its allies. Worse yet, the necessity of closer substantive integration of military plans with NATO would shatter France's shallow defense consensus and return the country to the ideologically polarized foreign policy debate of the Fourth Republic.

French defense policy remained essentially unchanged during the last half of the 1970s and the first half of the 1980s even though its underlying premises further eroded. Repeated demonstrations of unreliability on the part of the United States, combined with a steady military buildup by the Soviet Union, increasingly called into question the value of the U.S. defense commitment to Europe. Meanwhile, popular discontent in Germany with Alliance nuclear policy and dismay over the renewal of East-West tensions were beginning to undermine the other hidden assumption of French defense policy, namely, that Germany would continue to remain firmly integrated in NATO.

Mitterrand nevertheless began his first term as French president by reaffirming once again the key elements of Gaullist foreign policy. The Socialist government launched a major modernization of the French nuclear force and also attempted to reduce the constraints on French military freedom of maneuver that had grown up during the Pompidou and Giscard presidencies. Developments in Germany, however, gradually led the French government to begin reconsidering some of the elements of its defense doctrine. The rise of a German pacifist movement, Germany's continuing dedication to East-West détente, and the consolidation of Bonn's independent dialogues with Moscow and East Berlin were regarded in Paris as portents of a possible German drift toward neutralism. The German peace movement, which signaled an erosion in the German defense consensus, was extremely unsettling to the French political elite. Ultimately the fluidity of the situation prompted Paris to offer Germany additional symbols of French solidarity, including closer operational military cooperation and, in principle, consultations prior to the use of French nuclear weapons on German territory. Kohl's government, for its part, became progressively more interested in stronger defense ties to France as its confidence in the Reagan administration's economic and foreign policies eroded. The demise of the Soviet empire in Eastern Europe intervened, however, before any fundamental realignment of strategic relations among the United States, France, and Germany could occur.

Cold War Cooperation in Arms Procurement

In the area of arms procurement collaboration, the overall pattern among NATO'S major states during the Cold War was one of competition more than cooperation. Rather early in the postwar period, France began seeking national self-sufficiency in advanced weapons technology. This policy, which took shape in the final years of the Fourth Republic and was continued by de Gaulle, was part of France's larger effort to establish a continental bloc able to resist direct and indirect forms of American domination. After withdrawing from the NATO command structure, Paris continued to seek technological autarky on the grounds that France could remain outside NATO military integration only so long as it could produce its own armaments without dependence on American technology.

The effort to retain independence from U.S. weapons technology drove France toward a dual strategy of intra-European armaments co-production and aggressive exporting of French-made weapon systems. Initially France regarded West Germany as the ideal partner for armaments collaboration. Germany could make substantial financial, industrial, and technological contributions to joint weapon projects, yet the small size of the German arms industry and Bonn's desire to maintain a low profile on armaments production and exports would enable Paris to define the terms of co-production to its own advantage. French governments initiated two major efforts to draw West Germany into systematic arms production cooperation. These were the armaments triangle of 1957–1958 and the Elysée Treaty. Neither initiative succeeded as hoped.

France increasingly turned to arms exports to meet its needs, and during the 1970s sales of French weapons to foreign states grew rapidly. Arms exports came to play a major role for France in job creation, the technological advancement of industry, and balance-of-payments solvency following the oil price increases of 1973.[1] Because France could export arms freely only if they contained no components subject to American end-use restrictions, the growing economic dependence on arms exports coalesced with preexisting political objectives to strengthen France's quest for self-sufficiency in armaments technology.

In the 1980s, confronted with a renewed U.S. challenge to its arms export markets, France sought once again to strengthen the position of its arms producers through more systematic cooperation with Germany in the development and manufacture of advanced conventional weapons. But Germany had become more demanding about co-production arrangements, and systematic cooperation proved impossible to achieve. Paris therefore began to focus its efforts on bilateral arrangements with smaller European arms producers such as Spain and Belgium. The advantage of such arrangements was that they would allow France to share with others the costs of developing and producing new weapon systems, but would enable the French to continue to dominate design and production of the co-produced weapons.

In Germany, the pattern of armaments production differed somewhat from the French case. When Germany entered NATO in 1955, its arms industry had all but ceased to exist. Weapons manufacturers were not a powerful interest group in German politics, and many West Germans did not want their country to become involved again in the production of military equipment. Influential figures such as Ludwig Erhard advocated that Germany buy its arms from foreign suppliers on the basis of price and performance criteria.

Nevertheless, arms procurement policy in Germany as in France was governed from the first by political criteria rather than by the pursuit of military cost-effectiveness. During the large-scale rearmament of the late 1950s and early 1960s, Bonn's choice of fighter aircraft and other weapon systems was strongly shaped by the goal of increasing Germany's political weight in the Alliance. Since Germany's status in the Alliance was tied to its military contribution, Bonn invested heavily in nuclear-capable systems (such as the F-104 Starfighter) so that a Bundeswehr equipped with U.S.-owned tactical nuclear warheads would have the same importance for Western defense as American, French, or British forces.

From the beginning of its rearmament West Germany resisted so-called "offshore" purchases of advanced weapon systems. (Offshore purchases are those in which an entire weapon system is imported ready-made from a foreign manufacturer.) Instead, German governments typically negotiated arrangements in which as much of a given weapon system as possible would be produced in Germany under license, so that domestic industry would obtain employment and technical know-how through the procurement contract. Germany's behavior in this regard was similar to that of other industrial European states who bought major weapon systems from foreign producers.[2] Licensed production agreements, beginning in the late 1950s with German manufacture of the French Fouga-Magister trainer jet and Noratlas transport plane, followed in the 1960s by the much more ambitious licensed production of the F-104G fighter, caused the rise of a substantial military aeronautics industry in Germany where there had been none in 1955.

Unlike Paris, Bonn was typically quite willing to rely on U.S.-licensed technology for weapon components it could not produce itself. The French, if they could not produce a key component for a weapon themselves, would in most cases simply delay purchasing the weapon—for a decade, if necessary—until French arms producers had evolved the requisite technological capability. The Germans, by contrast, preferred to produce needed components immediately via an American license, thereby acquiring competence in the relevant technology. In the late 1970s, for example, the Germans favored equipping the European Fighter Aircraft with General Electric's F-404 engine and the Hughes APG-65 radar, both of which could be produced in Europe under license. Paris, however, insisted that the EFA's engine and radar be of French design. A similar dispute divided Paris and Bonn on the question of whether to equip the Franco-German combat helicopter with the TADS/PNVS targeting system produced by Martin Marietta or to wait until a comparable French system could be developed.

The difference in French and German willingness to rely on American weapons technology derived from their different defense policies. For the French, avoidance of U.S.-licensed technology was a precondition for unencumbered export of French-made arms, which in turn was both a major French economic interest and a precondition for France to avoid de facto reintegration into the NATO command structure. Bonn, by contrast, made no pretense of strategic independence from the United States. Since Germany's economic dependence on arms exports was less than that of France (particularly in the area of combat aircraft), the Germans could incorporate licensed American technology in their weapon systems without calling into question their entire defense policy edifice.

Once German industry had acquired the capability to design and manufacture a given type of weapon component, however, Bonn sought to preserve and further develop that capability through its subsequent arms procurement choices. Here again, the German pattern resembled that of other Western industrial states. Since France and Britain also sought to preserve the capabilities of their arms industries, weapons co-production among the major European states worked out badly or failed altogether in virtually every case where more than one participant in a proposed joint project possessed a well-developed capability for design and production of the envisaged weapon system. In negotiations on a Franco-German battle tank, for example, the preference by military and industrial interests on each side for a national design led twice to the failure of proposed joint projects, in 1963 and again in 1982. Similarly, the battle by France and Britain to be design leader for the European Fighter Aircraft finally caused France to withdraw from the program.

Government support for domestic arms makers contributed to the emergence of oversized armaments industries in all the major Alliance countries and to tremendous redundancy in NATO arms development and production facilities. Efforts by the major NATO states to reduce the economic burden imposed by their oversized arms industries led to growing dependence on arms exports, a trend that was most conspicuous in the French case but was also apparent in the United States, Germany, and Britain. As a result, competition among the major NATO countries for arms markets in Western Europe and elsewhere in the world grew more intense over time.

CHOOSING BETWEEN AUTONOMY AND POWER

For both France and West Germany, the Cold War was a period of gradual adaptation to the loss of great-power status. Although both countries initially entertained hopes of eventually recovering a great-power role in world politics, by the 1980s political leaders in France as well as Germany appeared to have given up such aspirations for good. Each of the two countries seemed fundamentally reconciled to the limits on its international power imposed by American and Soviet military predominance in the world arena. The consolidation of the Franco-German defense partnership, although one of the great accomplishments of Cold War European politics, never led to a genuine effort to create an autonomous European defense system.

In France, the military ambitions of the early Fifth Republic gave way over the years to a more modest agenda. For de Gaulle, the creation of a national nuclear force had been part of a larger plan to rebuild France's overall military capabilities into those of a major power. De Gaulle sought nuclear weapons not just for their political value as a strategic deterrent and a symbol of French grandeur, but also for their unparalleled enhancement of national firepower and war-fighting capabilities. He envisaged a Western Europe with enough military strength to justify its claim to a role in world politics on a par with the superpowers.

Subsequent French governments, although they continued to strengthen French nuclear capabilities, scaled down Gaullism's ambitions and redefined France's nuclear buildup as a predominantly political strategy. Although France eventually came to possess hundreds of nuclear warheads, it became clear over time that the military mission of France's armed forces was one of deterrence, not defense. Despite its growth and modernization, France's nuclear force, unlike the American and Soviet arsenals, lacked even a limited counterforce capability. It was an instrument of deterrence pure and simple, and both its strategic and tactical components were tailored accordingly. France's conventional forces shrank steadily in size, and their modernization lagged behind that of American, Soviet, and German forces. To the extent that French governments upgraded France's conventional forces, they concentrated investment disproportionately in a handful of elite units designed for small-scale military interventions in Francophone Africa or the Middle East. With each passing decade of the Cold War era, in other words, France's armed forces declined in their ability to defend against a Warsaw Pact military assault on Western Europe. France's deterrent posture came to depend almost wholly on deterrence-by-punishment, that is, the threat to retaliate against a Soviet attack by the bombing of Soviet population centers, rather than on any actual ability to defeat a Soviet invasion of French territory.

West Germany, for its part, moved even more sharply than France from a military to a political definition of security. Adenauer's "policy of strength" toward the Soviet Union, which hoped to use Western military superiority to extract concessions from Moscow, proved to offer Germany little political leverage in East-West relations. Bonn therefore gravitated in the 1970s to a policy based on the renunciation of military force as a means of resolving the political and territorial disputes left over from the war. In doing so, West Germany recognized that it had little chance of accomplishing its objectives in Eastern Europe through military strength. Greater long-run potential lay in a policy of deemphasizing the role of military power in European diplomacy, seeking to reduce East-West tensions in Europe, and building mutually beneficial trade relations between West Germany and the East European countries.

West Germany did, of course, also work steadily to maintain and upgrade its well-equipped armed forces. Successive West German governments unwaveringly supported German membership in NATO and an undiminished American military presence in Europe. Nevertheless, over time Bonn put progressively more emphasis on détente, and less emphasis on allied nuclear deterrence or conventional defense, as the means for overcoming the East-West divide. Whereas Germany's major political parties were initially at odds over détente, by the mid-1980s a new German consensus had formed which regarded the active pursuit of European détente as a cornerstone of West Germany's foreign policy.

The evolution of French and German security perspectives corresponded to the dynamics of the East-West bloc system. Since most of the military instruments of political influence were controlled by the two superpowers, France and Germany stood to gain by downplaying the military dimension of European security. The evolution in security perspectives also resulted in part from the inability of either Paris or Bonn to obtain cooperation with the other on its own preferred terms. Given the circumstances, abandoning great-power aspirations yielded a substantial payoff for both France and Germany. Withdrawing from the NATO military command enabled France to reap the fruits of rhetorical self-assertion on the world stage. At the domestic level, Gaullism's deliberately constructed mythology of national grandeur proved remarkably effective in helping France overcome its historically deep internal divisions. For Germany, meanwhile, *Ostpolitik* brought with it the restoration of traditional ties to Eastern Europe and reduced vulnerability to American pressures. As a result, the idea of a self-reliant West European defense system based on a Franco-German axis lost most of its appeal for Paris and Bonn.

In many respects, the long-term trend in bilateral Franco-German defense relations during the Cold War was toward closer and more cordial ties. There was nothing in this trend, however, to suggest a gradual movement toward eventual West European defense independence. From the late 1960s on, virtually all initiatives by Paris or Bonn for closer military ties were motivated by self-limiting objectives.

One such objective was the largely negative goal, shared by both France and Germany, of preventing the actions of the other from undermining its own security or strategic position. Thus on the German side, Adenauer consistently sought to use his personal ties to de Gaulle to deflect the general's quest for French national grandeur into arrangements that would instead promote European integration and Western unity. In the late 1960s, Willy Brandt tried to upgrade Franco-German strategic consultations in the hope of preventing France's policy of independence from obstructing East-West arms reduction negotiations. Helmut Schmidt and Helmut Kohl both tried to use the Paris-Bonn axis as a lever to influence French tactical nuclear doctrine in ways that would make it more consistent with NATO nuclear planning. On the French side, François Mitterrand made closer Franco-German consultations a major foreign policy priority precisely in order to intervene against what he saw as a neutralist trend in Germany that could imperil France's strategic position. In each of these instances, the impetus for cooperation came from the desire by one side to limit the real or potential damage to its security caused by the policies of the other. This essentially negative motivation did not carry within it any potential for the emergence of true West European military self-reliance.

The other primary motive for closer Franco-German military cooperation was the desire of French and German leaders for a greater ability to assert their own national interests vis-à-vis Washington. This was the origin of the French government's frequent initiatives in the area of Franco-German armaments cooperation, for example. It was the reason for Schmidt's proposal to Giscard for greater harmonization of French and German foreign policies, and for Kohl's increased attention to Franco-German defense ties in the aftermath of Reykjavik. None of these initiatives, however, was intended to lay the foundation for a self-sufficient European defense. All of them aimed primarily at reducing France and Germany's vulnerability to political pressures from the United States, and at reducing their domestic sensitivity to displays of U.S. unreliability, while remaining within the framework of a continued American commitment to Europe's defense.

Faced with a choice between power and autonomy, in other words, France ultimately decided to maximize its foreign policy autonomy rather than pursue a quest for strategic power that would have required it to submerge its national identity in a common Franco-German defense policy. Germany, for its part, found neither power nor autonomy to be attractive strategic options given its exposed position as a divided state on the front line of the East-West conflict. Instead, Germany's strategic perspective underwent a lengthy and in some ways difficult evolution leading to the abandonment of aspirations for an eventual restoration of German military might. By the late 1980s, a new domestic consensus had formed in Germany which favored a strategy of peaceful diplomatic and economic partnership with states to Germany's east as well as those to the west. Pursuing this policy involved progressively greater sacrifices of Germany's national strategic autonomy and military capability in exchange for the consolidation of peace at Europe's center.

THE LOGIC OF FUTURE FRENCH AND GERMAN STRATEGIC CHOICES

The end of the Cold War and the reunification of Germany revolutionized Western Europe's strategic environment. Even so, neither development seemed likely to have much impact on French or German strategic orientations. In the 1990s, French and German strategic perspectives remained heavily conditioned by the lessons of past strategic choices. Moreover, prevailing international conditions provided few incentives for either state to reconsider the essentials of its strategic posture.

This was especially the case for Germany. From a German standpoint, the active pursuit of détente with the East during the 1970s and 1980s had paid off handsomely. Through a consistent commitment to peaceful dialogue and security partnership with its Eastern neighbors, Germany had gradually helped persuade Soviet leaders that they could demilitarize their own strategy in Europe without inviting a renewal of German aggression. The apparent success of Germany's strategy in bringing about the end of the Cold War and achieving peaceful unification served only to deepen the domestic consensus in Germany on continued adherence to a "civilian power" approach.

In France, both political leaders and the general public viewed the strategy of national independence instituted by de Gaulle as a success, and after the end of the Cold War there remained a solid consensus in favor of continuing the strategy. However, the growing costs of advanced technology did cause Paris to begin modifying its policy of independence at the margins, mainly by accepting greater dependence on other West European states for military technology. French policy continued to be motivated by the desire to preserve as much strategic independence vis-à-vis the United States as possible, even though doing so required some transfer of military and technological competences from the national to the European level.

Although the demise of the Soviet Union and the withdrawal of Soviet military power from Eastern Europe had drastically altered Europe's political landscape, these changes were not of a sort likely to provoke a reconsideration of French or German strategic doctrines. Indeed, in post–Cold War Europe it was difficult to discern *any* powerful incentives for France or Germany to alter their existing strategic orientations. Certainly, ethnic conflicts in Southeastern Europe (such as the Bosnian civil war) provided little motivation for such a change. The havoc in Bosnia and elsewhere in the former Yugoslavia did not threaten Western Europe in a direct military sense, and as such it had little apparent effect on French or German strategic planning. Western Europe's most far-reaching reaction to the Bosnian situation, it seemed, was to accelerate the tightening of laws governing immigration and political asylum so as to reduce the influx of refugees from the former Yugoslavia or from other unstable regions in Europe.[3]

It also appeared unlikely that either France or Germany would change its basic strategic orientation in response to the prospect of continued cutbacks in the U.S. military presence in Europe. During the Cold War, some analysts had argued that a significant diminution of America's strategic protectorate over Europe would prompt the formation of an independent, self-reliant West European defense system.[4] With the end of the Cold War, such arguments seemed to lose most of their force. In the absence of a Soviet or Russian military threat, the presence of American troops in Europe was important more as a symbol of continuing U.S.-European security partnership than as a physical barrier to a military threat that had ceased to exist. As long as the Atlantic Alliance remained intact at the symbolic level, therefore, reductions in actual U.S. troop levels in Europe appeared unlikely in themselves to prompt the creation of a common European defense policy.

Under the conditions prevailing in Europe at the midpoint of the 1990s, neorealist predictions of emerging German nuclear ambitions and renewed German militarism seemed farfetched. Given that Germany's "civilian power" strategy was widely perceived in Germany as a resounding success and was the object of an increasingly solid domestic consensus, and given that the strategy appeared thoroughly viable under existing and anticipated strategic conditions, it seemed far more plausible to expect continuity rather than radical change in German policy. There was simply no material basis for predicting that Germany would jettison its civilian strategy and return to a policy of aggressive militarism. Also, in view of the complete absence of domestic or international incentives for it to acquire nuclear weapons, the probability that Germany would move toward development of a national nuclear force appeared to be nil.[5]

The logic of strategic continuity applied to France as well. Barring the emergence of a major new threat to Western Europe's physical security, motives for France to alter its strategic orientation significantly were simply not in evidence.

As 1995 began, important elements of Europe's future did of course remain undecided. For example, would France and Germany forge ahead with the process of political union, including the creation of a common defense policy, or had European integration already approached its feasible limit? Despite evidence of growing ambivalence among European publics, many French and German leaders remained committed to the ambitious goals laid out in the Maastricht agreements. Chancellor Kohl, for example, continued to emphasize his wish that European political union become "irreversible."[6] For Germany, using the process of integration to insure permanent peace among the European Union's members remained a principal strategic objective. The French, for their part, continued to seek enough economic and political integration in the EU to assure Europe's economic competitiveness vis-à-vis the United States and Japan. It was unclear, however, that the achievement of these key German and French strategic goals would necessitate the creation of a common European defense policy.

Whether the process of European political union went forward or not, Western Europe appeared unlikely to emerge as an independent, militarily powerful strategic actor on the world stage. If progress toward political union stagnated, France and Germany appeared most likely to continue adhering to the broad outlines of their existing national strategies, namely, symbolic independence for France and a civilian strategy for Germany. If France and Germany did move toward a common defense policy, on the other hand, there was little reason to think that their joint enterprise would incorporate either the strategic ambitions or the military capabilities of a true great power.

NOTES

1. Kolodziej, *Making and Marketing Arms*, pp. 170–79.

2. On this point see, for example, Daniel Todd and Jamie Simpson, *The World Aircraft Industry* (London: Croom Helm, 1986), chapter 6.

3. See *The New York Times*, August 10, 1993.

4. See, for example, Calleo, *Beyond American Hegemony*, pp. 182–83, 195.

5. Others who reach similar conclusions include Anderson and Goodman, "Mars or Minerva?"; Robert Gerald Livingston, "United Germany: Bigger and Better," *Foreign Policy*, Summer 1992, pp. 157–74; Peter Katzenstein," "Taming of

Power: German Unification, 1989–1990," in Meredith Woo-Cumings and Michael Loriaux, eds., *Past as Prelude: History in the Making of a New World Order* (Boulder, Colo.: Westview, 1993), pp. 59–81; Nicolas and Stark, *L'Allemagne*, pp. 147–49; Schlör, *German Security Policy*; W. R. Smyser, "Dateline Berlin: Germany's New Vision," *Foreign Policy*, Winter 1994–95, pp. 140–57; and Sperling, "German Security Policy."

6. Interview in *Le Monde*, October 1, 1994.

Selected Bibliography

Adenauer, Konrad. *Erinnerungen*. Stuttgart: Deutsche Verlags-Anstalt, 1965–1968, 4 vols.

Adrets, André (pseud.). "Franco-German Relations and the Nuclear Factor in a Divided Europe." In Laird, *French Security Policy*, 105–19.

Albrecht, Ulrich, Peter Lock, and Herbert Wulf. *Arbeitsplätze durch Rüstung?* Reinbek bei Hamburg: Rowohlt, 1978.

Anderson, Jeffrey J., and John B. Goodman. "Mars or Minerva? A United Germany in a Post–Cold War Europe." In Robert O. Keohane, Joseph S. Nye, and Stanley Hoffmann, eds., *After the Cold War*. Cambridge, Mass.: Harvard University Press, 1993, 23–62.

Armand, François (pseud.). "La relation avec l'Allemagne en matière de politique étrangère et de sécurité 1988–1992." *Relations internationales et stratégiques*, Spring 1993, 147–59.

Bahr, Egon. "Atomare Klassenunterschiede." *Der Spiegel*, February 13, 1984, 36–37.

Baring, Arnulf. *Im Anfang war Adenauer: Die Entstehung der Kanzlerdemokratie.* Munich: Deutscher Taschenbuch Verlag, 1971.

Bauer, Johannes. *Die deutsch-französischen Beziehungen, 1963–1969: Aspekte der Entwicklung nach Abschluss des Vertrages vom 22. Januar 1963*. Doctoral dissertation, Bonn, 1980.

Beaufre, André. *NATO and Europe*. New York: Knopf, 1966.

Bender, Karl-Heinz. "Les Forces Françaises en Allemagne: Ein Rückblick." *Dokumente*, 1993, no. 5, 398–401.

Benecke, Theodor, and Günther Schöner, eds. *Wehrtechnik für die Verteidigung.* Koblenz: Bernard & Graefe, 1984.

Berman, M. B., and G. M. Carter. *The Independent European Force: Costs of Independence*. Santa Monica, Calif.: Rand Corp., 1993.

Bittner, Gustav A. "Eine positive Bilanz." In Kaiser and Lellouche, *Deutsch-französische Sicherheitspolitik*, 113–28.

Blankenhorn, Herbert. *Verständnis und Verständigung: Blätter eines politischen Tagebuches, 1949 bis 1979*. Frankfurt am Main: Propyläen, 1980.

Bloes, Robert. *Le "Plan Fouchet" et le problème de l'Europe politique*. Bruges: Collège d'Europe, 1970.

Bode, Hans-Günter. *Rüstung in der Bundesrepublik Deutschland*. Regensburg: Walhalla und Praetoria Verlag, 1978.

Bodenheimer, Suzanne J. *Political Union: A Microcosm of European Politics, 1960–1966*. Leiden: A. W. Sijthoff, 1967.

Boyer, Yves. "Europe's Future Strategic Orientation." *Washington Quarterly*, Autumn 1993, 141–53.

Boyer, Yves. "Strategic Implications of the New Technologies for Conventional Weapons and the European Battlefield." In Catherine M. Kelleher and Gale A. Mattox, eds., *Evolving European Defense Policies*. Lexington, Mass.: D. C. Heath, 1987, 99–121.

Bozo, Frédéric. *La France et l'OTAN*. Paris: Masson, 1991.

Brandt, Willy. *People and Politics: The Years 1960–1975*. Boston: Little, Brown and Co., 1978.

Brauch, Hans Günter, ed. *Sicherheitspolitik am Ende?* Gerlingen: Bleicher, 1984.

Brauch, Hans Günter, ed. *Star Wars and European Defense*. New York: St. Martin's Press, 1987.

Bull, Hedley. "Civilian Power Europe: A Contradiction in Terms?" *Journal of Common Market Studies*, September/December 1982, 149–64.

Bundy, McGeorge, George F. Kennan, Robert S. McNamara, and Gerard Smith. "Nuclear Weapons and the Atlantic Alliance." *Foreign Affairs*, Spring 1982, 753–68.

Buteux, Paul. *The Politics of Nuclear Consultation in NATO, 1965–1980*. Cambridge: Cambridge University Press, 1983.

Cafruny, Alan W., and Glenda G. Rosenthal, eds. *The State of the European Community*, vol. 2: *The Maastricht Debates and Beyond*. Boulder, Colo.: Lynne Rienner, 1993.

Calleo, David P. *Beyond American Hegemony*. New York: Basic Books, 1987.

Camps, Miriam. *European Unification in the Sixties*. London: Oxford University Press, 1967.

Cannizzo, Cindy, ed. *The Gun Merchants: Politics and Policies of the Major Arms Suppliers*. New York: Pergamon, 1980.

Carlier, Claude. *L'aéronautique française, 1945–1975*. Paris: Lavauzelle, 1983.

Carton, Alain. "Coopération en matière d'armements entre la France et l'Allemagne." *Documents*, 1991, no. 4, 24–29.

Carton, Alain. "'Perceptions allemandes du plan Rogers': Les réactions officielles à la 'nouvelle doctrine' de l'OTAN en Europe." *Défense nationale*, July 1983, 55–72.

Chilton, Patricia. "French Nuclear Weapons." In Jolyon Howorth and Patricia Chilton, eds., *Defence and Dissent in Contemporary France*. New York: Croom Helm/St. Martin's Press, 1984, 135–69.

Chirac, Jacques. "Au sujet des armes nucléaires tactiques françaises." *Défense nationale*, May 1975, 11–15.

Chirac, Jacques. "La France et les enjeux de la sécurité européenne." *Défense nationale*, February 1988, 9–18.

Commission du Bilan. *La France en mai 1981*, vol. 5: *L'Etat et les citoyens*. Paris: La Documentation Française, 1981.

Couve de Murville, Maurice. *Une politique étrangère, 1958–1969*. Paris: Plon, 1971.

Cowen, Regina H. E. *Defense Procurement in the Federal Republic of Germany: Politics and Organization*. Boulder, Colo. and London: Westview, 1986.

Cowper–Coles, Sherard. "From Defence to Security: British Policy in Transition." *Survival*, Spring 1994, 142–61.

Daalder, Ivo H. *The SDI Challenge to Europe*. Cambridge, Mass.: Ballinger, 1987.

David, Dominique. *La Force d'action rapide en Europe: Le dire des armes*. Paris: Fondation pour les Etudes de Défense Nationale, 1984.

Les Déclarations du Président de la République sur la politique de défense et la politique militaire, juin 1974—décembre 1976. France, Premier ministre, Service d'Information et de Diffusion.

de Gaulle, Charles. *Discours et messages*. Paris: Plon, 1970, 5 vols.

de Gaulle, Charles. *Major Addresses, Statements and Press Conferences, May 19, 1958 to January 31, 1964*. New York: French Embassy, Press and Information Service, 1964.

de Gaulle, Charles. *Mémoires d'espoir: Le Renouveau, 1958–1962*. Paris: Plon, 1970.

de Gaulle, Charles. *War Memoirs*. New York: Viking, 1955, vol. 1.

de Ménil, Lois Pattison. *Who Speaks for Europe?* New York: St. Martin's Press, 1977.

Dörfer, Ingemar. *Arms Deal: The Selling of the F-16*. New York: Praeger, 1983.

Dreyfus, François-Georges. "RFA: Le péril national-neutraliste." *Politique internationale*, Autumn 1987, 185–200.

Dubos, Jean-François. *Ventes d'armes: Une politique*. Paris: Gallimard, 1974.

Dussauge, Pierre. *L'Industrie française de l'armement*. Paris: Economica, 1985.

Ehrenberg, Eckehart. *Der deutsche Rüstungsexport: Beurteilungen und Perspektiven*. Munich: Bernard & Graefe, 1981.

Ehrhart, Hans-Georg. "La sécurité européenne vue par le PS et le SPD." *Documents*, 1991, no. 5, 25–31.

Fabius, Laurent. "La politique de défense: Rassembler et moderniser." *Défense nationale*, November 1984, 7–17.

Flynn, Gregory. "The New France and Post–Cold War Europe: Paradigm Lost . . . ?" Paper delivered at the Annual Meeting of the American Political Science Association, September 1–4, 1994.

Födisch, Rolf. "'Fränkischer Schild'—Manöver des III. Korps der Bundeswehr." Österreichische Militärische Zeitschrift, 1986, no. 6, 529–40.

France, Ministry of Defense. Livre blanc sur la défense, 1994.

France, Ministry of Defense. Livre blanc sur la défense nationale, 1972.

Frank, Paul. Entschlüsselte Botschaft. Stuttgart: Deutsche Verlags-Anstalt, 1981.

Fricaud-Chagnaud, Georges. "L'Armée de Terre face à ses missions en Europe." Défense nationale, May 1983, 35–44.

Fursdon, Edward. The European Defence Community: A History. New York: St. Martin's Press, 1980.

Gallois, Pierre M. "French Defense Planning—The Future in the Past." International Security, Fall 1976, 15–31.

Gallois, Pierre M. Le renoncement. Paris: Plon, 1977.

Geiger, Wolfgang. "'Wenn Deutschland erwacht . . . ': Die 'deutsche Frage' aus Französischer Sicht." Die Neue Gesellschaft/Frankfurter Hefte, January 1990, 63–68.

Germany, Federal Ministry of Defense. White Paper on the Security of the Federal Republic of Germany and the Situation and Future of the Bundeswehr, 1994.

Gerosa, Guido. "The North Atlantic Cooperation Council." European Security, Autumn 1992, 273–89.

Gilpin, Robert. France in the Age of the Scientific State. Princeton: Princeton University Press, 1968.

Giscard d'Estaing, Valéry. "Allocution." Défense nationale, July 1976, 5–20.

Giscard d'Estaing, Valéry. Le pouvoir et la vie. Paris: Compagnie 12, 1988.

Glucksmann, André. La force du vertige. Paris: Grasset, 1983.

Gordon, Philip H. A Certain Idea of France. Princeton: Princeton University Press, 1993.

Gordon, Philip H. "The Normalization of German Foreign Policy." Orbis, Spring 1994, 225–43.

Grewe, Wilhelm. Rückblenden: Aufzeichnungen eines Augenzeugen deutscher Aussenpolitik von Adenauer bis Schmidt. Berlin: Propyläen, 1979.

Grosser, Alfred. La IVe République et sa politique extérieure. Paris: Armand Colin, 1961.

Grosser, Alfred. The Western Alliance. New York: Continuum, 1980.

Haftendorn, Helga. Sicherheit und Entspannung: Zur Aussenpolitik der Bundesrepublik Deutschland, 1955–1982. Baden-Baden: Nomos, 1983.

Haftendorn, Helga. Sicherheit und Stabilität: Aussenbeziehungen der Bundesrepublik zwischen Ölkrise und NATO-Doppelbeschluss. Munich: Deutscher Taschenbuch Verlag, 1986.

Haglund, David G. Alliance within the Alliance? Franco-German Military Cooperation and the European Pillar of Defense. Boulder, Colo.: Westview, 1991.

Hanrieder, Wolfram. *Germany, America, Europe*. New Haven: Yale University Press, 1989.

Hanrieder, Wolfram. "West German Foreign Policy, 1949–1979: Necessities and Choices." In Wolfram Hanrieder, ed., *West German Foreign Policy, 1949–1979*. Boulder, Colo.: Westview, 1980, 15–36.

Harris, Scott A., and James B. Steinberg. *European Defense and the Future of Transatlantic Cooperation*. Santa Monica, Calif.: Rand Corp., 1993.

Harrison, Michael M. *The Reluctant Ally: France and Alliance Security*. Baltimore: Johns Hopkins University Press, 1981.

Hartley, Keith. *NATO Arms Cooperation: A Study in Economics and Politics*. London: Allen and Unwin, 1983.

Heinemann, Irmgard. *Le Traité franco-allemand du 22 janvier 1963 et sa mise en oeuvre sous le général de Gaulle, 1963–1969*. Doctoral thesis, University of Nice, 1977.

Heisbourg, François. "Für einen neuen Anfang." In Kaiser and Lellouche, *Deutsch-französische Sicherheitspolitik*, 129–41.

Hernu, Charles. "Equilibre, dissuasion, volonté: La voie étroite de la paix et de la liberté." *Défense nationale*, December 1983, 5–20.

Hernu, Charles. "Face à la logique des blocs, une France indépendente et solidaire." *Défense nationale*, December 1982, 7–21.

Heyhoe, D.C.R. *The Alliance and Europe: Part VI—The European Programme Group*, Adelphi Paper 129. London: IISS, Winter 1976/77.

Hildebrand, Klaus. "Der provisorische Staat und das Ewige Frankreich: Die deutsch-französischen Beziehungen 1963 bis 1969." In Schwarz, ed., *Adenauer und Frankreich*, 62–81.

Hoffmann, Stanley. *Decline or Renewal? France since the 1930s*. New York: Viking, 1974.

Hoffmann, Stanley. "Thoughts on the French Nation Today." *Daedalus*, Summer 1993, 63–79.

Howard, Michael. "A European Perspective on the Reagan Years." *Foreign Affairs, America and the World 1987/88*, 478–93.

Institut Charles-de-Gaulle, ed. *L'aventure de la bombe: De Gaulle et la dissuasion nucléaire, 1958–1969*. Paris: Plon, 1985.

James, Robert Rhodes. *Standardization and Common Production of Weapons in NATO*. London: Institute for Strategic Studies, 1967.

Jobert, Michel. *L'autre regard*. Paris: Grasset, 1976.

Joffe, Josef. *The Limited Partnership*. Cambridge, Mass.: Ballinger, 1987.

Kaiser, Karl. *German Foreign Policy in Transition*. London: Oxford University Press, 1968.

Kaiser, Karl. "RFA: Un défi au consensus." In Pierre Lellouche, ed., *Pacifisme et dissuasion*. Paris: IFRI, 1983, 59–72.

Kaiser, Karl, and Pierre Lellouche, eds. *Deutsch-französische Sicherheitspolitik: Auf dem Wege zur Gemeinsamkeit?* Bonn: Europa Union Verlag, 1986. Pub-

lished in France as *Le couple franco-allemand et la défense de l'Europe*.
Paris: IFRI, 1986.

Kapstein, Ethan B. "America's Arms-Trade Monopoly." *Foreign Affairs*, May/June
1994, 13–19.

Katzenstein, Peter. "Taming of Power: German Unification, 1989–1990." In
Meredith Woo-Cumings and Michael Loriaux, eds., *Past as Prelude:
History in the Making of a New World Order*, Boulder, Colo.: Westview,
1993, 59–81.

Kelleher, Catherine M. *Germany and the Politics of Nuclear Weapons*. New York:
Columbia University Press, 1975.

Kiep, Walther Leisler. "The New Deutschlandpolitik." *Foreign Affairs*, Winter
1984/85, 316–29.

Kissinger, Henry A. "The Future of NATO." In Douglas J. Murray and Paul R.
Viotti, eds., *The Defense Policies of Nations*. Baltimore: Johns Hopkins
University Press, 1982, 121–25.

Kissinger, Henry A. "A Plan to Reshape NATO." *Time*, March 5, 1984, 20–24.

Kissinger, Henry A. *The Troubled Partnership*. New York: McGraw-Hill, 1965.

Kissinger, Henry A. *Years of Upheaval*. Boston: Little, Brown and Co., 1982.

Klein, Jean. "France, NATO, and European Security." *International Security*, Winter 1977, 21–41.

Klinker, Bruno. "Wehrtechnische Forschung." In Benecke and Schöner, *Wehrtechnik für die Verteidigung*, 72–119.

Kohl, Wilfrid L. *French Nuclear Diplomacy*. Princeton: Princeton University Press,
1971.

Kolboom, Ingo. "Der Blick Nach Osten—Von der französischen 'Détente' und
der deutschen 'Ostpolitik' zu einer gemeinsamen Öffnung nach Osten?"
In André Brigot, Peter Schmidt, and Walter Schütze, eds., *Sicherheits-
und Ostpolitik: Deutsch-Französische Perspektiven*. Baden–Baden: Nomos,
1989, 115–44.

Kolodziej, Edward A. "Europe: The Partial Partner." *International Security*, Winter
1980/81, 104–31.

Kolodziej, Edward A. *French International Policy under de Gaulle and Pompidou: The
Politics of Grandeur*. Ithaca: Cornell University Press, 1974.

Kolodziej, Edward A. *Making and Marketing Arms: The French Experience and Its
Implications for the International System*. Princeton: Princeton University
Press, 1987.

Krauss, Melvyn. *How NATO Weakens the West*. New York: Simon and Schuster,
1986.

Kreile, Michael. "Aufschwung und Risiko: Die Wirtschafts- und Haushaltspolitik
der Reagan-Administration." In Hartmut Wasser, ed., *Die Ära Reagan:
Eine erste Bilanz*. Stuttgart: Klett, 1988, 162–84.

Krell, Gert, Thomas Risse-Kappen, and Hans-Joachim Schmidt. "The No-First-
Use Question in West Germany." In John D. Steinbruner and Leon V.

Sigal, eds., *Alliance Security, NATO and the No-First-Use Question*. Washington, D.C.: Brookings, 1983, 147–72.

Krop, Pascal. *Les Socialistes et l'armée*. Paris: Presses Universitaires de France, 1983.

Laird, Robbin F. *France, the Soviet Union, and the Nuclear Weapons Issue*. Boulder, Colo.: Westview, 1985.

Laird, Robbin F., ed. *French Security Policy: From Independence to Interdependence*. Boulder, Colo.: Westview, 1986.

Laird, Robbin F., ed. *Strangers and Friends: The Franco-German Security Relationship*. New York: St. Martin's Press, 1989.

Lakoff, Sanford, and Randy Willoughby, eds. *Strategic Defense and the Western Alliance*. Lexington, Mass.: D. C. Heath, 1987.

Larrabee, F. Stephen. "The View from Moscow." In Larrabee, ed., *The Two German States and European Security*. New York: St. Martin's Press, 1989, 182–205.

Layne, Christopher. "The Unipolar Illusion: Why New Great Powers Will Arise." *International Security*, Spring 1993, 5–51.

Leimbacher, Urs. *Die unverzichtbare Allianz: Deutsch-französische sicherheitspolitische Zusammenarbeit 1982–1989*. Baden-Baden: Nomos, 1992.

Lellouche, Pierre. "France in Search of Security." *Foreign Affairs*, Spring 1993, 122–31.

Lellouche, Pierre, ed. *L'Initiative de défense stratégique et la sécurité de l'Europe*. Paris: IFRI, 1986.

Lerner, Daniel, and Raymond Aron, eds. *France Defeats EDC*. New York: Praeger, 1957.

Livingston, Robert Gerald. "United Germany: Bigger and Better." *Foreign Policy*, Summer 1992, 157–74.

Lorell, Mark A. *Multinational Development of Large Aircraft*. Santa Monica, Calif.: Rand Corp., 1980.

Louet, Henri. *Rapport d'information par la Commission de la défense nationale et des forces armées sur la coopération industrielle franco-allemande en matière d'hélicoptères de combat*. Paris: Assemblée Nationale, Troisiéme session extraordinaire de 1985–86, no. 249.

Löwenthal, Richard. "The German Question Transformed." *Foreign Affairs*, Winter 1984/85, 303–15.

Ludlow, Peter. *The Making of the European Monetary System*. London: Butterworth Scientific, 1982.

Maccotta, Giuseppe Walter. "Alcune considerazioni sulla Force de frappe: Le sue origini ed il suo significato politico." *Rivista marittima*, April 1982, 23–28.

Mahncke, Dieter. *Nukleare Mitwirkung: Die Bundesrepublik Deutschland in der atlantischen Allianz, 1954–1970*. Berlin: Walter de Gruyter, 1972.

Main de Boissière, Jean-Baptiste. "Le programme Eurêka." *Défense nationale*, December 1986, 133–48.

Mayer-Simeth, Dieter. "La peur de l'atome: Une nouvelle composante de l'âme allemande?" In Bernard Brigouleix and Joseph Rovan, eds., *Que devient l'Allemagne?* Paris: Editions Anthropos, 1986, 147–54.

Maull, Hanns W. "Germany and Japan: The New Civilian Powers." *Foreign Affairs*, Winter 1990/91, 91–106.

Mauroy, Pierre. "La stratégie de la France." *Défense nationale*, November 1983, 5–22.

McCarthy, Patrick, ed. *France-Germany, 1983–1993: The Struggle to Cooperate.* London: Macmillan, 1993.

McNamara, Robert S. "The Military Role of Nuclear Weapons: Perceptions and Misperceptions." *Foreign Affairs*, Fall 1983, 59–80.

Mearsheimer, John J. "Back to the Future: Instability in Europe after the Cold War." *International Security*, Summer 1990, 5–56.

Mechtersheimer, Alfred. *Rüstung und Politik in der Bundesrepublik: MRCA Tornado.* Bad Honnef: Osang, 1977.

Mendershausen, Horst. *Troop Stationing in Germany: Value and Cost.* Santa Monica, Calif.: Rand Corp., 1968.

Menon, Anand, Anthony Forster, and William Wallace. "A Common European Defence?" *Survival*, Autumn 1992, 98–118.

Ménudier, Henri. "Die deutsche Frage aus der heutigen Sicht Frankreichs." In Hannelore Horn and Siegfried Mampel, eds., *Die deutsche Frage aus der heutigen Sicht des Auslandes.* Berlin: Duncker & Humblot, 1987, 25–50.

Méry, Guy. "Une armée pour quoi faire et comment?" *Défense nationale*, June 1976, 11–34.

Meyer, Timm R. "Die Rüstungszusammenarbeit zwischen Grossbritannien und der Bundesrepublik Deutschland." In Karl Kaiser and John Roper, eds., *Die Stille Allianz: Deutsch-britische Sicherheitskooperation.* Bonn: Europa Union Verlag, 1987, 264–85.

Moens, Alexander. "American Diplomacy and German Unification." *Survival*, November/December 1991, 531–45.

Moïsi, Dominique. "French Foreign Policy: The Challenge of Adaptation." *Foreign Affairs*, Fall 1988, 151–64.

Moïsi, Dominique. "La France et la crise des euromissiles." *Défense nationale*, August-September 1983, 37–46.

Moravcsik, Andrew. "Negotiating the Single European Act: National Interests and Conventional Statecraft in the European Community." *International Organization*, Winter 1991, 19–56.

Morgan, Roger. *The United States and West Germany, 1945–1973.* London: Oxford University Press, 1974.

Müller-Roschach, Herbert. *Die deutsche Europapolitik, 1949–1977.* Bonn: Europa Union Verlag, 1980.

Newhouse, John. *De Gaulle and the Anglo-Saxons.* New York: Viking, 1970.

Nicolas, Françoise, and Hans Stark. *L'Allemagne: Une nouvelle hégémonie?* Paris: IFRI, 1992.

Noack, Paul. *Das Scheitern der Europäischen Verteidigungsgemeinschaft.* Düsseldorf: Droste, 1977.

Osgood, Robert E. *NATO: The Entangling Alliance.* Chicago: University of Chicago Press, 1962.

Paolini, Jérôme. "Les deux politiques européennes de François Mitterrand." *Relations internationales et stratégiques,* Spring 1993, 124–34.

Pearson, Frederic S. "Of Leopards and Cheetahs: West Germany's Role as a Mid-Sized Arms Supplier." *Orbis,* Spring 1985, 165–81.

Pearson, Frederic S. "Political Change and World Arms Export Markets: Impact on the Structure of West European Arms Industries." In Michael Brzoska and Peter Lock, eds., *Restructuring of Arms Production in Western Europe.* Oxford: Oxford University Press, 1992, 44–58.

Pleiner, Horst. "'Kecker Spatz—Moineau hardi'—Deutsch-französische Heeresübung 1987." *Österreichische Militärische Zeitschrift,* 1987, no. 6, 512–27.

Poirier, Lucien. *Des stratégies nucléaires.* Paris: Hachette, 1977.

Poirier, Lucien. "La greffe." *Défense nationale,* April 1983, 5–32.

Pond, Elizabeth. *Beyond the Wall.* Washington, D.C.: Brookings, 1993.

Pond, Elizabeth. "Germany in the New Europe." *Foreign Affairs,* Spring 1992, 114–30.

Pond, Elizabeth, and Kenneth N. Waltz. "Correspondence: International Politics, Viewed from the Ground." *International Security,* Summer 1994, 195–99.

Radoux, L. *France and NATO.* Paris: Assembly of Western European Union, Committee on Defence Questions and Armaments, June 1967.

Richardson, James L. *Germany and the Atlantic Alliance.* Cambridge, Mass.: Harvard University Press, 1966.

Risse-Kappen, Thomas. *The Zero Option: INF, West Germany, and Arms Control.* Boulder, Colo.: Westview, 1988.

Robin, Gabriel. "The German Problem Revisited." *Atlantic Quarterly,* Autumn 1983, 191–200.

Rogers, Bernard W. "Follow-on Forces Attack (FOFA): Myths and Realities." *NATO Review,* December 1984, 1–9.

Rotfeld, Adam Daniel, and Walther Stützle, eds. *Germany and Europe in Transition.* Oxford: Oxford University Press, 1991.

Roussel, Eric. *Georges Pompidou.* Paris: J. C. Lattès, 1984.

Rovan, Joseph. "Le problème allemand." *Défense nationale,* December 1982, 27–35.

Rovan, Joseph. "Réflexions sur la crise allemande." *Politique étrangère,* 1983, no. 1, 39–46.

Ruehl, Lothar. "Der Aufschwung der sicherheitspolitischen Zusammenarbeit seit 1982." In Kaiser and Lellouche, *Deutsch-französische Sicherheitspolitik,* 27–47.

Ruehl, Lothar. *La politique militaire de la Ve République.* Paris: Fondation Nationale des Sciences Politiques, 1976.

Rummel, Reinhardt, ed. *The Evolution of an International Actor: Western Europe's New Assertiveness.* Boulder, Colo.: Westview, 1990.

Sampson, Anthony. *The Arms Bazaar.* New York: Viking, 1977.

Sandholtz, Wayne. *High-Tech Europe.* Berkeley: University of California Press, 1992.

Schlesinger, James. "Reykjavik and Revelations: A Turn of the Tide?" *Foreign Affairs,* America and the World 1986, 426–46.

Schlör, Wolfgang F. *German Security Policy,* Adelphi Paper 277. London: IISS, 1993.

Schlotter, Peter. *Rüstungspolitik in der Bundesrepublik: Die Beispiele Starfighter und Phantom.* Frankfurt am Main: Campus Verlag, 1975.

Schmid, Günther. "Positionen in der Sicherheitspolitischen Diskussion und ihre Vertreter in der Bundesrepublik Deutschland." *Österreichische Militärische Zeitschrift,* 1983, no. 6, 504–13.

Schmidt, Helmut. *Menschen und Mächte.* Berlin: Siedler, 1987.

Schmidt, Peter. "The Franco-German Defence and Security Council." *Aussenpolitik,* 1989, no. 4, 360–71.

Schmidt, Peter. "French Security Policy Ambitions." *Aussenpolitik,* 1993, no. 4, 335–43.

Schmidt, Peter. *The Special Franco-German Security Relationship in the 1990s,* Chaillot Paper 8. Paris: Institute for Security Studies, 1993.

Schmückle, Gerd. *Ohne Pauken und Trompeten: Erinnerungen an Krieg und Frieden.* Munich: W. Heyne, 1982.

Schulz, Eberhard, and Peter Danylow. *Bewegung in der deutschen Frage? Die ausländischen Besorgnisse über die Entwicklung in den beiden deutschen Staaten.* Bonn: Europa Union Verlag, 1984.

Schütze, Walter. *Frankreichs Verteidigungspolitik, 1958–1983.* Frankfurt am Main: Haag & Herchen, 1983.

Schwartz, David N. *NATO's Nuclear Dilemmas.* Washington, D.C.: Brookings, 1983.

Schwarz, Hans-Peter, ed. *Adenauer und Frankreich: Die deutsch-französischen Beziehungen 1958 bis 1969.* Bonn: Bouvier, 1985.

Schwarz, Hans-Peter. "Das aussenpolitische Konzept Konrad Adenauers." In Klaus Gotto et al., *Konrad Adenauer: Seine Deutschland- und Aussenpolitik, 1945–1963.* Munich: Deutscher Taschenbuch Verlag, 1975, 97–155.

Schwarz, Hans-Peter. *Die Ära Adenauer: Epochenwechsel, 1957–1963.* Stuttgart: Deutsche Verlags-Anstalt, 1983.

Schwarz, Hans-Peter. *Die gezähmten Deutschen: Von der Machtbesessenheit zur Machtvergessenheit.* Stuttgart: Deutsche Verlags-Anstalt, 1985.

Schwarz, Hans-Peter. *Eine Entente Elémentaire: Das deutsch-französische Verhältnis im 25. Jahr des Elysée-Vertrages.* Bonn: Forschungsinstitut der Deutschen Gesellschaft für Auswärtige Politik, 1988.

Siegler, Heinrich. *Europäische politische Einigung: Dokumentation von Vorschlägen und Stellungnahmen, 1949–1968.* Bonn: Siegler & Co., 1968.

Sigal, Leon V. *Nuclear Forces in Europe: Enduring Dilemmas, Present Prospects.* Washington, D.C.: Brookings, 1984.

Silj, Alessandro. *Europe's Political Puzzle: A Study of the Fouchet Negotiations and the 1963 Veto.* Cambridge, Mass.: Center for International Affairs, Harvard University, 1967.

Simonian, Haig. *The Privileged Partnership: Franco-German Relations in the European Community, 1969–1984.* Oxford: Clarendon Press, 1985.

Smith, Dale L., and James Lee Ray. "European Integration: Gloomy Theory versus Rosy Reality." In Dale L. Smith and James Lee Ray, eds., *The 1992 Project and the Future of Integration in Europe.* Armonk, N.Y.: M. E. Sharpe, 1993, 19–44.

Smyser, W. R. "Dateline Berlin: Germany's New Vision." *Foreign Policy,* Winter 1994–95, 140–57.

Sorenson, Theodore C. *Kennedy.* New York: Harper and Row, 1965.

Sperling, James. "German Security Policy and the Future European Security Order." In Michael G. Huelshoff, Andrei S. Markovits, and Simon Reich, eds., *From Bundesrepublik to Deutschland: German Politics after Unification.* Ann Arbor: University of Michigan Press, 1993, 321–46.

Stanley, John, and Maurice Pearton. *The International Trade in Arms.* New York: Praeger, 1972.

Stares, Paul B. *Allied Rights and Legal Constraints on German Military Power.* Washington, D.C.: Brookings, 1990.

Stark, Hans. "France-Allemagne: Entente et mésententes." *Politique étrangère,* Winter 1993/94, 989–99.

Steinberg, James B. *The Transformation of the European Defense Industry.* Santa Monica, Calif.: Rand Corp., 1992.

Steinbruner, John D. *The Cybernetic Theory of Decision.* Princeton: Princeton University Press, 1974.

Stern, Fritz. "Germany in a Semi-Gaullist Europe." *Foreign Affairs,* Spring 1980, 867–86.

Stratmann, K.-Peter. "The Future of West European Security and Defence Cooperation—German Perspectives." In Peter Schmidt, ed., *In the Midst of Change: On the Development of West European Security and Defence Cooperation.* Baden-Baden: Nomos, 1992, 31–63.

Stratmann, K.-Peter. "A German View." In Hans Sjöberg, ed., *European Security and the Atlantic Alliance.* Stockholm: Swedish National Defense Research Institute, 1984, 41–50.

Strengthening Conventional Defense in Europe: Proposals for the 1980s. Report of the European Security Study. London: Macmillan, 1983.

Stromseth, Jane E. *The Origins of Flexible Response.* New York: St. Martin's Press, 1988.

Szabo, Stephen F. *The Diplomacy of German Unification.* New York: St. Martin's Press, 1992.

Talbott, Strobe. *Endgame: The Inside Story of SALT II.* New York: Harper and Row, 1979.

Taylor, Maxwell D. *The Uncertain Trumpet.* New York: Harper and Brothers, 1959.

Teltschik, Horst. *329 Tage.* Berlin: Siedler, 1991.

Thévenin, Pierre. "L'Institut de Saint-Louis." *L'Armement*, June 1984, 46–59.

Thygesen, Niels. "The Delors Report and European Economic and Monetary Union." *International Affairs*, Autumn 1989, 637–52.

Todd, Daniel, and Jamie Simpson. *The World Aircraft Industry.* London: Croom Helm, 1986.

Treverton, Gregory F. *The Dollar Drain and American Forces in Germany.* Athens, Ohio: Ohio University Press, 1978.

Valentin, François. "L'arête étroite." *Défense nationale*, May 1983, 45–56.

Valentin, François. *Une politique de défense pour la France.* Paris: Calmann-Lévy, 1980.

Vernet, Daniel. "France in a New Europe." *The National Interest*, Fall 1992, 30–38.

Waever, Ole. "Three Competing Europes: German, French, Russian." *International Affairs*, July 1990, 477–93.

Wahl, Albert, and Fritz Engelmann. "Wehrtechnik Luft." In Benecke and Schöner, *Wehrtechnik für die Verteidigung*, 163–227.

Waltz, Kenneth N. "The Emerging Structure of International Politics." *International Security*, Fall 1993, 44–79.

Wasserman, Sherri L. *The Neutron Bomb Controversy.* New York: Praeger, 1983.

Weisenfeld, Ernst. "Die Aussenpolitik Frankreichs." In Karl Kaiser and Hans-Peter Schwarz, eds., *Weltpolitik: Strukturen—Akteure—Perspektiven.* Bonn: Bundeszentrale für politische Bildung, 1985, 334–45.

Wettig, Gerhard. *Entmilitarisierung und Wiederbewaffnung in Deutschland, 1943–1955.* Munich: R. Oldenbourg, 1967.

Wilkens, Andreas. *Der unstete Nachbar: Frankreich, die deutsche Ostpolitik und die Berliner Vier-Mächte-Verhandlungen 1969–1974.* Munich: R. Oldenbourg, 1990.

Willis, F. Roy. *France, Germany, and the New Europe, 1945–1967,* revised and expanded edition. Stanford: Stanford University Press, 1968.

Wood, Pia Christina. "François Mitterrand and the Persian Gulf War: The Search for Influence." *French Politics and Society*, Summer 1992, 44–62.

Wulf, Herbert, ed. *Arms Industry Limited.* Oxford: Oxford University Press, 1993.

Yost, David S. *France and Conventional Defense in Central Europe.* Marina del Rey, Calif.: European American Institute for Security Research, 1984.

Yost, David S. "France in the New Europe." *Foreign Affairs,* Winter 1990/91, 107–28.

Yost, David S. *France's Deterrent Posture and Security in Europe.* Adelphi Papers 194 and 195. London: IISS, Winter 1984/85.

Yost, David S. "Franco-German Defense Cooperation." *Washington Quarterly,* Spring 1988, 173–95.

Yost, David S. "French Defense Budgeting: Executive Dominance and Resource Constraints." *Orbis,* Fall 1979, 579–608.

Zelikow, Philip. "The New Concert of Europe." *Survival,* Summer 1992, 12–30.

Ziebura, Gilbert. *Die deutsch-französischen Beziehungen seit 1945: Mythen und Realitäten.* Pfullingen: Neske, 1970.

Index

About the Author

STEPHEN A. KOCS is an Associate Professor, Department of Political Science, College of the Holy Cross, Worcester, MA. He has published articles on international relations theory and on the causes of war.

ISBN 0-275-94890-0

EAN

90000>

9 780275 948900

HARDCOVER BAR CODE